*The*

# 99% INVISIBLE

## CITY

# The
# 99% INVISIBLE
# CITY

### A FIELD GUIDE *to*
### THE HIDDEN WORLD
### *of*
### EVERYDAY DESIGN

## ROMAN MARS AND KURT KOHLSTEDT

HOUGHTON MIFFLIN HARCOURT
BOSTON · NEW YORK

2020

*For all you plaque readers*
*and curious urbanists*

Copyright © 2020 by ROMAN MARS

For information about permission to reproduce selections from this book,
write to trade.permissions@hmhco.com or to Permissions,
Houghton Mifflin Harcourt Publishing Company, 3 Park Avenue,
19th Floor, New York, New York 10016.

hmhbooks.com

*Library of Congress Cataloging-in-Publication Data*
Names: Mars, Roman, author. | Kohlstedt, Kurt, author.
Title: The 99% invisible city : a field guide to the hidden world of everyday design
/ Roman Mars and Kurt Kohlstedt.
Other titles: Ninety-nine percent invisible city : a field guide to the hidden world
of everyday design
Description: Boston : Houghton Mifflin Harcourt, [2020] | Includes bibliographical
references and index. | Summary: "A beautifully designed guidebook to the unnoticed
yet essential elements of our cities, from the creators of the wildly popular 99%
Invisible podcast"— Provided by publisher.
Identifiers: LCCN 2020023323 (print) | LCCN 202002332 (ebook)
| ISBN 9780358126607 (hardback) | ISBN 9780358396369 | ISBN 9780358396383 |
ISBN 9780358125020 (ebook)
Subjects: LCSH: Cities and towns—Miscellanea. | Public works—Miscellanea.
Classification: LCC NA9050 .M29 2020 (print) | LCC NA9050 (ebook)
| DDC 720—dc23
LC record available at https://lccn.loc.gov/2020023323
LC ebook record available at https://lccn.loc.gov/2020023324

*Book design by* RAPHAEL GERONI
*Illustrations by* PATRICK VALE

Printed in the United States of America
DOC 10 9 8 7 6 5 4 3
4500810416

# CONTENTS

# INTRODUCTION

THE WORLD IS FULL OF AMAZING THINGS. WALK AROUND any major city and you will find soaring skyscrapers that inspire awe, bridges that are marvels of engineering, and lush parks that provide respite from the concrete landscape. There are travel guides for all of that. This, however, is a guide to the overlooked and ordinary: the boring stuff. The truth is that the mundane objects we pass by without noticing or trip over without thinking can represent as much genius and innovation as the tallest building, the longest bridge, or the most manicured park. So much of the conversation about design centers on beauty, but the more fascinating stories of the built world are about problem-solving, historical constraints, and human drama.

This has always been the worldview of the *99% Invisible* podcast. Since 2010, we have told stories about all the thought that goes into things most people don't think about. Our name references the everyday objects that are invisible because of their everydayness, but it also refers to the invisible parts of things you *do* notice. In the case of something like the Chrysler Building, the aesthetics and architecture of the massive Art Deco tower are only 1% of the story. It's our mission to tell you the hidden parts of the story: the speed of its construction, the building's place in the great Manhattan skyscraper race, the iconoclastic architect who designed it, and his daring, secret strategy to beat out the competition at the last possible moment. As beautiful as the Chrysler Building is, the *99% Invisible* part is the best part.

In this book, unlike the podcast, we get the opportunity to show you pretty images (illustrated by Patrick Vale) that help tell the hidden history and development of these designs. That said, this guide is not meant to be an encyclopedia that provides a few rote paragraphs about the inventor and origin story of each object. You have Wikipedia for that. This is about breaking down the cityscape into its more fascinating subparts. Rather than tell you about the first traffic light, we'd rather tell you about the most *interesting* traffic light in the world: the one in Syracuse,

New York, that has the green light above the red light as a display of Irish pride. Instead of recounting the construction of the jaw-dropping Brooklyn Bridge, we introduce you to the aesthetically mundane Can Opener bridge in Durham, North Carolina, which has an uncanny history of shearing off the tops of tall trucks trying to pass underneath. The Brooklyn Bridge represents an incredible advancement in engineering, but Durham's Norfolk Southern–Gregson Street Overpass illustrates the perils of sclerotic modern transit bureaucracy, something citizens bang their heads against every day.

Like the best-intentioned urban planners, we have laid out a path for you as we walk together through this inevitably incomplete guide to the city. We take you through the things you never noticed as well as the things you always notice but might not understand—from massive top-down municipal infrastructure made by trained planners at their desks to bottom-up citizen interventions created by urban activists. However, there's no reason why you can't pick and choose the path through this book that suits your own journey—create a personal desire path, a favorite subject in the *99% Invisible* universe. Desire paths emerge when people trample on the grass to cut a route to the place they want to go when urban planners have failed to provide a designated paved walkway. These spontaneous trails are shaped by pedestrians who are effectively voting with their feet. Most of the desire paths you encounter in a city trace the shortest distance between two points, often to cut corners, but many others are there just because people want to take a path less traveled. Once a desire path is created, it frequently become self-reinforcing: others begin following these newly formed routes, which increases their visibility and perpetuates their usage.

So as you make your way through your own city or one you're visiting, carry this book with you, flip through, find a story, and settle in. If you are in a city, you will probably find some analog to the thing we're talking about even if the specific example being discussed is in London or Osaka or beautiful downtown Oakland, California.

This is your guide to decoding the built world in whatever city you find yourself. Once you learn about all the designs in this book, you will look at the world in a radically different way. You will exalt in curb cuts, shake your fist at bench armrests, and tell the person walking next to you that the orange spray-painted markings on the street mean there are telecommunication lines just below the surface.

*You are*

*about to see*

*stories*

*everywhere,*

# YOU

# BEAUTIFUL

# NERD.

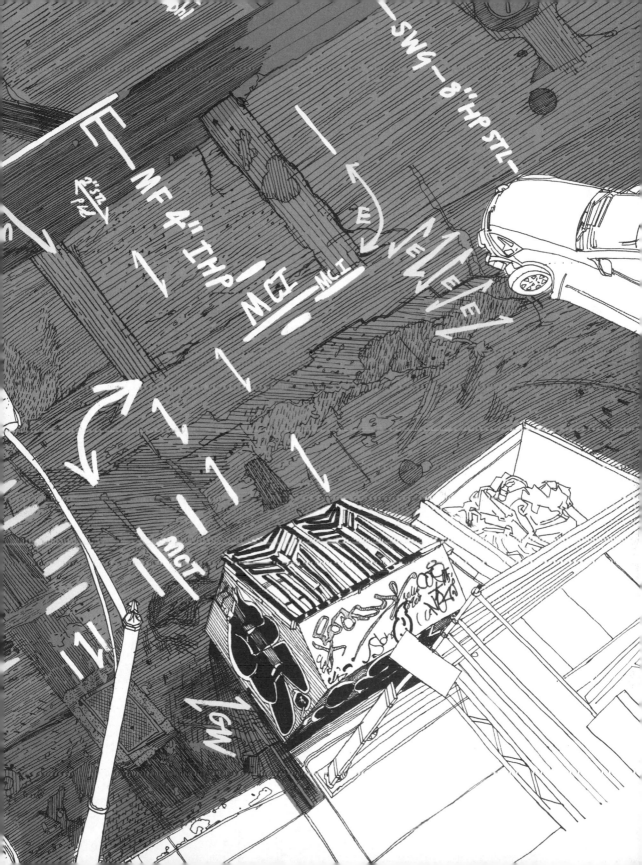

*Chapter 1*

# INCONSPICUOUS

**T**HERE IS A HIDDEN WORLD OF DESIGN all around you if you look closely enough, but the cacophony of visual noise in our cities can make it hard to notice key details. There are street markings that protect you from being blown to bits, tiny safes affixed to building exteriors that can help save occupants in a fire, and ornamental flourishes that may seem like mere decoration but actually work to hold entire brick buildings together. Amid all of this, there are also myriad incremental odds and ends that simply accumulate through people forever reshaping a city to fit their needs. Decoding these more subtle aspects of the cityscape can also help you gain insight into the people who make cities what they are, most of whom are just trying to live their lives, but some of whom are actively trying to save yours.

PREVIOUS: *Spray painted utility codes to mark underground hazards in Oakland*

# UBIQUITOUS

O NCE YOU START TO SEE THEM, you'll never understand how you hadn't noticed them before. On any given city street, there are design details scattered everywhere that are meant to establish boundaries or protect you on an everyday basis and in cases of emergency. Even obscure notations created and used by specialists contain layers of information written onto the built world that can be read by anyone who knows how to decipher them.

LEFT: *Sidewalk markers, a breakaway post, and emergency access box*

# Official Graffiti

## *Utility Codes*

Careless or uninformed digging around cables and pipes can cause everything from major utility outages to gas leaks—or, as in the case of a 1976 incident in California, a gigantic explosion that leveled half a city block. One fateful day in June of that year, workers were excavating a stretch of Venice Boulevard in Los Angeles when someone accidentally cut into a hidden petroleum pipeline. The pipe ruptured, and pressurized gas ignited into a fireball that engulfed passing cars and adjacent businesses. More than two dozen people were killed or injured as a result of this error. This wasn't the first or last tragedy of its kind, but the enormity of this particular disaster helped catalyze the codification of critical color-coded utility markings that are so omnipresent today. If you are in a US city, look down and you will see colorful official street graffiti everywhere; these markings are a guide to the networks of pipes, wires, and tubes crisscrossing below you.

The Los Angeles explosion spurred the creation of DigAlert, a nonprofit designed to help prevent future such tragedies in Southern California. Today, excavators in the region are required to mark out their work areas with white paint, chalk, or flags, and reach out to DigAlert; the organization then identifies and contacts companies with utilities running through the site so their technicians can go out and mark off potential hazards. Locators sent out by these companies can employ cable avoidance tools to establish or confirm the positions and depths of things below the surface. Ground-penetrating radar and devices to detect metals or magnetic fields help pinpoint concrete pipes, plastic tubes, and metal cables. Potential subsurface hazards are then highlighted using standardized colored-coded markings.

Over the decades, services similar to DigAlert have formed across the United States. To simplify things, the FCC designated 811 as a federal phone number in 2005 to connect excavators with these organizations. In general, anyone excavating on public property is required to contact a regional alert organization before proceeding, though private property owners are encouraged to reach out as well. According to a recent DIRT (Damage Information Reporting Tool) report, tens of thousands of accidents could be avoided each year if everyone called when planning to dig, drill, blast, or trench.

For clarity and consistency, US utility companies rely on Uniform Color Codes developed by the American Public Works Association when mapping out subterranean utilities on surfaces above. On city streets today, you can see the spectrum of safety colors that have been formalized and revised over the decades by the American National Standards Institute:

> **R e d:** electric power lines, cables, and conduit
>
> **O r a n g e:** telecommunications, alarm and signal lines
>
> **Y e l l o w:** gaseous or combustive materials including natural gas, oil, petroleum, and steam
>
> **G r e e n:** sewers and drain lines
>
> **B l u e:** potable water
>
> **P u r p l e:** reclaimed water, irrigation, or slurry lines
>
> **P i n k:** temporary markings, unidentified facilities, or known unknowns
>
> **W h i t e:** proposed excavation areas, limits, or routes

While the use of different colors provides general information about what's below, notations including lines, arrows, and numbers are also needed to keep track of details about the locations, widths, and depths of specific hazards. Here, too, standards are helpful, and there are organizations dedicated to helping coordinate and disseminate these. Among other functions, the nonprofit Common Ground Alliance maintains an exhaustive best practices guide for "underground safety and damage prevention." Documents like this one also provide useful explanations and diagrams for curious urbanists looking to decode street markings.

Some enthusiasts take things a step further and create more expansive guides. Artist Ingrid Burrington's book, *Networks of New York*, contains more than one hundred pages on just one color category of utility in one city: the orange that designates network infrastructure in the Big Apple. Her volume dives deeply into the history of competing telecoms, but it also lays out practical examples for identification like an arrow flanked by the letters *F* and *O,* which together indicate the path of a fiber optic line directly below a stretch of pavement. In the wild, such markings are sometimes accompanied by numbers indicating depths, names identifying associated utility companies, and abbreviations referring to the types of materials in play, such as *PLA* for plastic pipes.

Different countries have their own national, regional, and local conventions, too, which can be more or less official. In a *BBC News* article, journalist Laurence Cawley scratches the surface of London's underground utilities with some local examples, including ones that illustrate how intuitive certain codes can be. A number next to a *D* often indicates depth, for instance. For electrical lines, *H/V* means high voltage, *L/V* denotes low voltage, and *S/L* stands for street lights. For gas lines, *HP* refers to high pressure, *MP* to medium pressure, and *LP* to low pressure. Some markings are harder to understand at first glance, like a looping infinity symbol used to indicate the beginning or end of a proposed project area—a counterintuitive use of a character normally applied to things without beginnings or ends.

Biodegradable paints are typically employed to create the variously colored letters and symbols sprayed by specialists onto the streets and sidewalks of our cities. These odd hieroglyphics are then either erased in the course of excavations or simply left to fade over time, slowly making room for newer, more vibrant squiggles when the next project rolls around. While they last, though, such markings provide essential information to diggers as well as ephemeral windows for the rest of us into the complex systems running right beneath our feet.

# INITIALED IMPRESSIONS

## *Sidewalk Markings*

AS THE COUNTRY'S ORIGINAL CAPITAL AND THE BACKDROP for many key moments of American history, the city of Philadelphia is lousy with important era-defining monuments and plaques, whose grandeur can make subtler and less dramatic markers easy to miss. Amid the many statues standing in squares and tablets affixed to buildings are a series of enigmatic plaques embedded in sidewalks. The etched or embossed messages on these metal plaques read like abstract spatial koans or urban poems advising pedestrians that "Space within building lines not dedicated" or "Property behind this plaque not dedicated."

In property law, dedicating means giving over to another party—the public, for example. The wording on these plaques varies, but the basic message of these so-called easement markers is the same: you pedestrians are welcome to walk here for now, but just a heads-up—this is actually private property. To define such areas, long thin rectangular plaques are often arrayed to form a dashed demarcation line along the boundary of the property while right-angled variations are used to define the corners.

In a 2016 *PlanPhilly* article, reporter Jim Saksa explains that "the plaques are used when the property lines don't align with the building's physical dimensions or the dimensions of any sort of fencing, landscaping or other improvements that would clearly mark a boundary between the public right-of-way and private property." In other words, a passerby might assume a property line ends at a fence or hedge or the edge of a building when the actual property line might run through a sidewalk instead.

Easement laws can give people limited rights to cross other people's land but can also allow for different forms of adverse possession. As Saksa explains the concept, if someone uses a piece of property "blatantly, consistently and exclusively for a long, statutorily set amount of time—21 years in Pennsylvania—then they own it." In the case of these prescriptive easements in Philadelphia: if private owners fail to explicitly mark out their territory, someone could eventually argue they have forfeited ownership. That's why you'll see these markers embedded in sidewalks both there and in other cities. The plaques ensure that the public knows that this particular patch of sidewalk belongs to the property owner even if they allow the public to walk on it for now.

Such plaques only scratch the proverbial surface of the sidewalk etchings that comprise a cityscape. There are, of course, the ubiquitous informal markings made less than legally by ordinary citizens, like so-and-so + so-and-so with a heart around it scratched into drying concrete sidewalks. But there are formal marks, too, and not just for easements. Among the semi-permanent declarations of love, you'll find elegant signatures in many cities that were left by the construction companies that laid the sidewalk.

In California's Bay Area, sidewalks in cities like Oakland feature stamps or plaques dating back to the early 1900s when concrete began to take off as a cheap and robust alternative to brick or board walkways. Many sidewalk stamps that remain date back to the 1920s through the postwar era of rapid urban expansion. Some are wrapped with decorative borders and include construction dates, addresses, phone numbers, and even union numbers. A curious individual could write down the stamped union number, go to the union office, and look up the name of the individual who smoothed out that patch of concrete fifty years before.

In places like Chicago, these markers are ubiquitous and detailed because they are required to be under municipal law: "Before the top or finishing of concrete walks has set, the contractor or person building the walk shall place in such walk in front of each lot or parcel of property a stamp or plate giving plainly the name

and address of the contractor or person building the walk and the year in which the work was done." In turn, these markings end up becoming physical archives of urban development, telling the histories of cities and city-building businesses, and outlining tales of neighborhood construction and expansion. In the sidewalks of Berkeley, California, there are markings representing the evolution of a family business over decades. A Paul Schnoor stamp might show a date of 1908 while over in a newer neighborhood, you'll find a Schnoor & Sons stamp, presumably a rebranding that took place when the next generation began working for their dad. If you encounter an even more recent construction project, you can actually find a Schnoor Bros. mark that recalls the era after dad retired and the boys took over.

In some cases, concrete installers have effectively turned sidewalks into signage, too, naming streets at intersections, lending them additional wayfinding functions. This hasn't always gone well for cities, though. Back in 1909, an article in the *Calgary Herald* titled "Calgary Can't Spell" lamented prominent misspellings like Linclon and Secound Avenue etched into the sidewalks. The piece pressed for the prevention of "any further occurrences of the disgraceful spelling with which the names of our streets and avenues are unfadingly imprinted in the walks of stone," admonishing that "workmanship such as this might be tolerated in ramshackle frontier towns, but cannot be in Calgary." In response, municipal workers were instructed to tear out the offending slabs and thus spare this proud Albertan city further embarrassment. In San Diego and other cities, old sidewalk stamps (at least ones that are spelled right) are actively protected—construction workers are supposed to work around them wherever possible when tearing up and replacing sidewalks so these small pieces of urban history can be preserved.

These days, many cities no longer require markers on new sections of sidewalk. Some bureaucratic killjoys even mandate that contractors get a permit to sign their work, and they significantly limit the size of signature stamps—after all, these represent free and durable advertising that can last for decades or longer. But more important for us, sidewalk markings tell a rich story about who made our built environment, down to the individual worker who got down on his knees to make a piece of land smooth and walkable for generations of people. You can learn so much from reading sidewalk markings—especially when they're spelled right.

# PLANNED FAILURE

## *Breakaway Posts*

POSTS THAT HOLD UP SIGNS, STREET LIGHTS, AND UTILITY lines need to be strong and durable enough to withstand winds, storms, tsunamis, and earthquakes. Every so often, though, these same posts are called upon to do something crucial but fundamentally at odds with their everyday function: they need to break easily on impact. If hit by a fast-moving vehicle, posts need to come apart in just the right way in order to reduce damage and save lives. Engineers have spent a lot of time attempting to resolve this apparent paradox.

One of the ways to get robust posts to break properly is called a "slip base" system. Instead of using a single continuous post, a slip base approach joins two separate posts close to ground level using a connector plate. This joint allows the pair to break apart at an intended juncture. It works basically like this: a lower post is put in the ground, then an upper post is attached to it using breakaway bolts. These bolts are made to fracture or dislodge when the post gets hit hard enough, so the upper post gets knocked over while the lower post passes safely under the moving vehicle. When everything works as designed, such posts can also help slow down a vehicle and minimize damage. Subsequent infrastructure repair becomes easier as well—in many cases, a new upper post can simply be bolted onto the undamaged base post below it, which requires less material and work. The critical plate-to-plate connections underpinning slip systems can be obvious to the naked eye or tucked away under plate covers.

The connector plates of inclined slip bases take this basic engineering design a step further by being tilted at an angle relative to the ground and optimized for hits from an assumed direction of impact. Instead of simply sheering sideways, posts are actually launched up into the air on impact, ideally landing behind the car that hit them. In slow-motion crash test videos, signs arc up, twirl overhead, then land on the road surface once the vehicle has passed beneath it. The downside is that if the post is hit from an unexpected direction it might not break away at all.

Straight or angled slip bases can work in isolation, but they can also be paired with hinged upper connections that help preserve infrastructure and save lives. The telephone lines running along the tops of utility poles can in some cases help hold up a pole even if a vehicle crashes into it. Instead of falling over (potentially onto a vehicle or into a lane of traffic), a telephone pole can be designed to break off at its base and then swing up and out of the way before coming to a stop and hanging in place while the cables linking it to neighboring poles hold it up temporarily.

Slip bases and hinge systems aside, different kinds of breakaway posts can be found all over the built environment. Many of the world's stop signs are supported by joined metal posts. Their joints work differently, but the basic idea is the same: two post sections are connected in a way that makes it easier for them to break apart. An in-ground post is matched with an aboveground insert post that is designed to bend or break on impact. Once you spot them, it becomes hard to unsee these common solutions to the perpetual problem of cars crashing into signs.

People generally tend to think that the development of safer cars is what protects them in their vehicles, which is true to an extent. Quality wheels provide traction, sturdy frames resist damage, seat belts and airbags keep passengers secured and cushioned, and safety glass is designed to break into less harmful shards. In the end, though, car design and construction are just a few variables within a larger safety equation. The engineering of things people crash into plays a less conspicuous but critical role in our safety as well.

# A Little Safer

## *Emergency Boxes*

EVEN THOUGH THEY ARE GENERALLY POSITIONED AT EYE level directly adjacent to entryways and are adorned with reflective red stripes, Knox Boxes are easy to overlook. Like Kleenex, Dumpster, or the once-trademarked escalator, Knox Box is the common brand name associated with a generic thing: in this case, the rapid entry access boxes affixed to all kinds of urban architecture. When disaster strikes, these urban safes go from being functionally invisible to highly essential in an instant.

Seconds count in an emergency, so getting inside a building quickly and safely is critical. Knox Boxes offer a simple solution: when emergency personnel respond to a call and arrive on site, they use a master key or code to unlock a rapid entry access box and retrieve its contents. Inside a typical box is another key or code for accessing that specific building. So firefighters essentially have a skeleton key that opens all of the boxes in their area. With that one key, they can effectively gain entry to the huge array of buildings they are charged to protect, including apartments, stores, office complexes, art museums, and more.

There are various types of Knox Boxes. Some boxes work like small safes, providing access to a single key or set of building keys. There are also more advanced ones that flip open to reveal control panels with more complex functionality. Some have switches that allow responders to disable power or gas lines or sprinkler systems in cases of false alarms.

In the absence of at least a basic access box, firefighters and paramedics would have to wait to be let in or physically break into buildings, leading to injuries and

damaged property. In light of potential broken-down doors, busted-up windows, or burned-down buildings, adding a small box to the outside of a building seems like a smart option.

From a security perspective, these access boxes may sound like a perfect opportunity for a burglar to go on a robbery spree, but building owners and key users are aware of the risks and take precautions. Some building managers also tie their boxes to larger security alarm systems that will trigger when anyone accesses them. As for the master keys that open the boxes, some fire departments employ tracking functionality to avoid losing them or letting them fall into the wrong hands. Though cities and businesses don't always agree on the necessity of having Knox Boxes, many people feel that the rewards outweigh the risks, so you can spot these clever little boxes everywhere.

# CAMOUFLAGE

THERE ARE BEAUTIFUL PIECES OF civic infrastructure that feed the soul—from ancient ornate aqueducts to structurally expressive modern bridges. Generally speaking, though, most infrastructure doesn't get this royal treatment. Rather than making an exhaust port or an electrical substation into a flamboyant display of modern engineering, we often do the next best thing: we hide them. The camouflaging of everything from oil derricks to cell phone towers can be so devious and varied, it can sometimes be difficult to distinguish between what's real and what isn't.

LEFT: *Fake facade in front of a subway exhaust opening in Paris*

# THORNTON'S SCENT BOTTLE

## *Stink Pipes*

INITIALLY ENVISIONED AS AN OPEN PUBLIC SPACE BY THE aptly named architect Francis Greenway, Sydney's Hyde Park is Australia's oldest park. In the late 1700s, this open space had been primarily used by locals to graze animals and gather firewood. Over time, the area became a place where children played and cricket matches were held. In the 1850s—as the city and neighborhood around it continued to evolve—grass, trees, running water, and monuments were added. The park became increasingly formal and grand, a place for political orations and official gatherings for visiting royalty. One of its most outstanding features from that era is a towering obelisk.

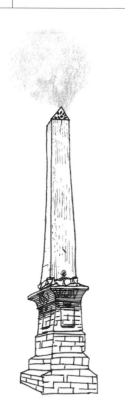

Inspired by Cleopatra's Needles—a series of ancient Egyptian relics now in London, Paris, and New York—the Hyde Park Obelisk was unveiled in 1857 under the tenure of Sydney mayor George Thornton. The roughly fifty-foot-tall monument sits on a twenty-foot-tall sandstone base; its tapered sides are wrapped in sphinxes and serpents. Locals were so enamored with their revamped park and its exotic centerpiece that after the mayor gave his speech at the unveiling "he was carried on the shoulders of stalwart men" to a nearby hotel, according to one newspaper account.

As the fervor died down, however, people began to notice a strong, unpleasant smell wafting off this otherwise impressive monument, which led it to become known by another name: Thornton's Scent Bottle. The tower's noxious emissions were not accidental but a product of its actual design intent. Like many other seemingly innocuous sculptures in cities around the world, this obelisk served two primary purposes: one aesthetic and one functional. It was not just an impressive display of cosmopolitan splendor but a means to vent gases from the city's underground sewer system.

The idea of using a grand monument to ventilate a sewer may seem strange, but the city's sewage system was a new technology for Australia at the time. On the functional side, engineers had developed two basic types of sewer vents—educt and induct. The induct drew in air while the educt allowed lighter gases back out. Pressure, odor, and disease had to be addressed in the system, so they were addressed in style, starting with the Hyde Park Obelisk's eductive design. The resulting obelisk is both infrastructure and landmark. Since its erection, the obelisk has been the subject of several modifications and repairs, but it has mostly been preserved in its original form.

The precedent of the Hyde Park Obelisk inspired other early ornate brick ventilation shafts around Sydney. In other major cities, sewage exhaust designs can be a bit more of a mixed bag—many so-called stink pipes around London are relatively utilitarian affairs. Some are dressed up a bit to look like monuments or lampposts, but most could be mistaken for rusted flagpoles. The Sydney obelisk, meanwhile, is still in use today, though its function has shifted slightly. It is now used as a vent for stormwater runoff rather than the smelly city sewer system. It's now a monument in its own right, too, having been added to the New South Wales State Heritage Register in 2002. In the end, this faux monument to Cleopatra became a real monument to modern cities and the way they have adapted to new kinds of infrastructure.

# EXHAUSTIVE OUTLETS

## *Fake Facades*

THE CONTROVERSIAL *EHEKARUSSELL* SCULPTURE IN Nuremberg, Germany, features sets of larger-than-life bronze figures arrayed around a low pool that depict the ups and downs of domestic married life. From young love to the death of a spouse, the vivid scenes on this "marriage merry-go-round" capture a lifetime of joys and sorrows, passions and pains, in explicit ways that many local residents were not excited to confront on leisurely strolls through the historic city. The dramatic sculpture serves an even more notable purpose beyond aesthetics, though; it's placed strategically to conceal an exhaust port for one of the city's U-Bahn lines. Completed in the 1980s, this installation is a relatively recent example in a long tradition of subway ventilation camouflage, infrastructure that runs the gamut from small and sculptural to huge and architectural.

When the world's first urban underground railway system opened in 1863, British civil engineers knew that venting the tunnels would be essential to keeping passengers healthy and happy—or, at the very least, alive. At the time, trains used condensers to cool steam and reduce emissions, but they still needed open-air stretches to vent exhaust. The Metropolitan Railway, which would later become the London Underground, began excavating routes using a cut-and-cover approach with this in mind. Section by section, the ground was dug up to lay tracks and then covered back over except in select segments left open for ventilation. As the routes were planned out, they inevitably carved through areas that had already been built up. Among the buildings standing in the way of the London Underground were 23 and 24 Leinster Gardens, situated right in the middle of a row of historic homes in a posh neighborhood. Here, however, route developers saw a site-specific opportunity.

Instead of leaving a gaping ventilation hole in the ground, which would not go over well in upmarket Bayswater, a facade was erected at the Leinster Gardens site to match the adjacent mid-Victorian houses. Largely indistinguishable from the neighboring buildings, with fluted Corinthian columns flanking a grand front entrance and balustraded balconies cantilevering out above, it looks like a house, but this grand display is only about a foot deep. Behind it is a gaping hole in the ground with braces and metal struts that stabilize the opening and prop up the facade. While the overall effect is largely convincing, especially at a distance, there are clues in the camouflage suggesting something is amiss. Knock on the door and no one will answer—as pizza delivery drivers sent there by prank callers have discovered. The biggest giveaways, though, are the gray painted rectangles where one would expect to see windowpanes. This is a flaw that betrays similar structures around the world.

Passing by 58 Joralemon Street in Brooklyn, New York, it would be easy to dismiss the three-story brick structure as just another Greek Revival residence in a row of similar homes. It has many of the same features as its neighbors: its height and proportions are similar and there is a staircase leading up to a distinctively framed front door. The longer one looks at the front, however, the more it becomes apparent that this is no ordinary building. The windows and the muntins, frames, and lintels

around them are all jet black. This building is, in fact, a ventilation vector for the subway line running underneath it as well as an emergency egress point for passengers should something awful happen on the train below. In this case, the building is real, but it has been gutted and repurposed. Whether they are purpose-built or adapted, such structures present a fun puzzle, a site-specific mystery like a trompe l'oeil rendered in three dimensions.

# C<small>ATALYTIC</small> D<small>IVERTERS</small>

## *Ventilation Buildings*

B<small>UILT IN THE</small> 1920<small>S TO CONNECT</small> N<small>EW</small> Y<small>ORK AND</small> J<small>ERSEY</small> City, the Holland Tunnel wasn't the first underwater tunnel, but it was an exceptionally ambitious project for its time. Carving out the tunnel through mud and bedrock was part of the challenge, but the more daunting task was to accommodate a huge number of gas-guzzling cars and trucks continuously spewing their poisonous exhaust. Skeptics were concerned that ventilating such a long span would be impossible, resulting in dangerous if not deadly conditions for drivers.

Project engineers worked with government agencies and universities to address this colossal engineering challenge and prove the proposed tunnel's safety to the public. A test tunnel hundreds of feet long was enclosed inside an abandoned mine to try out ventilation strategies. Additionally, a group of Yale University student volunteers spent hours in airtight chambers while researchers pumped carbon monoxide inside to determine human tolerances and side effects. (Oh, to be a student in the early 1900s!) Researchers concluded that air would need to be pushed through the tunnels at nearly one thousand cubic feet per second to keep drivers and passengers from asphyxiating. Thanks to an abundance of cautious engineering, the air quality in the tunnel would turn out to be better than it was on many surface streets in New York City. (To be fair, that is setting quite a low bar.)

The key to this ventilation system lies not only in the tunnel itself but also in a series of buildings surrounding it that stick high up into the air and still operate today. A pair of concrete ventilation-shaft structures flank the Hudson River along the shore while two more in the river stand more than one hundred feet above the water. These four structures are equipped with dozens of huge intake and exhaust fans that can replace the entire volume of air inside the tunnel every minute and a half.

Engineer Clifford Holland, the tunnel's namesake, may be the project's most famous contributor, but Norwegian architect Erling Owre designed these critical ventilation buildings. Considering that he was creating a glorified exhaust port, Owre really went above and beyond, making not just functionalist frameworks but also designing works of cutting-edge architecture. "Owre brought a Scandinavian sensibility to the drafting table—minimalism, craftsmanship, form," explains John Gomez, founder of the Jersey City Landmarks Conservancy. "He would have been schooled in the traditional ... [the] Romanesque, the Byzantine and the Gothic—but also the newly established Bauhaus in Germany, Russian Constructivism, and the architecture of Le Corbusier and Frank Lloyd Wright."

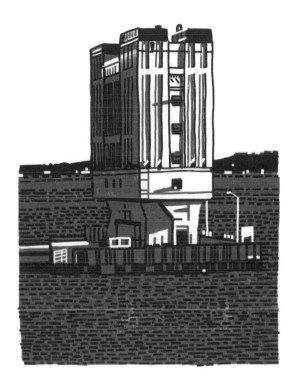

Synthesizing these influences, Owre's approach to the Holland Tunnel project was groundbreaking, with its "spectacular steel girders, colossal poured-in-place concrete columns and yellow cathedral brick," writes Gomez, "all expressed through slender strings of rounded arches, corbeled courses, glass louvre panels, small gargoyle heads and striking cantilevered bases." The resulting buildings looked bold and contemporary, like Frank Lloyd Wright's Larkin Administration building or a library or some kind of civic center. They were a fusion of architecture and infrastructure, and a harbinger of the coming car age that embodied an elegant transition into Modernism and, of course, New Jersey.

# Neighborhood Transformers

## *Electrical Substations*

RANGING IN APPEARANCE FROM MODEST SINGLE-FLOOR cottages to multistory mansions, there's no single aesthetic feature common to the buildings that both house and hide Toronto's regional energy infrastructure. Walls, roofs, doors, windows, and landscaping help create the illusion that these are ordinary buildings, but there are telltale signs that there is more to the story.

Toronto Hydro was established in 1911, the same year that electrical power from the massive new generators at Niagara Falls first lit up the city's downtown streets. New substations were needed to connect this natural powerhouse to people's homes and convert raw energy into usable power for consumers along the way. Convincing citizens to accept ugly masses of metal and wire in their neighborhoods would have been a challenge, though, so a series of architects were hired to develop alternatives.

Some of the first pre-Depression electrical substations were constructed to be aesthetically pleasing and quite large. These were grand affairs built of stone and brick and adorned with decorative flourishes made to mimic civic institutions like museums or city halls. Then, in the post–World War II residential construction boom, smaller substations started to proliferate and take the form of more modest houses that fit naturally into domestic surroundings.

Most of these house-shaped substations were variations on a half-dozen base models designed to fit into different kinds of neighborhoods. Over the twentieth century, Toronto constructed hundreds of these structures that spanned an aesthetic spectrum from ranch-style houses with asymmetrical rooflines supported by post-and-beam construction to faux-Georgian mansions with gabled roofs and triangular plinths above their doors.

Usually, "breakers and voltage dials are located in the main part of the house," explains local journalist Chris Bateman, while "unsightly heavy equipment necessary for converting high voltage electricity to a current suitable for domestic consumption [is] usually in a brick building at the rear." Inside, the utility of these buildings is obvious. They are packed with equipment and a smattering of chairs for visiting engineers. But even on the outside, there are subtler hints that these buildings are not what they appear to be.

Many of these residential-looking substations feature windows or doors that seem out of place or overly industrial for a house, while others feature landscaping that is often a little too perfectly designed and maintained. In some cases, neighborhoods have changed, and surrounding buildings have gotten bigger, dwarfing the cozy-looking little wood or brick substation structures and causing them to stand out more. Arrays of security cameras around their perimeters are also obvious clues, as are city or utility company vehicles parked in their driveways. There is also the more general and uncanny sense of déjà vu that builds up over time from seeing nearly identical fake houses over and over again in different locations.

Toronto Hydro has stopped adding new residential-looking substations and has even started tearing some down as new technology has made them obsolete and occasionally dangerous. One actually exploded in 2008, resulting in a fire and a local power outage, which, naturally, concerned citizens living next to similar structures. Area residents are likely to see fewer of these over time—or at least ones still housing infrastructure. In fact, some substations have since been repurposed and transformed into the very houses they were designed to imitate.

# Cellular Biology

## *Wireless Towers*

WHEN ENGINEERS AT BELL LABS FIRST ENVISIONED A modern wireless communications network in the 1940s, they imagined relay towers that would provide continuous coverage by passing calls from tower to tower as people moved between zones. As commercial cellular towers began to sprout up in the 1970s, diagrams depicting their coverage areas looked like blobby plant or animal cells pressed up against one another—hence the name "cell phones."

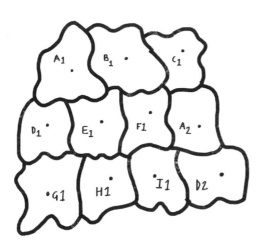

$O_i$: $i$TH CELL USING CHANNEL SET Q
● : TRANSMITTER LOCATION

The engineers developing these systems and drawing these illustrations presumably never guessed that many of the actual towers in this network would later be designed to also mimic nature, disguised as various species of trees to make them more inconspicuous.

As mobile phones became more popular in the 1980s, more and more cellular network towers had to be built, most of which were relatively utilitarian and industrial-looking affairs. This naturally led to predictable NIMBY (not-in-my-back-yard) criticisms from area residents who saw these additions as eyesores. Thus, an array of camouflage techniques emerged in parallel with this expanding technology, pioneered by companies like Larson Camouflage in Tucson, Arizona. This particular firm was well positioned to shift into a new industry; for years, the company had faked natural environments, building faux landscapes with artificial rocks and greenery for Disney parks as well as

pseudo-wild settings for museum exhibits and zoos. Larson debuted their first faux tree towers in 1992, just a few years before the legal landscape around cell towers underwent a big shift.

The Telecommunications Act of 1996 restricted the ability of communities to regulate the placement of towers by telecom companies, which was frustrating to municipal governments. Unable to fully control or block construction outright, some areas responded with ordinances requiring new towers to be camouflaged. Suddenly, aesthetic subterfuge went from desirable to mandatory. Some new towers were hidden entirely out of sight inside of tall architectural elements, like the steeples of churches, while others were integrated with structures like water towers or flagpoles that were either extant or purpose-built to serve as part of the disguise. Still, there were many places where these kinds of obvious human artifacts would stand out, so the idea of cell towers looking like trees really began to take root.

In the decades that followed, business flourished for these camouflage companies as cell phone usage proliferated. Larson expanded its range of trees to blend into different regional environments. The single-pole cell tower is often called a monopole so, naturally, the first cell tower Larson disguised as a pine tree was called Mono-Pine. This was soon followed by Mono-Palms and Mono-Elms—they even made ones that look like saguaro cacti. Today, there are hundreds of thousands of cellular towers across the United States, many of which are camouflaged in some way by companies like Larson.

Some of these fakes are well disguised, but others stand out in part because of costs and other challenges. Camouflage can add more than $100,000 to cell tower construction prices, leading frugal clients to skimp on branches. Adding more branches costs more in itself but also adds more weight, necessitating a sturdier trunk and thus additional expense. Cell towers also have to reach high to function well, which can make them look awkward in groves of trees half their height. In the flat landscape of Las Vegas, some faux-palm towers can be seen from miles away. And, of course, seasonal change in many places can make these camouflaged towers stick out more. Faux pines may remain evergreen like their natural neighbors, but deciduous lookalikes become freakish oddities when the real trees around them shed their leaves.

In the end, some semi-camouflaged towers can ironically wind up standing out more than bare-bones, functionalist steel ones would, falling into a kind of botanical "uncanny valley" between natural trees and utility poles. Camouflaging towers as trees is clever, but there is arguably something simple, honest, and clear-cut about more functionalist tower designs. Things don't have to look natural to be beautiful. But setting aesthetic judgments of functionalist industrial chic and ungainly faux greenery aside, it can be fun to keep an eye out for the fakes.

# RESOURCEFUL ARTIFICE

## *Production Wells*

STANDING MORE THAN 150 FEET TALL, THE SO-CALLED Tower of Hope on the campus of Beverly Hills High School started out as a bland concrete spire. A few decades ago, a layer of colorful mural art was added to this structure, but even with this attempt to beautify the towering enclosure, it stood out as strangely tall and apparently functionless in the landscape. Behind its tapered walls, though, sat an array of machinery installed to harvest hundreds of barrels of oil a day and large volumes of natural gas. For years, these outputs fueled the school's annual operating budget, though the presence of the tower grew more controversial over time.

The phenomenon of urban drilling in the Los Angeles area is neither new nor limited to posh neighborhoods. In the 1890s, what was then a small town of around fifty thousand people became the center of an energy boom. By 1930, California was responsible for a quarter of the world's oil output. In some places, metal oil derricks pumping crude out of the ground were set so close to one another that their legs overlapped. Across large swaths of LA, this equipment was packed in, creating what looked like artificial forests of denuded trees. Strange, science fiction–worthy landscapes of tall towers served as backdrops for beachfront activities, creating uncanny juxtapositions of industrial-age machinery alongside scenes of carefree recreation. Easily forgotten amid film-centric nostalgia for the fashionable and carefully staged Golden Age of Hollywood was a nakedly industrial and roughshod rush to extract black gold from beneath the city's surface.

Over time, many derricks and pumpjacks were removed as oil patches dried up and operations were consolidated. Those that remain can be found in the parking lots of fast food restaurants, fenced off alongside homes and highways, hidden behind rows of trees alongside parks, or even tucked into sand traps at fancy golf courses. Taller operations, like the one in Beverly Hills, are often dressed up to look like chimneys or clad in the shells of bland office building facades. Many are acoustically camouflaged, too, with sound-dampening materials.

Some newer operations have also moved offshore to oceanic rigs and artificial islands, including a particularly prominent chain located near Long Beach. The THUMS Islands are the only decorated oil islands in the United States, taking the scale of such camouflage to the next level. These tropical-looking faux utopias boast distinctive and flashy buildings surrounded by palm trees and sound-mitigating landscape elements. The original name of THUMS was an acronym for Texaco, Humble (now Exxon), Union Oil, Mobil, and Shell, but the chain was later renamed the Astronaut Islands, which seems fitting given the space-age look of their architecture.

These islands were constructed in the 1960s using hundreds of tons of boulders from a nearby natural island as well as millions of yards of material dredged from

the San Pedro Bay. Around $10,000,000 was spent on what was termed "aesthetic mitigation." This part of the project was overseen by theme-park architect Joseph Linesch, who had experience crafting elaborate artificial landscapes for Disneyland in California and EPCOT Center in Florida. The quirky camouflage structures were described by one critic as "part Disney, part Jetsons, part Swiss Family Robinson," and their disguises largely work, in part because they are mostly seen from afar. The structures on the islands can easily be mistaken for buildings in an offshore hotel complex or luxury resort. Drillers have pumped more than a billion barrels of oil from this patch during the past half century, all while hiding in plain sight out on the water.

Back on the mainland, however, the once-booming LA oil industry has slowed. Over the decades, production from the Tower of Hope dwindled to around 10% of its peak output. A few years back, Venoco, which managed the derrick, filed for bankruptcy, leaving the fate of the tower in limbo. Meanwhile, California has turned more toward green energy, which has led to a decline in the practice of harvesting fossil fuels in the middle of metropolises. At some point, no amount of camouflage can provide enough cover for something if the thing being camouflaged no longer serves the public interest.

SEA LEVEL VIEW

# ACCRETIONS

A S CITIES AGE, THEY GET USED AND abused by the people who live in them. We sometimes patch what we damage, but other times we let things fall apart. As a result, most urban environments are a hodgepodge of haphazard fixes and odd vestiges. Yet pointless leftovers and accumulated remnants are just as much a part of the city as thoroughly considered, still-functional functional objects. Such imperfect items are not always the prettiest examples of what we can make, but they perfectly represent our flawed and complex humanity.

LEFT: *Anchor plates, love locks, and constructive reuse*

# Seeing Stars

## *Anchor Plates*

Metal stars set against white mortar stripes along red-brick facades could at first seem like patriotic expressions, especially in a city like Philadelphia. However, these metal plates that dot many of the historic row homes there and in other cities around the world are not strictly decorative—in fact, they serve a vital structural function.

In many old brick row houses, floor and roof joists run side to side, connecting load-bearing party walls that run perpendicular to the street. As a result, the front and back facades of these homes aren't very well connected to core building supports. The problem, explains Philadelphia architect Ian Toner, "is that sometimes these end walls can start to bulge outwards, since they're only connected to the rest of the houses at their edges." The risks can become even more serious in cases where poor-quality lime mortar was used by builders. Shifting foundations, gravity, and time can exacerbate the dangers and threaten these buildings; in some cases, there is even a risk of catastrophic collapse.

If bricks are already bulging, they may need to be pushed back into place, but that's only the first step. A common engineering retrofit used to stabilize such structures involves bolts or tie rods and anchor plates. A rod can be run through the bricks and threaded into the joists behind them to create a better structural connection between the facade and the interior supports. On the outside, tension rods are braced by what amount to big wide washers, which spread loads across adjacent bricks.

A star shape is a logical choice for these kinds of wall anchor systems because points reaching out in multiple directions help distribute loads. Stars also work well aesthetically because they can be rotated and still look good. But squares, octagons, circles, and other more elaborate and ornate shapes can also be found on historic brick and other masonry buildings around the world.

These types of retrofits reveal a lot about how buildings used to be constructed, the deterioration that comes with age, the changes in safety standards, and differences in local conditions that require certain interventions. In places like the Bay Area where seismic activity requires extra masonry reinforcement, anchor plates help keep bricks from falling off facades during earthquakes. Whatever their shape or function, wall anchors can be lovely additions to an exterior brick wall, and they are certainly more attractive than the alternative: a pile of bricks.

# SCARCHITECTURE

## *Urban Infill*

AS CITIES EVOLVE, ARCHITECTURE OFTEN EXPANDS TO fill in abandoned routes originally designed for cars, trains, or other forms of transportation. Once roads or tracks are gone, the voids that remain are sometimes rendered solid in the form of new buildings, their edges conforming to the shapes of forgotten thoroughfares. The result is a kind of architectural scar tissue—as if the built environment were filling in and healing old wounds. At street level, the effect can be subtle. Individual buildings may feature an unusual angle here or curve there, but when seen from above, larger patterns emerge that span blocks or even entire neighborhoods. Such scars are especially noticeable when they are set against the comprehensive planning schemes of urban grids.

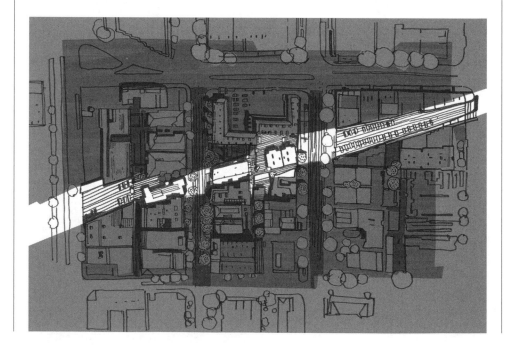

In growing industrial cities, trains often left impressive marks in their wake. Across a whole section of Berkeley, California, a number of homes are aligned not with the street like their neighbors but with a slash carved by an old right-of-way for the Union Pacific Railroad. Here and in other places, central rail lines fell into disuse, and the empty spaces they left behind became valuable real estate destined for reuse. Infill architecture retains the shapes of old voids, inadvertently preserving large traces of local urban history.

"The notion that every city has these deeper wounds and removals that nonetheless never disappear is just incredible to me," Geoff Manaugh writes of similar "ghost streets" in Los Angeles. "You cut something out—and it becomes a building a generation later. You remove an entire street—and it becomes someone's living room." Repurposed routes can shape open spaces as well, including parking lots, greenways, and linear parks. Whatever form infill takes, these layers become a sort of urban palimpsest. Parts of cities get erased and overwritten, but you can often still see evidence of what came before. In modern rectilinear cities, scars are often more obvious and exceptional. In older cities around the world, though, layers of scar tissue can build up over time to the point where it becomes hard to tell when and how the cuts happened. Taken together, these curious traces can tell stories of iteration around cities once wrapped by walls, devastated by disasters, or simply divided by railroad tracks.

# LINES OF SIGHT

## *Relay Nodes*

THE CENTURYLINK BUILDING IN MINNEAPOLIS IS A MODestly elegant skyscraper in the city's skyline. It has a relatively uniform granite exterior with long vertical lines that are a hallmark of the Art Deco style. "It was an all-Minnesota project" when it was built in the 1930s, recalls James Lileks of the *Star Tribune*—its stone was "from Kasota and Morton, the cement was from Duluth, and the steel was sourced from the Mesabi Range." The building was already a regional icon when a bold new crown standing multiple stories high was installed on top of it in the 1960s, changing its function and its appearance for decades to come. Wrapping around the top of the structure, this new microwave antenna array positioned the building on the forefront of then-modern technology. With this addition, the structure became a key node in a vast and unprecedented line-of-sight communications relay network designed to span the entire country, remnants of which can still be seen on rural mountaintops and urban towers today.

Telephone service first came to Minneapolis in 1878, facilitated by a switchboard located in city hall, right across the street from the future site of the CenturyLink Building. A network that started with just eleven lines ballooned to nearly two thousand within a decade. By 1920, close to 100,000 lines were in service, and a new dedicated space was needed. The Northwestern Bell Telephone Building, the initial name of the CenturyLink Building, was constructed with switchboards, offices, mechanical rooms, and space for around one thousand employees. But technology continued to evolve and phone service continued to expand.

Responding to increased demand for long-distance service and the rise of home televisions in the 1950s, AT&T rolled out a new technological solution. Their system of microwave relay towers would transmit information from coast to coast, bouncing signals from tower to tower across the United States. It was the largest network of its kind at the time and was technologically advanced in its use of wireless microwaves, which made it easier and faster to deploy than conventional transmission wire. Huge directional antennas the size of SUVs conveyed phone conversations and television signals from the era of the Kennedy assassination through the resignation of Nixon. Like interstate highways and railways, communication via microwaves required long direct paths and shaped cities accordingly.

In the 1990s, AT&T sold off most of what remained of this network. Largely obsolete in today's world of fiber optics, satellites, and wireless internet, many of the towers have been taken down or retrofitted to serve cellular data functions. Some of the more remote buildings between cities that once formed the backbone of this transcontinental network have been bought by private owners and turned

into vacation cabins or doomsday bunkers. Others serve as emergency communication network backups in rural areas.

In Minneapolis, it was announced in 2019 that the crown of microwave relays on the CenturyLink Building would be coming down. A design feature once hailed as "modernistic" and lauded in a 1967 article for its role in improving "the over-all appearance of the rooftop, the silhouette of the building and the skyline of the city" was destined to be dismantled and removed. "When the antenna is gone," laments Lileks, "the building will likely look a little more solemn and serious," stripped of its "flamboyant headgear."

In other cities, remnant relays still in place can be easy to miss among HVAC outcroppings, satellite dishes, and other miscellanea sticking up from urban rooftops. Once their distinctive shape is familiar, though, they go from being easy to overlook to being hard not to notice. Some leftover arrangements hide in plain sight, too—so integrated into the visual design of prominent rooftops that removing them would reshape skylines. So, strangely enough, some of these derelict relays are actively maintained for the sake of appearances.

# THOMASSONS

## *Maintained Remains*

WALKING TO LUNCH WITH SOME FRIENDS ONE DAY IN 1972, Japanese artist Genpei Akasegawa noticed an oddly useless staircase alongside a building. A few steps led up to a landing, but there was no door at the top where he would have reasonably expected to see one. What struck him as particularly curious, though, was that the railing running along these stairs to nowhere had been recently repaired. Despite serving no function, the stairs were apparently being kept in working order. On further excursions, Akasegawa began to notice more and more inexplicably maintained features like this in the built environment.

Cities are forever evolving, with new structures being added and old ones getting torn down, renovated, or expanded. In the process, small bits and pieces get left behind, vestiges of former iterations: utility poles without wires, empty pipes, useless staircases. Such remnants are usually removed or left to decay, but sometimes they are cleaned, polished, repaired, and repainted despite their utter lack of purpose.

Akasegawa was entranced by these curiosities—items with no function that were still maintained. He considered them a kind of art, so he began writing irreverently about these objects in a countercultural photo-magazine column.

Readers soon started sending him photos of other examples from around the world, which he evaluated by their degree of uselessness and the recency of their apparent maintenance. In 1985, he published a book collecting a number of these images and his reflections on them.

By this time, Akasegawa had coined a term for these leftovers, one that to a casual observer might seem to come out of left field. He called them *Thomassons*—after Gary Thomasson, a talented American baseball player who played for the Los Angeles Dodgers, the New York Yankees, and the San Francisco Giants before moving to Japan to play for the Yomiuri Giants, Akasegawa's favorite team. Thomasson was paid a lot to move and work overseas, but once there, everything changed. He went from being an all-star to nearly setting the all-time strikeout record in Japan's Central League in 1981. He remained in a rut until his contract ran out. He wound up mostly sitting on a bench while making a lot of money for doing nothing. He was useless but maintained.

As the concept became more widespread, Akasegawa came to have mixed feelings about using the word *Thomasson* to signify a useless but maintained object. He had a lot of respect for Gary Thomasson and didn't want to offend the player's fans or family. But the name stuck, and in the end, Thomasson achieved a certain status as an eponym that other baseball players could only dream of. Thomassons are also delightful to find, so one could argue that the association isn't as negative as it might seem at first. Thomassons are treasures waiting to be discovered and analyzed—whether or not they are art, they are an intriguing lens through which to look at and understand change over time.

# ACCUMULATIVE CONTROVERSY

## *Love Locks*

THE POPULARITY OF LOVE PADLOCKS (ALSO KNOWN SIM-ply as love locks) can be traced back to the story of a schoolteacher named Nada and an army officer named Relja in the small Serbian town of Vrnjačka Banja. The couple pledged their love to each other while standing on a local bridge before Relja went off to fight in World War I. While battling the Central Powers in Greece, however, Relja found a new flame and married her instead. Nada, as the story goes, died from grief in the wake of this betrayal. A tradition was born of this tragedy: local couples began to etch their names onto padlocks, attach them to the bridge, and throw the key into the water, a symbolic and public act sealing their commitment to each other. When the poet Desanka Maksimović heard the story, she memorialized the tale in a poem that would spread the practice.

Today in Vrnjačka Banja, metal railings along the "Bridge of Love" are covered in loads of padlocks of different shapes, sizes, colors, and materials that are engraved or otherwise marked with names, dates, and messages. Around the world, love locks can be found on bridges, walls, fences, and monuments, especially in famously romantic cities like Paris, Rome, and New York.

People love love locks, but cities are often a bit more on the fence about them. In the Australian capital of Canberra, love locks were removed in 2015 for fear of weighing down a bridge; later that year in Melbourne, 20,000 locks were clipped and stripped from a bridge when cable wires began to sag under the extra weight. In Paris, the Pont des Arts pedestrian bridge struggled under the burden of 700,000 locks until authorities began removing entire panels covered with them. Here and elsewhere, acrylic and glass panels have been installed below railings to foil the placement of additional locks.

What began as a simple gesture of romance has become a global (if sometimes controversial) activity. In some cities, love locks are considered vandalism, and if lovers are caught affixing them, they may be greeted with a fine. In other places, locks are actively encouraged with structures specially built to support them. There are dedicated chains for affixing locks of love strung along parts of the Great Wall of China, for instance—indeed, some believe that love locks have their roots in ancient China, not modern Serbia. Meanwhile, fake metal trees were put up next to a popular bridge in Moscow to give people an alternative place to attach locks. Approaches like this echo the treatment of graffiti in some cities where special mural-making walls are presented as alternatives to illegal vandalism. Like kissing the Blarney Stone in Ireland or sticking a wad of gum on a rather gross wall in Seattle, putting up a lock may seem like a novel lark, but when a lot of people line up to do the same thing, such traditions can lose their romantic appeal.

# SPOLIA OF WAR

## *Constructive Reuse*

DURING WORLD WAR II, MORE THAN 600,000 STEEL stretchers were assembled by British authorities to be deployed in the aftermath of German air raids. These stretchers were designed to be strong and durable but also easy to disinfect in the wake of a gas attack. After the war, though, a surplus of them remained, which led the London County Council to put them to surprising use throughout the city—not as monuments or memorials but as railings along the edges of various estates. Most are black with wire mesh and curved supports that served to raise the stretchers off the ground. These curves make them easy to identify in the wild. Stretchers turned on their sides, suspended between vertical support posts, and arrayed in rows effectively form long fences in places like Peckham, Brixton, Deptford, Oval, and other parts of South and East London. Exposed to the elements, though, many are deteriorating.

"Some local authorities have removed sets of railings in recent years due to their degradation," according to the Stretcher Railing Society. This organization aims to get other people as excited as they are about repurposed World War II stretchers by cataloging locations around the city and getting local councils involved in preservation efforts. They argue that "these railings are an important part of our heritage and should be preserved as an integral element in the fabric of these iconic mid-century housing estates."

These aren't the first or only tangible reminders of past wars around the United Kingdom. Some old pillboxes and bunkers have been converted into sheds and homes. Entire sea forts around the British coast have been turned into private island retreats, pirate radio stations, and even one high-profile micronation called Sealand. More common and less obvious, though, are smaller recycled bits and pieces, like stretcher railings or bollards made from ship cannons.

Bollards are short posts and have been used for centuries to moor ships, manage urban traffic, and help keep pedestrians safe from carriages and later from cars. Historically, most bollards were made of wood, but as early as the seventeenth century, old metal cannons half-buried in the ground began to serve as robust alternatives.

In England, there are tales of Royal Navy ships bringing French cannons back from the Napoleonic Wars and planting them as trophies in East London dockyards, but this reuse was actually about economics, not celebrating victories. Many of the reused cannons were made of iron and deemed unsuitable for recycling because of their low scrap value; when more valuable cannons were captured, they were usually melted down for their constituent metals.

Converted cannons can still be found sticking out of streets and sidewalks around Britain, often serving as traffic barriers or survey markers. Around the world, people pass by cannon bollards all the time—these stalwart remnants can be found shielding building corners in Halifax, Nova Scotia, and protecting pedestrians from cars along the sidewalks of Havana, Cuba. Long after most cannons were melted down or otherwise recycled, cannon-style bollards have continued to pop up in cities, including ones that were not made to be used as weapons at all. The aesthetic has caught on, and as a result, it can be hard to tell the real cannons from the fakes—but they are all real bollards.

Urban reuse is as old as cities. Wherever there has been long-term human habitation, there are instances of spolia, from the Latin *spolia,* as in the "spoils" of war. Historically, the term has been used to refer to stone that has been taken from one demolished structure and then incorporated into something new. As with metal stretcher railings or cannon bollards, such reuse can be driven by practicality. After all, why manufacture something new when one can loot it from the felled ranks of one's vanquished foes? The etymology of spolia may seem morbid, but archeologist Peter Sommer offers a more positive takeaway. He observes that "we all accept that visual artists, writers, poets or musicians, even scholars, build their creations on the works of those before them, often incorporating and 'reusing' their source material." Spolia, he suggests, have functioned in a similar fashion throughout human history.

Today, the idea of repurposing historically significant artifacts in works of new architecture would generally be frowned upon by most architects and art historians, not to mention a lot of everyday citizens. Nobody would advocate stripping the Pantheon for parts or turning it into a Dunkin' Donuts. Even Postmodernists who sought to bring back variety and delight by using historical styles and ornamentation drew inspiration rather than actual physical material from ancient works. Much of what we see in cities around the world is relatively new, fabricated to fit its current function. Amid these newer constructions, though, many of the building blocks of our built environments are older than they may first appear, having been refitted to serve new purposes across generations of urban evolution.

*Chapter 2*

# CONSPICUOUS

I T'S OFTEN SAID THAT GOOD DESIGN IS invisible. When designed objects are functioning properly, they work without calling attention to themselves. However, some things are designed specifically to be seen. The job of warning signals, plaques, flags, and the like is to communicate something important: *You need to stop! Safety is this way! You are in Chicago!* When they fail to get noticed, they fail to do their job. The very best visual signals communicate an incredible amount of meaning with a quick glance in their direction.

# IDENTITY

T HE CHARACTER OF A CITY OR neighborhood is often established through a haphazard array of independent actions by a variety of actors. A new café opens on the block. A Victorian home gets renovated with bright colors. A yearly block party brings all the neighbors together. Zooming out, though, there is a broader layer of top-down municipal efforts that serve to create a specific civic identity. If you ask us, the best place to start is a good flag.

LEFT: *Miss Manhattan figure at public library branch in New York City*

# VEXILLOLOGY RULES

## *Municipal Flags*

POCATELLO, IDAHO, HAD THE WORST CITY FLAG IN THE
United States. At least that was the verdict of a 2004 survey of 150 city flags conducted
by the North American Vexillological Association. Vexillology is the study of flags,
and like most fields where the stakes are quite low, opinions can be very intense.
Even at a glance, though, it's easy to see why respondents were unenthusiastic

about this particular specimen. As Roman Mars
explained in a widely circulated 2015 TED talk,
the flag of Pocatello was a complete mess of colors, shapes, and fonts that was made even worse
by the inclusion of distracting trademark and
copyright symbols. Of course, one could argue
that any judgment about flag design is bound to
be subjective, but in his booklet *Good Flag, Bad
Flag: How to Design a Great Flag,* vexillologist
Ted Kaye lays out some solid rules of thumb.

There are five key principles of good flag design according to Kaye, many of
which can also be applied to all kinds of other designs: (1) keep it simple, (2) use
meaningful symbolism, (3) use two or three basic colors, (4) no lettering or seals,
and (5) be distinctive or be related. In other words, a good city flag should be simple
but memorable, easy to recall, and usable at different scales. It should also feature
colors, patterns, and graphics that are meaningful and distinctive, with elements
relating to local history or civic identity.

Most people know the flag of their country. Many are also familiar with state
flags, at least their own. City to city, though, some flags are more well known than
others. The Chicago city flag is widely flown on municipal buildings but has also
permeated the public consciousness due to its striking design. It features two blue

horizontal stripes across a white field with an array of four six-pointed red stars running across the middle. The blue stripes represent water, specifically Lake Michigan and the Chicago River, while the four stars represent key moments in the city's history: the founding of Fort Dearborn;

the Chicago Fire; the Columbian Exposition, which people remember because of the White City; and the Century of Progress International Exposition, which few people remember at all.

The Chicago flag checks a lot of "good design" boxes. It is simple, symbolic, distinct, and iconic. Chicagoans from all walks of life display the flag, from punks to police. Of course, basic city pride could be the reason for all this heraldic display, but Ted Kaye notes that there can be a positive feedback loop between city flag design and civic pride. It's not just that people love the city and therefore love the flag but also that people love the city *more* because the flag is so cool. Part of the reason the Chicago flag can be found all over town is that it is so well designed that it can be deployed as a whole or in part at various scales. You'll see the six-pointed stars on coffee cups and T-shirts and even as tattoos.

Understanding the strengths of the Chicago flag may explain the relative absence of the San Francisco flag in its home city. The flag of San Francisco features a phoenix rising from the ashes, which alludes to the fires that devastated the city in the 1800s. While the symbolism is bold, its relevance is not unique. Atlanta also burned to the ground and immortalized a phoenix on its flag, and there is another American city with a phoenix prominently on its flag: a

city called Phoenix. Both the Atlanta and the Phoenix flags are superior to San Francisco's, which has a detailed illustration that would be hard to draw from memory and thus violates flag design principle number one regarding simplicity. Its depiction of the mythical bird somehow manages to look crudely illustrated and overly complicated at the same time. The flag also features a flapping ribbon adorned with Spanish phrases in small print, which are hard to read at a distance. Even worse, the city's name is spelled out in bold blue letters at the bottom. "If you need to write the name of what you're representing on your flag," asserts Ted Kaye, "your symbolism has failed."

While national flags face international publicity and scrutiny and are thus generally well designed, the process can be a bit more informal and haphazard at regional, state, and city levels. Without experience to draw on or criteria to work from, there is a tendency for people to design local flags using a hodgepodge of available municipal symbols. It is quite common for flags to be composed simply of the city seal on a solid blue background. These are what vexillologists would call a SOB, short for "seal on a bedsheet." Seals are meant to be stamped on paper and contain details that can only be deciphered up close, making them a poor choice for flags that are often seen at a distance and prone to flapping in the wind. This misappropriation of city symbolism resulted in the hot mess that was the Pocatello flag, wherein a city marketing logo was taken out of context and plopped onto a white background, trademark symbol and all, and then declared the flag.

When the aforementioned TED talk shined a spotlight on this particular flag, Pocatello took the negative publicity in stride, turning it into an opportunity to generate a better design. "Over the past year," reads a city press release from 2016, "Pocatello has received national attention for our city flag design," which experts had deemed "the worst city flag in the United States." In response, "community leaders and elected officials have taken note and a new City of Pocatello ad hoc committee will be working to create a new flag for Pocatello." In the end, competing designs were evaluated, and a finalist dubbed Mountains Left was selected to become the official replacement. The new flag features three geometrically abstracted red mountains set on a field of blue. On top of the highest peak sits a golden compass rose, which symbolizes the historical importance of transportation to the region, while a blue line running through the base of the peaks represents the Portneuf River. The design works. It has simple forms and colors, but it's distinctive and symbolic.

Many other cities around the United States are in various stages of flag redesigns as well, some driven by grassroots efforts organized by engaged citizens, many of whom cite *99% Invisible* as the catalyst for their campaigns. No city wants to be the next Pocatello, thrust into the spotlight for bad flag design. Still, it can be hard to get municipalities on board. When city leaders say that they have more important things to do than worry about a city flag, Ted Kaye responds to them with the argument that "if you had a good city flag you would have a banner for people to rally under to face those more important things." Bad city flags go unused, ceding visual branding territory to sports teams and corporate interests, which come and go. When city flags are done well, they are remixable, adaptable, and powerful long-term tools for civic engagement as well as sources of local pride.

# PUBLIC BODIES

## *Civic Monuments*

IN THE STATUARY OF NUMEROUS CITIES, THERE IS A recurring figure who has gone by many names, including *Star Maiden, Mourning Victory,* and *Priestess of Culture.* Yet all of these likenesses were based on a single woman: Audrey Munson. All over New York City, in particular, there are statues of her in various poses and states of undress: at the main branch of the public library, she leans against a white horse; at the intersection of Fifty-ninth Street and Fifth Avenue, she perches atop a fountain; on 107th and Broadway, she reclines on a bed; and on top of the Manhattan Municipal Building, she stands unusually tall, cast in gold. More than thirty statues at the Metropolitan Museum of Art were made in Munson's likeness. She adorns dozens of memorials and bridges and buildings all over this metropolis. Although her body has been immortalized in monumental works of iron and marble, her name has been largely forgotten. In the early twentieth century, however, Munson was a star who would come to be called America's first supermodel.

Like so many supermodels that would come after her, Audrey Marie Munson was scouted on the streets of the Big Apple, where she and her recently divorced mother had moved for a fresh start. One bright spring morning in 1907, a photographer approached Munson and asked if she would pose for some portraits. Her mom was invited to accompany her. These initial photo shoots were fully clothed affairs. After some success, Munson was introduced to the famous sculptor Isidore Konti. He, too, was interested in hiring Munson for his work, but for this endeavor she would have to pose "in the altogether," meaning naked. She and her mother agreed. For decades, the resulting sculptural set of three muses, each patterned after Munson, sat in the lobby of the Hotel Astor. Looking back, she called this series "a souvenir of my mother's consent."

Munson's reputation grew as she began to work for other famous artists in New York, leading her to be nicknamed Miss Manhattan by the *New York Sun*. She was known for being able to evoke a complete mood with her posture and expression—she was also known for being able to hold a pose for a really long time. Munson worked closely with the artists, learning their temperaments and familiarizing herself with their work. Her popularity grew partly in proportion to the rise of the Beaux Arts style in architecture, which incorporated a lot of ornamentation and sculpture. As this movement spread west, Audrey's likeness followed, and her image soon adorned capitol buildings and monuments on both coasts. At the 1915 Panama–Pacific International Exposition in San Francisco, three-quarters of the statues on the grounds were modeled after her. There was even a visitors' map highlighting all of their locations.

Once out west, Munson wound up in Hollywood, where filmmakers consistently cast her to play a model. Unfortunately for any potential acting career, her skill at evoking a mood and conveying rich emotions seemed to end the moment she broke pose. She was so stiff in front of the camera that she was given an acting double in some cases, a kind of low-risk stunt double who would play her part when her character was in motion, so it's no surprise that she was not destined to be a breakout film star.

As Modernism came into fashion, the decorative intricacies of the Beaux Arts style became a less popular choice for new buildings. This signaled the end of an era for Miss Manhattan. Munson eventually moved to upstate New York and spent the rest of her life between her mother's home and then, following a suicide attempt, various mental institutions.

This model's very public body had come to represent truth, memory, civic fame, the stars, and even the universe in statues and sculptures. Ultimately and tragically, the inspirational figure herself was hidden away for nearly two-thirds of her life. Still, that glorious first third immortalized Audrey Munson and placed her all over American cities, observed and admired by people who largely know nothing about her. Munson is only one of many largely unknown figures with their own life stories whose likenesses have outlasted them in cities around the world.

# FONTS OF KNOWLEDGE

## *Historical Plaques*

SEVERAL YEARS AGO, WHILE WRITER JOHN MARR WAS speaking at the Smith Memorial Student Union building at Portland State University, he asked the audience if anyone knew how the building got its name. The audience was stumped, which led him to relay the story of a young Michael Smith, who helped lead the College Bowl trivia team to an underdog victory in 1965, then tragically passed away from cystic fibrosis shortly after graduating. When asked how he knew this local story of university history, Marr explained that he had read it on a plaque prominently placed right outside the building where he was speaking and that his motto is to "always read the plaque." It's a mantra that has an obvious literal meaning, but it's also another way of reminding ourselves to constantly be on the lookout for stories embedded in our built environments.

Plaques can also bring about a new appreciation for everyday objects. In the Mission District of San Francisco, observant passersby can discover the heroic history behind a fire hydrant that sits on an otherwise ordinary sidewalk. In the wake of the 1906 earthquake that shook San Francisco, a great blaze swept through the city. Many of the water mains failed and other lines ran dry, but one hydrant continued to function. This bit of infrastructure is credited with saving the Mission District from total destruction. Today, the hydrant has been painted gold and its importance has been further memorialized with an adjacent plaque. The small marker tells a huge city-defining tale of tragedy and triumph and highlights a moment in time that reshaped a metropolis.

Different countries and cities have different rules about where official plaques can be located, how they are shaped and sized, and what they are allowed to commemorate. In some places, standardized materials, colors, and fonts help citizens and tourists identify official plaques, like the blue plaques administered by English Heritage for sites within Greater London. These round markers designate places occupied by famous historical persons and sites of significant events. They adorn the homes of cultural icons like Charles Dickens, Alfred Hitchcock, John Lennon, and Virginia Woolf.

It's important to note that plaques and historical markers don't always tell the full and literal truth. In James Loewen's book *Lies Across America,* the author points out that historical markers often say as much or more about the era they were dedicated in as they do about the specific times, places, and people they are ostensibly there to commemorate. Many markers in the American South that whitewash slavery are very much products of the turn of the twentieth century when the backlash against progressive Reconstruction was in full force. Markers in the West and elsewhere often ignore the perspective of Native Americans in favor of white colonialists' points of view.

Plaques have a lot to say about the cities they inhabit, both directly and indirectly. The edict "always read the plaque" is a great way to engage with the built environment and all the stories embedded in it, but it doesn't mean every story embossed in metal is the real or entire story—curious plaque readers should keep a critical eye on the (proverbial) fine print.

# DISTINGUISHED FEATURES

## *That Fancy Shape*

IT'S A SIMPLE SHAPE, BUT IT'S EVERYWHERE FROM fast-fashion handbags to ornate cathedral windows. A quatrefoil is easily identified as a symmetrical four-leaf clover minus the signature stem. The simple beauty of this shape is often used to convey a sense of style and sophistication—a fancy shape signifying a fancy person or neighborhood. Arrays of quatrefoils fill in the complex decorative facades of Gothic Revival architecture and the windows of old Victorian and Mission-style homes as well as cottages in Newport, Rhode Island, and the Washington National Cathedral. If you look closely enough, you can spot them in the repeating decorative patterns on metal railings, concrete bridges, and other everyday structures as well.

The word *quatrefoil* comes from the Anglo-French *quatre* (four) and the Middle English *foil* (leaves). These were first combined into a single word in the fifteenth century, but the shape dates back even further. Examples can be found in the city of Constantinople during the Byzantine Empire as well as in ancient Mesoamerica, where it was used to symbolize elements including clouds, rain, and the crossroads between celestial realms and underworlds.

Christy Anderson, an architectural historian who teaches at the University of Toronto, has traced more recent Western uses of the design back to Islamic architecture, which has a long tradition of distilling organic shapes into geometrical forms. The quatrefoil eventually made its way to Europe via the Silk Road in the patterns of carpets, velvets, and silks shipped to Europe as luxury objects.

Once in Europe, quatrefoils maintained their shape but shifted in usage and meaning. They were incorporated into stone tracery around big glass windows, which conveyed a sense of wealth in part because they were challenging to craft. Churches began to incorporate quatrefoils into reliefs, tracery, and other ornamentation, lending them religious associations bolstered by geometric similarities to the Christian cross. The symbol rose and fell in popularity throughout the years, finding different meanings in different periods and contexts. The quatrefoil was popular in Gothic and Renaissance buildings, then later in Gothic Revival architecture as the Industrial Revolution sparked a reactionary interest in ornate and organic preindustrial forms.

"In the second half of the 19th century," explains Anderson, there were a lot of "architects and designers who created pattern books of designs, which could be used by architects, masons, craftsmen—really in any field." Artisans drew on guides like Owen Jones's *The Grammar of Ornament,* which were packed with examples from all over the world—Chinese, Indian, Celtic, Turkish, Moorish, and more. Jones's book and others like it abstracted the ornamentation, taking it out of context and turning it into raw material for design inspiration that could be deployed in new materials and places. And designers have done just that, employing forms like the quatrefoil both in physical architecture and infrastructure as well as in graphic designs of all kinds.

Jones started off his 1856 book with a list of thirty-seven propositions for the creation of good decorative design. These were principles he envisioned for the arrangement of form and color in the creation of architecture and the decorative arts. For the most part, this introduction is easy to overlook compared to the dazzling patterns that follow, but the thirteenth proposition offers insight into the power of the quatrefoil: "Flowers or other natural objects should not be used as ornaments," wrote Jones, advocating instead for "conventional representations founded upon them sufficiently suggestive to convey the intended image to the mind without destroying the unity of the object they are employed to decorate." In short, abstraction is the key. When nature is rendered mathematical, something chaotic and organic is turned into something regular, comprehensible, repeatable, and ultimately beautiful. Given the proliferation of the quatrefoil, he may have been onto something. Whatever the reasons, the simplified quatrefoil has indeed become ubiquitous and coveted, a persistent symbol of luxury and high style.

# SAFETY

OUR CONTEMPORARY WELLBEING owes much to medical breakthroughs like antibiotics and vaccines, but a case can be made that the warning lights, traffic signals, road markers, and safety symbols that dot the built landscape also do their part to keep you in one piece. As the world has sped up and new invisible dangers have emerged, visual designs have evolved to keep up.

---

**LEFT:** *Traffic lights, retro-reflective studs, and recognition patterns at night*

# MIXED SIGNALS

## *Traffic Lights*

AT AN OTHERWISE QUITE ORDINARY-LOOKING INTERSECTION in Syracuse, New York, sits an upside-down traffic signal. It is the only one of its kind in the United States, and it's been curiously exceptional ever since it was erected in the early 1900s. At the time, traffic signals with their now-conventional red-over-green light configuration were a relatively new development. So when a new traffic signal came to the corner of Tompkins Street and Milton Avenue in Tipperary Hill, a neighborhood named after a county in Ireland, some locals were greatly offended by the placement of the Unionist color red over the Irish color green.

There ensued a heated back-and-forth battle over this intersection. By most accounts, a normal light was installed, tempers flared, and stones or bricks were thrown by vandals to break the red lights. This cycle repeated over and over each time the lights were fixed. Eventually, neighborhood alderman John "Huckle" Ryan stepped in and successfully petitioned to have the city invert the signal. The state, however, overturned the decision and decreed that the light should be righted once more, thus prompting a resumption of hostilities. Finally realizing the futility of resistance, officials caved and left the lights upside down for good.

In 1994, the city of Syracuse broke ground on a memorial park at one corner of the intersection. At a glance, it looks like a typical pocket park made up of conventional materials and landscaping, but closer inspection reveals a series of clues about what Tipperary Hill Memorial Park, also known as Stone Throwers' Park, was designed to commemorate. A family of sculptures situated near the street corner features a father figure pointing up at the intersection while his son, standing adjacent, carries a slingshot tucked into his bronze back pocket. Part of the park is also paved with bricks boasting the names of local donors, many of which are conspicuously Irish. The flag of Ireland flies above the park as well, hoisted up on a green flagpole. In case that was all still too subtle, the park is also partially wrapped in a green fence adorned with ornamental shamrocks. Clearly, this location has come to be a significant place for the neighborhood. The flip of the signal was a small but meaningful concession that highlights the inexorable links between culture and infrastructure.

Halfway around the world in Japan, traffic signals have also been shaped by cultural factors in a highly visible way: many go signals there are a bluish green. "Historically, there has been significant overlap in the Japanese language as it pertains to green (*midori*) and blue (*ao*)," writes Allan Richarz in an article for *Atlas Obscura.* "Blue—one of the four traditional colors originally established in the Japanese language along with red, black and white—historically encompassed items that other cultures would describe as green," he explains, which resulted in a kind of "grue" or "bleen." Objects like apples that would be green in English are referred to in Japanese as being blue—and this includes traffic lights.

Notably, Japan is not a signatory to the Vienna Convention on Road Signs and Signals, a multilateral treaty systemizing road signs, markings, and lights across dozens of countries. Instead, Japanese stoplights have been labeled blue in official documents for nearly one hundred years despite clearly being what in many languages would be called green at the outset. Color vision tests for Japanese drivers even use red, yellow, and blue. For decades, there was debate over whether to make the lights a truer blue to reflect the language or convert them to green to reflect international standards. They split the difference instead.

"Ultimately," writes Richarz, "a novel solution was employed. In 1973, the government mandated through a cabinet order that traffic lights use the bluest shade of green possible—still technically green, but noticeably blue enough to justifiably continue using the *ao* nomenclature." Even now, "while modern Japanese allows for a clear delineation between blue and green, the concept of blue still encompassing shades of green still remains firmly rooted in Japanese culture and language."

Regardless of what "grue" or "bleen" says about a place and its people, the lines humans draw on color wheels are not fixed, inevitable, or universal. It may seem surprising that Syracuse and Japan would flout the usual red, yellow, and green convention when it comes to their traffic lights, but from another perspective, it's more surprising that there is any conformity at all.

# VISIBILITY AIDS

## *Retroreflective Studs*

AS HIS BROTHER CECIL TOLD THE STORY, INVENTOR PERCY Shaw was driving through the fog one night in 1933 on the way home from his favorite pub, the Old Dolphin in Clayton Heights, when a cat's glowing eyes saved his life. When Shaw spotted the cat along the shoulder of Queensbury Road, he corrected his car's path and avoided a treacherous drop-off. At the time, Shaw and other drivers relied on the reflectivity of metal tramlines set into the road to keep them on the straight and narrow when visibility was poor. On this occasion, however, the lines had been pulled up either for repair or perhaps permanently. Around England, trams were increasingly being displaced in favor of more automobile traffic, resulting in the loss of a crucial (if unintentional) kind of wayfinding device.

Shaw, who had been a tinkerer all of his life, became inspired by this turn of events and started to work on a road visibility solution he fittingly dubbed "cat's eyes."

Shaw's invention involved two reflective glass beads peeking out at drivers from inside a rounded cast-iron shell. These clever devices not only reflected light but also focused it, directing illumination back toward drivers. And they were self-cleaning—as cars drove over them in or after rainfalls, a rubber wiper pressed up against the glass and polished its surface. Poking up above the pavement, these devices also acted as reminder bumps in the road that alerted drivers who might be drifting into oncoming lanes of traffic.

Shaw set about testing his work in a less-than-legal fashion by using his earlier experiences as a paver to dig up stretches of local road and deploy his prototypes. He was eventually able to interest some municipalities in his design, but adoption was slow until the blackouts of World War II. Suddenly, nighttime road visibility was more essential than ever. Shaw was invited to visit Whitehall and was ultimately funded to create 40,000 units per week, which changed his fortunes virtually overnight. These "cat's eyes" remained popular for a long time in the United Kingdom partly because they work well in foggy weather. In other parts of the world, road markers have evolved along other paths, reflecting different regional conditions.

In postwar America, a rapid increase in car traffic and associated collisions in California led the state's Department of Transportation to develop what became known as Botts' dots, named for Dr. Elbert Dysart Botts, who worked on them for Caltrans. These round bumps were made for visibility, but their physical elevation also helped them to function like rumble strips. Early versions were made of glass and nailed or tacked to the ground through holes in their tops, but these tended to break or come loose, which led to exposed nails and punctured tires. The design was improved upon thanks in part to the development of better adhesives. In 1966, the California State Legislature mandated the use of the dots on all freeways in areas where it didn't snow, which led to more than 25,000,000 being placed across the state in the decades that followed. Recently, however, California has shifted gears again, phasing out Botts' dots, which, despite design improvements, still need regular replacement. Newer thermoplastic striping is now widely used as it is both cheaper and can be melted right

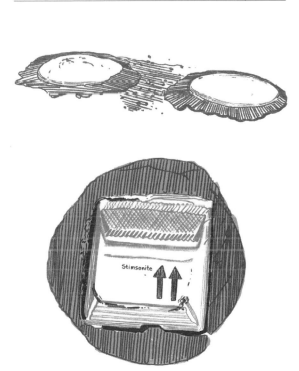

into roads so it lasts longer. In some places, markers have gone even higher tech with solar-powered designs and LED variants that actively blink.

Bright raised pavement markers (or RPMs) of different hues are often used to bolster the visibility of other markings, like white and yellow to reinforce lane lines, but they can serve more specialized purposes, too, like marking pullover spots for police officers along highways. Blue RPMs are employed in some cities to cue firefighters to the presence of roadside hydrants. Green ones can be used by emergency vehicles to locate access points, including entrances to gated communities, or by utility companies to find critical installation locations for rapid access. The angled sides of raised markers—many of which ramp up slightly, flatten out, then ramp back down—can also send different messages in different directions. Red on one side can indicate to drivers that they are going the wrong way while white on the other side lets them breathe a sigh of relief once they turn around and start heading in the right direction.

For his part in all of this, Percy Shaw remains something of a local legend in his hometown of Halifax. His "cat's eyes" design won national awards and earned praise from the British royal family, and his former home is adorned with a blue commemorative plaque. But Shaw was never too flashy with his fame and fortune. He traveled the world for work but preferred to come home, tinker around, and host modest parties. One of the few signs that he had become a man of means was his new luxury car. He was often observed being driven by a chauffeur in a Rolls-Royce Phantom to and from his favorite pub along the very road that had once inspired his most famous creation.

# CHECKERED PAST

## *Recognition Patterns*

THE STEREOTYPICAL POLICE CAR IN THE UNITED STATES looks something like this: white doors and a white roof that contrast starkly with black front and rear panels, fenders, hoods, and trunks. "The black and white look just represents law enforcement," explains Janice Crowther, a public information officer for the Dallas Police Department. "It's a sharp and smart look and since few (non-law enforcement vehicles) are black and white, they really stand out." While some departments continue to use this traditional palette, others have taken advantage of different color options and vinyl printing technologies to try out alternative approaches. In and beyond the United States, checkered patterns have become increasingly popular for law enforcement vehicles, the origins of which can be traced back to the early decades of cops driving around in cars.

The use of checkered patterns by police forces has roots in Scottish heraldry, traditional tartans, and one particularly progressive police chief in northern Britain. "Around the time of the First World War and shortly thereafter," according to the Glasgow Police Museum, "a number of Scottish Police forces, whose officers wore black peaked caps, sought ways to make their officers easily identifiable from the bus drivers and other local officials, who wore identical caps." At first, they added white cap covers in order to stand out, but these proved difficult to keep clean. So, starting in the 1930s, police in the city of Glasgow began using a black-and-white checkered cap band to stand out from other public servants. This specific pattern was brought into the realm of law enforcement by Sir Percy Sillitoe.

As chief constable of Glasgow, Sillitoe would make a name for himself by breaking up the city's notorious razor gangs (named for their weapon of choice) and modernizing his department with wireless radios. He would later go on to become the director general of MI5, the United Kingdom's internal security service. None of that, however, left a global legacy that rivaled his introduction of a simple tartan pattern to modern policing. "Strictly speaking," clarifies the Scottish Register of Tartans, "it isn't a tartan and Sir Percy Sillitoe . . . didn't design it." In fact, "it had existed for about 100 years as a Heraldic symbol in many Scottish coats-of-arms," explains the Register, and "Highland soldiers are said to have woven white ribbons into their black hatbands, thus creating a chequered effect." From these glengarry bonnets came the design used by officers under Sillitoe's watch, which featured a checkered pattern three rows high.

Variations on the so-called Sillitoe Tartan have since spread to police and emergency services vehicles around the United Kingdom as well as Brazil, South Africa, Iceland, and other countries around the world. In some places, the basic pattern is still black-and-white or blue-and-white, but there are myriad other color combinations. Such patterns are also often used by emergency services on official garments including vests and hats. Different colors can also convey different information that varies depending on location. In Australia, blue-on-white checkerboard patterns have been used by state, territory, national, and military police vehicles—even the official flag of the Australian Federal Police is framed with a Sillitoe border. Meanwhile red, yellow, and orange combinations have been used by other emergency services. Departments of transportation and corrections as well as volunteer rescue organizations have incorporated variants of the Sillitoe Tartan as well. In Western Australia, at least one ambulance service has adopted a newer design approach, employing what are known as Battenburg markings, which can look similar to Sillitoe patterns at a glance.

Like Sillitoe patterns, Battenburg markings are checkered, but instead of three rows of alternating tones, they are generally limited to just one or two rows with larger blocks of white, black, or other colors. Battenburg markings were developed for use on patrol cars by the Police Scientific Development Branch (PSDB) in the 1990s following a mandate to maximize both the recognizability and the visibility of police vehicles across the United Kingdom. The pattern's name comes from the fact that it looks a lot like a cross-section of a Battenberg cake.

By this time, the Sillitoe pattern had already spread to police forces in England and Wales, so checkered patterns were a familiar sight across much of the United Kingdom, but this classic three-rowed design was also found to have certain limitations. As intensive care paramedic and pattern enthusiast John Killeen summarizes, "Sillitoe is a recognition pattern, not a high-visibility marking scheme." While helpful for distinguishing between different kinds of emergency vehicles up close, smaller Sillitoe squares can be harder to differentiate and see clearly from long distances. In addition to recognizability, official vehicles require visibility both while they are in motion and to help reduce roadside collisions when police cars pull over along the sides of streets and highways.

In developing Battenburg markings, the PSDB experimented with and ultimately chose larger squares of bright yellow and blue to be the building blocks of their new pattern. Yellow is easy to see during the day while blue provides contrast but also functions as "the last colour to be visualised before human vision changes from colour to monochromatic shades of gray as darkness falls" according to Killeen.

SILLITOE

BATTENBURG

Both hues were also made retroreflective for greater visibility at night. Fortuitously, blue and yellow (or gold) were also already familiar to citizens because of their long association with police uniforms across much of England, which made the rollout of a blue-and-yellow checkered pattern more palatable to officers as well as the public, in turn fulfilling a key criteria of the PSDB's mandate.

In UK testing, the PSDB further found that so called full Battenburg patterns consisting of two horizontal rows performed well against neutral rural backdrops while single-row half-Battenburg solutions worked better in cities. In some other places, however, checkered patterns have gotten out of hand. Problems arise, argues Killeen, when designers try to get too creative. "Very few agencies dig deeply into visibility and conspicuity research to maximise safety aspects in their choice of design." They often come up with strange hybrids, "a rainbow cake mixture located somewhere between Sillitoe, Battenburg and fluorescent formats." There are cases in which these designs are taken to dazzling extremes and span not just one, two, or three rows but are stacked from top to bottom on the sides of vehicles, then sometimes also overlaid with text. Having too many squares can lead to vehicles being harder to pick out and identify rather than easier.

Sir Percy Sillitoe helped open the door to the wide variety of options now used around the world, but cities still need to think locally, too. Rather than adopting a pattern like Sillitoe or Battenburg just because it works well in other places and is cheap and easy to copy, police and other emergency departments would be well served by taking cues from the United Kingdom and creating criteria before making designs and then testing the results. In the absence of a more complete redesign and testing process, places like Dallas have perhaps wisely chosen to stick with more traditional and familiar patterns, painting vehicles with large sections of black and white.

# MEMORABLE
# BUT MEANINGLESS

## *Warning Symbols*

THE WORLD IS FULL OF ICONS THAT WARN US TO BE AFRAID— to stay away from this or not do that. Many of these are easy to understand because they represent something recognizable like a simplified fire icon or a stick-figure person slipping on a wet floor. Others, however, warn us of dangers that are harder to visualize and thus are more difficult to represent or communicate about visually.

Biological threats are often insidiously invisible, sometimes microscopic, and frequently odorless and tasteless, which makes them hard to symbolize in anything but an abstract way. Still, rooms and packages containing dangerous microorganisms or viruses or toxins need to have high-visibility warnings. Before a unified design standard was developed, scientists working with dangerous biological materials faced a dizzying array of warning labels that varied from one laboratory to the next. US Army laboratories employed an inverted blue triangle to designate biological hazards while the US Navy used a pink rectangle—even within the military, there was no shape or color consistency. Meanwhile, the Universal Postal

Convention called for a white snake-wrapped staff on a violet field to be used when transporting biological materials.

This lack of a consistent warning symbol was of increasing concern to the Dow Chemical Company in the 1960s. They were developing containment systems for dangerous biological materials with the National Institutes of Health (NIH), and they worried that the variety of designs being used was contributing to accidental infections of laboratory personnel, which could lead to even bigger disasters. In 1967, with these concerns in mind, Charles L. Baldwin of Dow and Robert S. Runkle of the NIH co-published a critical paper in *Science* that called for the broad adoption of the biohazard symbol we know today.

To arrive at this design, the project team first drew up a set of six criteria. The symbol should be striking as well as easily recognized and recalled. At the same time, it had to be unique and unambiguous so it wouldn't be confused with other symbols. For practical reasons, it had to be a shape that could be stenciled onto containers. It needed to have some symmetry as well so it would be identifiable in different orientations. Finally, it had to be inoffensive, a design that wouldn't have negative or problematic associations for any ethnic or religious groups.

In the absence of something familiar and visible to connect the graphic with, the designers sought to avoid accidental associations and create new ones instead. "We wanted something that was memorable but meaningless," Baldwin later explained in an interview, "so we could educate people as to what it means." With that guiding principle in mind and their criteria in hand, the team at Dow set about developing potential candidates. In order to ensure that the final symbol was indeed both memorable and meaningless, the project engineers and designers took their six semifinal solutions to the public for some real-world testing.

Three hundred people from twenty-five cities were shown an array of the six test symbols alongside eighteen commonly used symbols that included Mr. Peanut, the Texaco star, the Shell Oil symbol, the Red Cross logo, and even a swastika. Participants were asked to identify or guess the meaning of each. Their responses were then translated by the researchers into a "meaningfulness score." One week later, those same participants were shown an array of sixty symbols that included the original twenty-four plus thirty-six more. They were asked to recall which symbols they had seen in the first round of the study, and their answers were then used to create an associated "memorability score."

At the end of the test, one design stood out from the rest, having achieved the top score in both categories from among the six competing designs. The winning candidate was both the easiest to remember and the hardest to associate with any

particular meaning. This symbol met or exceeded the various other initial criteria as well. Even though the form was complex, it was not only easy to stencil but also could be drawn with only a straightedge and compass. Its trefoil design was another asset; a three-leafed shape with three-way symmetry can be stuck or stenciled onto a surface in any orientation and still be easily recognized if a marked barrel or box gets turned on its side or upside down. Rendering it in bright orange against a contrasting background made it easy to see, too.

Though ostensibly free of associations, the biohazard symbol arguably benefited from its similarity to the trefoil ionizing radiation warning symbol developed a number of years prior. This simpler predecessor was created at the University of California, Berkeley. Nels Garden, who was head of the Health Chemistry Group at the Radiation Laboratory at the time, later recalled that "a number of people in the group took an interest in suggesting different motifs, and the one arousing the most interest was a design which was supposed to represent activity radiating from an atom." In hindsight, one could make a case that this trefoil symbol began to establish visual associations between three-leaved iconography and serious dangers.

But in the 1960s, the biohazard symbol was still new and abstract, so the next step was to attach meaning to the still-meaningless form by associating it with a set of use cases. It "shall be used to signify the actual or potential presence of a biohazard," advised Baldwin and Runkle in 1967, "and shall identify equipment, containers, rooms, materials, experimental animals, or combinations thereof which contain or are contaminated with viable hazardous agents." The authors also defined and clarified the term *biohazard* as referring to "those infectious agents presenting a risk or potential risk to the well-being of man either directly through his infection or indirectly through disruption of his environment." Of course, people had to actually use the design broadly for it to be successful. Fortunately, research groups at the US Army Biological Warfare Laboratories, the Department of Agriculture, and the NIH agreed to test the new symbol for six months. Once it was adopted by the CDC (Centers for Disease Control and Prevention) and OSHA (the Occupational Safety and Health Administration), it quickly became the standard in the United States and has also gained traction internationally.

Many signs in our built environments are designed to be visual analogues of physical phenomena. This symbol, however, works by being distinctive, compelling, and complex while also remaining easy to remember. Its success ultimately hinges on the design maintaining a safe distance from other familiar emblems, shapes, and symbols. These days, however, its compelling distinctiveness may also be a drawback—it's just a little too cool! The symbol has made its way onto shirts, mugs, sunglasses, helmets, sports bags, stickers, and other everyday objects.

Baldwin expressed concern about this trend, recalling a confrontation with the organizer of a seminar on biohazards: "As gifts for the participants, he devised a beautiful tie with little biohazard symbols all over it. This got me upset, and I sent him kind of a nasty letter saying this symbol was not designed to be used sartorially." Baldwin's reaction may seem harsh, but it was grounded in a legitimate and serious concern: the more popular the symbol becomes outside of its intended use cases, the less effective it will be at saving lives by alerting people to actual biological hazards. Take the Jolly Roger, for instance, which was once one of the most feared symbols in the world, representing things like death, pirates, and poison. Now, though, a skull and crossbones is more often associated with blockbuster movies or Halloween accessories than actual danger.

Designing a danger symbol that retains its meaning over time is surprisingly difficult as physicist and science fiction author Gregory Benford knows from experience. Benford was invited to work on a special endeavor launched in the

1980s by the US Department of Energy. They wanted his assistance with the Waste Isolation Pilot Plant (WIPP), a massive storage site for radioactive waste in the southeastern plains of New Mexico. Benford was brought in to help calculate the probability that someone or something would intrude on the site for as long as it remains dangerous—approximately the next ten thousand years. As it turns out, few symbols retain their meaning for that long. A warning design like a skull and crossbones or the biohazard symbol wouldn't work; people might not understand it or think it marked something of value—like buried treasure.

Engineers, anthropologists, physicists, and behavioral scientists of a group known as the Human Interference Task Force proposed different design solutions to this fundamental problem of warning sentient beings ten thousand years in the future. One approach involved illustrating cause and effect across a series of panels arranged like a newspaper comic strip to indicate the dangers of tampering with a radioactive site. This strategy, however, assumed people of the far future would understand causality between frames and read from left to right, which even today isn't universal. Other designers focused on creating warnings in the built environment itself. They drew up imposing landscapes with features like spike fields and giant pyramids that capitalized on natural human instincts of fear and discomfort. But no one could be sure whether these structures would be perceived as terrifying or fascinating.

In 1984, the German *Journal of Semiotics* published a series of proposed solutions from various scholars. Linguist Thomas Sebeok suggested a kind of atomic priesthood. In his scenario, an exclusive political group would use its own rituals and myths to preserve knowledge of radioactive areas across generations much like any religion does. Meanwhile, French writer Françoise Bastide and Italian semiotician Paolo Fabbri advocated another solution involving genetically engineering bioluminescent cats that would glow in the presence of radioactivity. By creating songs and traditions about the danger of these glowing felines, the warning would theoretically be preserved by one of the oldest relics of civilization we have: culture.

Amid all of these ideas and proposals, there is no definitive or certain solution to the problem of warning our descendants far into the future. In the meantime, designing clear and inclusive symbols will continue to be a fundamental part of how we keep people safe in the present. Culture will change, as will the ways people communicate visually, so our warning symbols will have to change along with us. Presumably, this includes the biohazard symbol now found on ties, lighters, T-shirts, bicycle helmets, and your favorite coffee mug.

# SIGNS OF TIMES

## *Shelter Markers*

IN THE MIDDLE OF THE COLD WAR, THE TOWN OF Artesia, New Mexico, constructed a very unconventional version of a very conventional building: a subterranean elementary school. The "roof" of the Abo school was topped with asphalt at ground level, which served as a playground. Little boxy unassuming buildings on the surface opened up to stairwells that took students below. The children would spend their days in underground classrooms full of desks and chalkboards. But farther down the otherwise ordinary-looking hallways was a morgue, an array of decontamination showers, and a stockpile of food and medicine. In the event of a nuclear attack, more than two thousand people from the area could pile into the school-turned-bunker to seek refuge. When the space reached capacity, its steel doors would be slammed shut. Even the school's mascot fit its surreal subterranean location: the Abo Gopher.

The project was ambitious for the time, but it also anticipated a sweeping call to action in a nation full of fear during the Cold War. "To recognize the possibilities of nuclear war in the missile age," argued an impassioned President John F. Kennedy in the summer of 1961, "without our citizens knowing what they should do and where they should go if bombs begin to fall, would be a failure of responsibility." Tensions were high, and potential war with the Soviet Union loomed large. So Kennedy instructed Congress to fund a project "to identify and mark space and existing structures [both] public and private that could be used for fallout shelters in case of attack"—in effect, more places like Abo. Those shelters should then be stocked with "food, water, first aid kits, and other minimum essentials for our survival."

Following Kennedy's directive, a nationwide survey was undertaken by the Army Corps of Engineers to identify potential shelter sites. To create signage for this new national system of shelters, the Corps turned to a low-level administrator named Robert Blakely. Blakeley had fought in two wars and worked for the Veterans Administration, but he had also studied landscape architecture at the University of California, Berkeley, in the 1950s.

Put in charge of this project, Blakely took a practical and hands-on approach. The signs should be metal, he figured, so they would be durable, and the color scheme needed to be simple but visible so it could guide people even in the dark heart of a panicked metropolis threatened with a nuclear attack. So he tested out different symbols and tried out various reflective paints in his basement. In the end, he came up with a set of three yellow triangles circumscribed by a black circle, which bore a strong resemblance to radiation warning symbols that were also trefoiled and often similarly colored. Block-lettered words would reinforce the message: FALL-OUT SHELTER. Space on the sign was left to add the specific capacity of a given shelter. Letters and numbers aside, one could argue that this choice of symbol was potentially problematic—a nuclear radiation warning is effectively the opposite of a fallout shelter invitation and confusing the two could be seriously hazardous. If anyone had such concerns at the time, however, they were ignored in the rollout of this design.

More than a million of these signs were soon being fabricated and attached to architecture around the country, including schools and churches as well as offices, apartment complexes, and government buildings. There was also a surge of interest in backyard and basement fallout shelters from private citizens to the point where salesmen sold them door-to-door. Businesses with experience constructing things like swimming pools saw an opportunity and pivoted to specializing in shelter excavation and construction. Meanwhile, the fallout shelter placards designed by Blakeley were widely deployed to mark out both existing and purpose-built structures that could serve as emergency refuges for hordes of frightened American citizens.

In an era when the world seemed destined for nuclear war, fallout shelter placards became tangible and widespread signs of either hope or despair depending on one's perspective. As it spread throughout built environments, the design came to be interpreted and used in different ways. For some, it was part of an essential precautionary program that could help save lives in a disaster scenario; if things looked grim, these signs would lead people to places with some cover and basic necessities. For others, they became a countercultural icon used in antiwar protests. Critics saw shelters as harbingers of a more militarized America—a nation of concrete hovels that would become a dystopian wasteland even if some people survived a nuclear assault. Like the nuclear disarmament symbol, more commonly known as the peace symbol, it was a sign of the times.

More dramatic and extreme shelters like the Abo school became the focus of poignant criticisms by those concerned about Cold War escalations. Even the Soviets piled on, with a Moscow newspaper condemning the town for indoctrinating its people by priming them for the inevitability of war. For Artesia, though, the calculus was relatively straightforward. The town was looking to build a new school, and the Office of Civil Defense agreed to pay for the added cost of making one that could also serve as a fallout shelter, so they went along with it. Kids went about their school days largely unaware of how unusual the design of their educational institution was. For Robert Blakely, too, shelter-related design was not a big deal in his life—it was just another project in a long career of military and civil service, something that fortunately never amounted to more than a symbolic gesture.

# SIGNAGE

THE VAST MAJORITY OF THE GRAPHIC designs crowding your visual field are advertisements. It's probably okay to ignore most of them. That's not exactly the typical *99% Invisible* mindset, but if you don't block out all the mass-produced garbage, you might not notice the truly idiosyncratic commercial designs that add so much character and vibrancy to a city.

LEFT: *Hand-painted graphics, neon lights, and production placards*

# BROAD STROKES

## *Hand-Painted Graphics*

FOR MOST OF THE TWENTIETH CENTURY, PROFESSIONAL sign makers fundamentally shaped the look and feel of cities by hand. Building by building, sign by sign, they carefully drew letterforms for barbershop windows, sandwich boards, and even municipal street signs. These professionals were called mechanics, not artists, because their job was to create signs that were functional, not artistic. In some cases, a sign being beautiful or boastful might be part of that function, but in many everyday situations, like speed limit or stop signs, legibility, clarity, and simplicity were crucial.

To experts and aficionados, there are telltale hints that reveal the skill level of a given sign painter. A master letterer could use a squirrel-hair brush to create a rounded letter like an *O* in just a few strokes while neophytes might take dozens of passes and use a lot more paint to get it done. Speed, too, was essential for getting projects completed. With piecework like sign painting, a mechanic had to work fast to pay the bills, often painting signs while hanging off the side of a building in inclement weather. It was a tough trade, and not just physically or aesthetically. Sign making involved a lot of hustle and salesmanship. Some painters took their skills on the road, traveling from place to place and convincing local businesses to hire them on the spot. A typical large American city had a few dozen professionals trained in the specific styles and strokes of the trade, as well as the techniques for transferring small drawings onto bigger surfaces.

Sign painting didn't disappear entirely with the proliferation of illustration software and other new technologies, but innovations like the vinyl plotter did turn the industry upside down. With the advent of large-scale printers, making a sign became relatively simple. A user could input a series of letters and expect a precise output of those same letters writ large in any font desired. Vinyl letters were also arguably easier to maintain; they wouldn't wear down with repeated window washings like hand-painted equivalents did. By the mid-1980s, machines had begun to dominate the sign-making landscape, lowering the bar to entry and making sign design and manufacture more accessible to anyone, whether or not they could actually design a beautiful sign. For better or worse, the look of cities changed, and traces of this effect can be seen in the films made before, during, and after the paradigm shift.

But many vintage hand-painted signs are still around today. "Older signs in particular have a certain staying power," argues Laura Fraser in an article for *Craftmanship Quarterly*. Signs, she writes, "shape much of the aesthetic character of our cities and landscapes, creating a visual archeology of where we live." Even when their commercial function fades, they tell stories of bygone eras. "Each decade, and each region, has its own look and feel: Ouija board fonts, bold black enamel letters, winking cartoon characters, jazzy cut-outs, bubbles and stars, curlicues and winding flowers, or sleek, minimal designs."

With every new technology, there is a backlash, and for every trend, there is an eventual countertrend. These days, new hand-painted signs are found more and more frequently around fancy boutique stores, cozy coffee shops, hip food trucks, and high-end grocers. Their more organic lettering has a certain appeal based in nostalgia, but there may be something else contributing to their prevalence as well. The imperfections, brushstrokes, and individuating marks subconsciously cue the viewer that there was a real person behind the process and that this person cared to make something both functional and beautiful.

# TUBE BENDERS

## *Neon Lights*

THE SKYLINE OF BEAUTIFUL DOWNTOWN OAKLAND, California, is defined by various towers during the day, but at night, there is one that shines far brighter than the rest. Tall and thin, the Tribune Tower is clad in sandy brick and topped with a copper-coated mansard roof. What really sets it apart, though, is the glowing neon. On each of its four sides, TRIBUNE is spelled out in bright red letters. This text is paired with a set of four neon-illuminated clocks that tell the time with glowing numbers and hands. Prominent and well maintained, the neon stands out not only because of its brightness but also because of its rarity as a design element in contemporary construction. For a time, though, neon was the norm, its flickering presence lighting up cities around the world, traces of which can still be seen today.

Neon gas was discovered in 1898 by scientists Sir William Ramsay and Morris Travers. They derived the name from the Greek word *neos* ("new"), and it didn't take long for this new discovery to spark new technologies. The use of neon in signage was pioneered by a Frenchman named Georges Claude in the early 1900s, whose first commercial creation was a barbershop sign in Paris. In the 1920s, his company, Claude Neon, introduced neon signs to the United States. By the 1930s, neon had spread around the world; there were twenty thousand neon advertisements in Manhattan and Brooklyn alone, most of them made by Claude Neon.

The ingredients of a neon sign are simple: glass, electricity, and gases, most of which are drawn from the air we breathe. Red has long been a popular color choice for neon signs in part because it is the natural color of burning neon. Blue is popular, too, though this color is achieved by using argon gas brightened with a bit of mercury, so it's not technically "neon." Other colors are achieved by mixing other gases and materials or adding a phosphor powder coating on the inside of the glass tubes.

Neon was initially used to adorn high-end venues and fancy restaurants, but as it proliferated, cultural interpretations changed. Over the decades, as suburbs expanded and downtowns began to decline, neon increasingly became a symbol of seedy establishments and a flickering metaphor for urban loneliness. The gaudy brightness over a sketchy nightclub or crackling, flickering lights on the side of a diner were associated with vice and decay. In pictures from the 1950s, San Francisco's Market Street looks as bright and flashy as the Vegas Strip. Then, in the '60s, efforts to clean up and beautify the area led to the removal of most of its neon signs. The same story played out in other cities, including New York, also once a neon metropolis. In some places, such as Hong Kong, restrictive ordinances have contributed to the incremental removal and replacement of many neon signs.

At the same time, many historians, preservationists, artists, and other creatives continue to advocate for neon on historical as well as aesthetic grounds. "There is nothing like neon," muses John Vincent Law, a longtime neon contractor in Oakland who, among other things, maintains the Tribune Tower's lights. "Other light sources," he argues, "don't have that fuzzy, otherworldly look to it that you get with neon." He understands criticisms of neon, though, acknowledging that some people "have considered it to be cheesy and ugly and representative of some dying commercialism that they found unpleasant."

Despite today's thriving LED market, neon is enjoying a modest resurgence. There is still work for "tube benders," craftspeople who manually heat and flex straight glass tubes into letters and other shapes. These benders typically get glass from manufacturers in four-foot-long tubes and then draw out a pattern for how they will bend it, often working outward from the center of letters or shapes. They then heat up the tubes and vacuum out impurities before filling them with gas and fusing them to electrical sources. It is expensive, difficult work, which is part of the reason that broken neon signs tend to be replaced with LEDs.

Most large works of neon seen along city streets are painstakingly produced one letter at a time, usually by local benders. Even neon signs mass-produced in China are mostly twisted into shape by hand. When they break, it's expensive to call in a bender to make repairs or craft replacements, so you might find nonworking neon lights more often than not. Even the famous Tribune Tower went dark for years. Eventually, though, new owners had the clockfaces repainted and restored, and John Law was brought on to keep the neon lights illuminating these features going, maintaining a guiding star in the center of Oakland.

# SKY DANCERS

## *Inflatable Figures*

THEY DANCE CRAZILY ALONGSIDE STREETS AND SIDE-walks at car dealerships, gas stations, and shopping malls, heralding blowout sales and grand openings. As they rise and fall, flop and flail, these animated advertisers are all but impossible to ignore. They have various names and take different forms, but these inflatable figures with their slim arms and painted-on faces usually consist of a vinyl column set atop a fan. They are joyfully exuberant or extremely tacky depending on one's taste. Some cities are populated with tons of such figures while others, like Houston, have outlawed them. Per a 2008 municipal ordinance, they were determined to "contribute to urban visual clutter and blight [that] adversely affects the aesthetic environment."

One could imagine these tube figures being the brainchild of a used car dealer playing with leaf blowers and plastic bags in an attempt to drum up business, but their actual history is much longer, richer, and stranger. It started with Peter Minshall, a renowned Caribbean artist born in 1941. Minshall made a name for himself creating larger-than-life puppets that would dance through the streets to the beat of a steel-drum band. His work was featured in the book *Caribbean Festival Arts,* a copy of which wound up in the hands of someone on the steering committee for the Olympic Games.

For the opening ceremonies of the 1992 Olympics in Barcelona, Minshall worked on dramatic outfits and performances that incorporated versions of these giant puppets. A few years later, he found himself in the United States collaborating with other artists on designs for the opening festivities of the 1996 Olympics in Atlanta. That's when it came to him: inflatable tubes in the shape of figures that, when powered by fans from below, could dance like people did in his home country of Trinidad and Tobago. To make these Tall Boys work, though, he would need help.

Peter Minshall called up Doron Gazit, an Israeli artist who had worked on previous Olympic Games designs. Gazit had a long history with inflatables that started with making and selling balloon animals on the streets of Jerusalem. The duo's resulting design looked much like the tube figures you see around the world today except that they were bipedal and way bigger. The festive displays and performances of the 1996 Olympics came and went, but the figures persisted.

In the wake of the games, Doron Gazit took out a patent on what he called Fly Guys and began to license rights to other companies to make and sell them for various commercial purposes. Today, there are more than just Tall Boys and Fly Guys out in the world. There are also Air Dancers as well as Air Rangers, the latter of which are like scarecrows, designed to deter animals from invading farms and eating crops. Instead of smiley faces, these have angry features and sharp teeth. The LookOurWay company explains that their "dynamic unrepeatable dancing motion keeps birds away time after time." Aspects of this commercialization, however, became a point of contention.

According to Peter Minshall's account, he got a call from a fellow artist informing him that Doron Gazit was selling versions of the design they had worked on. For his part, Gazit says his lawyers told him that taking out a patent and selling derivative figures was appropriate because Minshall would not be considered an inventor in the eyes of the law. Peter Minshall and Doron Gazit both agree that the dancing inflatable figures were Minshall's idea, and they both agree that Gazit turned that idea into a reality. However, they disagree about whether or not it was ethical for Gazit to get a patent on it without informing Minshall, who wishes he had been consulted beforehand. Minshall remains glad overall, though, to see the figures out and about, bringing a traditional dance style from Trinidad and Tobago to the streets of cities around the world. Behind the erratic movements of these gaudy balloon men advertising low, low prices is a cultural artifact celebrating the rhythms of a nation.

# OUTSTANDING DIRECTORS

## *Production Placards*

LASHED TO FENCES, STRAPPED TO STREET LIGHTS, AND taped to traffic cones, a bright layer of Los Angeles signage blends in for locals but stands out for everyone else. These yellow signs help the many citizens of LA who work in the entertainment industry get around town every day, pointing casts and crews toward filming locations for various productions. Like official detour signs, they are generally spaced and situated so that a person can get where they are going using only the signage as a guide. With more than ten thousand signs produced per year, these placards are so common that a visitor could mistake them for city-sanctioned signage, which they aren't—not technically, at least. The city generally ignores them because they serve the film industry, which drives the local economy.

The format of these signs has evolved and become more formalized over time. In decades past, production workers would just scrawl words and arrows on whatever materials they had at hand. These days, a typical sign features a cryptic word, phrase, or acronym written in black both above and below a black directional arrow set against a bright yellow backdrop. The top characters appear forward and upright while the bottom ones run upside down and backward. The design makes sense upon reflection: each sign is modular and can be flipped in order to point left or right. In either orientation, one version of the text remains legible—at least as legible as it can be on the prefabricated eighteen-by-twenty-four-inch placards.

The text is usually a code name meant to be meaningless to anyone not in the know. Real titles could lead fans and press to secret filming locations, although sometimes crafty film buffs do crack the code. CORPORATE HEADQUARTERS was used to identify locations for the *Star Trek* reboot until fans figured it out, at which point new signs were printed with WALTER LACE as a replacement code. In some cases, the names contain insider hints that someone working on a show or movie would recognize but otherwise would be hard to decipher. People familiar with the classic comic book character Captain America might realize that FREEZER BURN is a subtle reference to this fictional World War II hero who spent decades frozen in ice before reemerging in the present. The fake names have to be distinctive to function but not overly humorous; if they are too strange or entertaining, the signs tend to get stolen. These placards have become a part of the cultural fabric of LA and have even starred in their own music video. To the tune of "L.A. Plays Itself" by YACHT, the viewer is driven past a series of black and yellow signs spread out across the Los Angeles area and spelling out the lyrics to the song.

In the modern world of digital maps, such signage might seem redundant, yet it is more popular than ever according to Jim Morris, co-owner of JCL Traffic Services, the main producer of these yellow signs. He explains that they serve an inherently valuable function in the fast-paced world of film. People working on a movie are given call sheets with location maps and times the night before. The problem is that locations aren't always places that can be plugged into a GPS system on a mobile device, and looking at a printed map or set of directions while driving is not particularly safe. Some locations are obscure, unlisted, or sprawl out over large areas, which further com-

plicates things. So yellow signs are essential to get people where they need to go, particularly if they have to travel to multiple places over the course of a day.

The obviousness of these signs could seem counterintuitive given the aim of keeping locations under the radar and allowing industry workers to film in peace. However, as Morris points out, the sheer volume of filming that happens in Los Angeles helps alleviate this potential problem. Few people are interested in following uncertain coded trails when there are so many shoots going on just about anywhere. Fanatics, Morris also notes, tend to find their way to target locations one way or another, so the lack of signs will not stop the diehards anyway.

There is no rulebook specifying that the signs have to be this way, but deviating from the standard yellow sign design tends to create problems for the rotating casts and crews forever crisscrossing the City of Angels in their cars. Morris recalls a client who asked for blue signs with white letters: "We made about three hundred of those one time, and after about three days, they were back," he says. The client demanded new ones and complained, "Everyone's driving right by these things. You can't see them! Everyone's looking for the yellow signs."

# MINDED BUSINESSES

## *Absent Advertising*

LIKE MANY CITIES, SÃO PAULO USED TO BE LITTERED with advertisements, but unlike many cities, this one also had a mayor with a bold plan to do something about it. In 2006, Gilberto Kassab proposed a sweeping clean-city law to reduce visual pollution and get rid of all kinds of excessive commercial graphics. Lei Cidade Limpa targeted more than ten thousand billboards as well as hundreds of thousands of ostentatious business signs, many of which cantilevered out over sidewalks and streets, competing for attention. The law forbade ads on buses and taxis, and even made it illegal to hand out promotional flyers. In the end, the passage of this legislation would do more than just reshape the visual experience of the city—it would also reveal some dark realities hidden under São Paulo's colorful veneer.

When it was announced, there was a lot of public support for the new legislation from citizens who were frustrated with private companies being able to endlessly brand public spaces. Predictably, though, business leaders with vested interests in their ad space fought back. Corporate lobbyists argued the ban would be bad for the economy and compromise real estate values. They also tried to appeal directly to everyday citizens whose taxes might have to pay for removing old posts that would no longer be supporting billboards. There was even an argument that illuminated ads helped people to safely navigate the city streets at night. Clear Channel Outdoor, one of the world's biggest outdoor-advertising companies, went so far as to sue the city, claiming the ban was unconstitutional.

In the end, advertising advocates lost and the law passed. Businesses were given ninety days to comply with its dictates or be fined. The process of removing ads transformed the entire look of the city, in some cases revealing lovely old buildings and surfacing beautiful architectural details. Local journalist Vinicius Galvao described his hometown to WNYC's *On the Media* as "a very vertical city," but noted that before the law "you couldn't even [see] the architecture . . . because all the buildings . . . were just covered with billboards and logos and propaganda." Suddenly forced to attract customers and clients without big signs, many business owners repainted their buildings with bright colors. Streets once crowded with overhanging signs attached to faded facades looked completely different.

In a city already known for its murals and graffiti, cleaning up ads from the sides of buildings also inadvertently freed up fresh new canvases for street artists to work on. Enthusiastic municipal workers, however, were at times overzealous when enforcing the clean-city law. Certain public murals were wiped clean, including ones that were officially sanctioned. The partial removal of one two-thousand-foot-long work in particular sparked local outrage as well as global press coverage. Eventually, with public support, the city created an official registry to protect key pieces of street art, which were now more visible than ever.

Aesthetics and art aside, there were some weightier unintended consequences to this law: advertisements, as it turned out, had been quite literally papering over some serious problems. Stripping away huge billboards alongside major roads ended up exposing poverty-stricken favelas. People had long driven by entire shantytowns without really noticing them because some of these neighborhoods had been visually fenced off by ads. Billboard removal forced people to bear witness to extreme wealth disparities. In addition to favelas, factory windows that had once been obscured by ads became visible, revealing that many workers inside were not only operating in very poor working conditions but were also living in these industrial buildings because they couldn't afford homes. In other words, the absence of colorful ads helped uncover problems or, viewed optimistically, highlighted opportunities for urban improvement.

This move to reduce advertising in public spaces is not unique to São Paulo, though few cities have taken bans quite as far as this one. Some places are selective about the formats of ads allowed or put restrictions on advertising content. Several US states prohibit billboard ads entirely, including Alaska, Hawaii, Maine, and Vermont. The mayor of Beijing specifically banned public ads for things like luxury apartments, which were seen to encourage self-centered and overindulgent lifestyles. Paris has also cracked down on big visual advertisements. A few years back, Tehran temporarily replaced some ads with art, a process that has long played out in other cities, though not always with official consent.

Meanwhile, some advertisements have been reintroduced to São Paulo, but the city is taking things slowly and carefully this time around. Interactive search-engine ads were installed at some bus stop shelters to allow residents to look up weather conditions for their destinations. The idea was that businesses that want to advertise also need to provide a useful public service. In addition, the advertisers had to agree to take care of the shelters. Other similar ideas have emerged at larger scales, like allowing thirty-two LED billboards to be put up, each associated with a major São Paulo bridge that marketers would have to fix up and maintain as part of the deal. Perhaps it is overly optimistic, simplistic, or too soon to tell, but there is something refreshing about advertisements that once covered over urban problems being employed to help solve them instead, though this kind of incremental privatization of public infrastructure could create new problems, too.

# Chapter 3

## INFRASTRUCTURE

**T**HE MOST IMPORTANT PHYSICAL PART of any civilization is its infrastructure—things like roads, bridges, and dams. Big impressive structures that involve special opening ceremonies (where people in suits cut ribbons with oversized scissors) tend to garner the most attention. There are also equally important but less glitzy varieties of infrastructure that are worth investigating, like the systems that provide clean water and take away our waste. Executing complicated, important projects like these requires extensive coordination, planning, and lots of money—it's pretty much why government was invented and one of the few remaining things that people of all political persuasions can agree on as being a good thing for government to do. When infrastructure works, it is the physical embodiment of the amazing things we can make when we work together. When infrastructure fails, it reveals the cracks in the system where we can improve.

PREVIOUS: *Chicago River reversed for waste management purposes*

# CIVIC

**C**ITIES MIGHT NOT ALWAYS FUNCTION as smoothly as we might wish, but given the number of different people working to keep them going, well, it's pretty amazing that they work at all.

LEFT: *Messy realities of overlapping municipal service obligations*

# BUREAUCRACY INACTION

## *Incidental Bridge*

THERE IS A RAILROAD BRIDGE IN DURHAM, NORTH CAR-
olina, that has become famous for scraping the tops off trucks that dare to pass
beneath its tracks. Nicknamed the Can Opener or the 11-foot-8 Bridge, the Norfolk
Southern–Gregson Street Overpass was designed to allow safe passage for vehicles up to around twelve feet tall, which probably seemed like more than enough
overhead when it was constructed in 1940. Over the years, though, trucks got taller,
and more and more trucks hit the bridge. Despite the implementation of a series
of bright signs, flashing lights, and other warnings that a driver's too-tall vehicle
is about to be loudly decapitated, these collisions kept happening.

Local resident Jürgen Henn was working in a nearby building when he began to
notice the high frequency of incidents involving the bridge. In 2008, he installed a
video camera to document the collisions. Since then, he has captured and posted
more than one hundred videos online. These short films capture a delightful
spectrum of mayhem, at least for those inclined toward infrastructural schaden-
freude. Especially tall trucks are stopped entirely by the bridge and bounce back
like a person hitting their head on a kitchen cabinet. Shorter vehicles slide under
with a painful screeching sound. In cases where the vehicle height is just right (or
just wrong) entire tops are peeled back like a sardine can, hence the Can Opener
nickname. After watching dozens and dozens of these incidents, one starts to
wonder how such an obvious problem can go unfixed for so long.

The railroad, the city, and the state have all taken actions to reduce incidents
involving the bridge over the years, but they've had limited success. The railroad
installed a crash beam to keep trucks from hitting the bridge itself. This protected
their infrastructure and any freight or passengers traveling overhead, but it didn't
do a lot for the trucks down below. For its part, the city of Durham installed a sup-
plemental array of warning mechanisms, including three low clearance signs posted

at each of three intersections in advance of the bridge. A pair of smaller roadside signs with a stated height limit of eleven feet, eight inches were also put up, which shaved a few inches off the actual limit to introduce another safety buffer. At one point, the state of North Carolina also installed a sign that warned OVERHEIGHT WHILE FLASHING with blinking orange lights directly in front of the bridge. Trucks, however, continued to crash into the beam, so the sign was removed in 2016 and replaced with a higher-tech variant with an LED display reading OVERHEIGHT MUST TURN that was linked with sensors to detect approaching oversized vehi-

cles. This system was integrated with a new traffic signal, so when the sensors were tripped, the stoplight would turn red. The idea was to give truck drivers more time to notice the warning sign before plowing ahead. Despite this more sophisticated intervention, how- ever, the bridge continued to claim and maim trucks.

Since no amount of warnings seemed sufficient, other solutions were considered over the years, including raising the bridge, lowering the street, or redirecting truck traffic entirely. The railroad long argued that raising the bridge would require sig- nificant regrading on both sides and potentially cost millions of dollars. Lowering the street was also deemed impractical because a sewer main ran directly below it. Installing a low-clearance bar in advance of the bridge or otherwise redirecting overheight traffic away from the area entirely would be challenging—delivery trucks need to be able to drive right up to the bridge and then turn in order to access a set of nearby restaurants. Rerouting them just wasn't feasible.

Finally, after years of delays and buck-passing, a work crew converged on the site in October of 2019 to do the improbable and raise the bridge. What was once the 11-foot-8 Bridge is now more or less a 12-foot-4 Bridge according to new road-flanking height limit signs, though according to Jürgen Henn's measurement, the actual clearance is around twelve feet, eight inches. For the not-so-low cost of half a million dollars, the North Carolina Railroad Company jacked up their tracks as much as they could without impacting nearby crossings on either side of the Can Opener. But this height still won't accommodate every truck—the state permits vehicles up to thirteen feet, six inches. Sure enough, a metal chunk of truck can be seen getting knocked off and hitting the street below in a video posted by Henn just a few weeks after this "fix" was enacted.

For decades, the Can Opener has represented a perfect storm of financial limitations, physical challenges, and political bureaucracy conspiring against a complete and permanent design solution. Even now that the bridge has been raised, it may still prove to be a flawed piece of infrastructure and persistent nuisance. All cities have things like this—ill-fitting byproducts of conflicting priorities that trip up citizens (or scrape up their vehicles)—but few are as large, troublesome, or widely shared on the internet as this one.

# GOOD DELIVERY

## *Postal Service*

SIX DAYS A WEEK, TEAMS OF PACK MULES WEIGHED DOWN with letters and packages make a two-and-a-half-hour trek into the Grand Canyon. These heroic beasts deliver mail to the Supai post office located more than two thousand feet below the rim of the canyon. This particular postal route was established in 1896 to serve the people on the Havasupai reservation, and it's one of the most remote nodes in a network of more than thirty thousand post offices around the United States. Some are grand structures that span entire city blocks; others are small and tucked away in the backs of rural general stores (or in canyons). Remote postal centers illustrate how far the USPS has gone to connect people through a national network we have come to take for granted. What started as a basic service ultimately became a driving force behind various critical types of modern infrastructure.

Throughout the ages, governments and powerful people of means have figured out ways to communicate over long distances, but for most of that time, these systems were used only by an elite few. The postal system of early colonial America was no different. The Crown's post was established by the English monarchy and used primarily for communications between each colony and England. Initially, the colonies weren't particularly interested in communicating with other colonies. Like fractious siblings, they primarily sought attention from the motherland. When commoners needed to send messages, it was typical to ask travelers to pass them along. This informal relay system evolved in the absence of more robust and official alternatives.

Benjamin Franklin was one of the early postmasters for the British Crown, at first working within the limited system that existed at the time. In that capacity, he traveled to every northern colony to see how the system might be improved, and he started to view the colonies as one nation instead of a bunch of disparate places. At a meeting of colonial representatives in Albany, New York, in 1754, Franklin proposed a plan for uniting the colonies and allowing them to elect their own officials rather than being governed by ones appointed by the monarchy. At the time, the idea was a nonstarter. Twenty years later, though, rhetoric about American self-governance was spreading, and revolutionaries in the colonies knew they would need something other than the Crown's post as a means to communicate their radical ideas.

So in 1774, the Second Continental Congress created a postal service based on a belief that communication (including a free press) should be free of government interference. As the American Revolution got underway, this network helped patriots communicate and kept the general populace informed. Before they had the Constitution or even a Declaration of Independence, Americans had the post, which bolsters the argument implied in the title of the book *How the Post Office Created America* by Winifred Gallagher. Her account emphasizes the vital role of the postal service in and beyond the founding of the United States.

After Americans gained independence from England, there was a push to use the post to circulate newspapers, as the founding fathers believed that a literate population was a crucial part of a healthy, functioning democracy. In 1792, Congress passed the Postal Service Act, which established new routes for mail delivery and lowered shipping rates for newspapers. The act was then signed into law by President George Washington. New publications of all political stripes took advantage of this affordable distribution system.

As it expanded, the postal service also served to stimulate the growth of roads and other infrastructure. Settlers in new communities would petition for post offices, which brought with them not just increased communication but also new routes of transportation. The addition of a post office could strengthen a settlement that could grow into a town that might eventually become a city. Post offices were also hubs of activity—without home delivery, people were always coming and going.

Post offices evolved into essential American institutions, particularly with the advent of prepaid postage. Payment on delivery had often resulted in piles of mail that recipients weren't willing to pay for, a paradigm that shifted when senders were forced to pony up cash in advance. Standardization made it possible for people to send letters around the United States for the same price no matter the distance. Lower costs and simplified rates helped spawn a letter-writing boom, particularly among women, which in turn changed post offices as well.

Post offices had historically been social spaces for men, where it was not uncommon to find liquor, prostitutes, and pickpockets. Eventually, post offices added special windows for ladies so they could pick up their letters without coming into contact with these unseemly elements. This was one step on a long path toward transforming post offices into more respectable spaces. By the mid-1800s, tens of thousands of post offices across the country were ferrying newly invented "greeting cards" (an instant hit) alongside political newspapers and other mail.

The spread of the postal service continued to enable the spread of radical ideas, too. Abolitionists advocating for the end of slavery used newspapers sent by post as their platform. Then, in the 1860s, as the Civil War was fought over slavery, the American post bifurcated for a time, with mail delivery ceasing between the North and South. The Civil War's unprecedented death toll also helped inspire another great innovation of the US Postal Service: home delivery. It was too painful and personal for mothers and wives to receive news of the death of a loved one in public post offices, so mail carriers started delivering letters directly to families so they could read the bad news in the privacy of their own homes.

In the American West, where the network was slow to fill in, short-lived services like the Pony Express were quickly replaced by telegraphs and train delivery. Train cars effectively became mobile post offices where workers sorted and processed mail while on the move. Trains revolutionized the mail, but mail also revolutionized the trains. Starting in the mid-1800s, subsidies from the post office to secure space for mail provided regular income for train networks and helped the rail system expand at a rapid pace. Postal subsidies also kept the aviation industry aloft after World War I. With passenger flights still in their infancy, early airports and aircraft were bolstered by this source of support.

Over the past few decades, Congress has imposed new financial rules that have proved to be a significant burden to the postal service. Private competitors, meanwhile, have taken on some of the roles traditionally played by post offices, such as package delivery. But despite all of these changes, the postal service continues to play a critical role in American society. Unlike private competitors such as FedEx and UPS, the USPS cannot pick and choose which places get serviced based on profit. It is obliged by its universal service obligation to "ensure all users receive a minimal level of postal services at a reasonable price." This means providing daily pickups and deliveries to every community in the country, even if that community is located at the bottom of the Grand Canyon.

# WATER

THE HEALTH AND GROWTH OF A CITY is inexorably linked to water. Clean water must be available and dirty water needs to be removed. The importance of this cannot be overstated, but it's easy for it to escape our notice. Water is often a driving force behind the locations of cities, but it also shapes and limits their physical boundaries. As the climate changes, this fluctuating relationship will have a profound effect on the lives of city dwellers that will be increasingly impossible to ignore.

LEFT: *Ornately embossed manhole cover featuring Osaka Castle*

# ROUNDING DOWN

## *Manhole Covers*

THERE IS A LOVELY METAL MANHOLE COVER IN OSAKA, Japan, that looks more like an ornate woodblock print than a utilitarian municipal disk. On it is a relief of the Osaka Castle wrapped in blue waves and white cherry blossoms that was commissioned to commemorate the hundredth anniversary of Osaka becoming a municipality. The design is striking, but this artistic approach is not unique to one city or celebration in Japan. Colorful illustrations of flowers, animals, buildings, bridges, boats, mythical heroes, and rising phoenixes adorn stylized manhole lids across the country.

Japanese cities have had various kinds of sewage and drainage infrastructure for more than two thousand years, but subsurface systems with standardized access points are still a relatively modern phenomenon. In the wake of standardization came a growing interest in creativity. According to a Tokyo-based association of manhole cover makers, the rise of more expressive covers started in the 1980s with a ranking construction ministry bureaucrat named Yasutake Kameda. At the time, slightly more than half of Japanese households were connected to municipal sewer systems. Kameda wanted to raise awareness of these vital subsurface utilities in part to get locals on board. After all, it's difficult to levy the taxes required to improve and expand these networks when they are unseen and underappreciated.

To Kameda, manhole covers seemed the obvious target for a visibility campaign— a surface expression of an otherwise underground and largely invisible system. He began encouraging towns and cities to develop and deploy location-specific motifs. Soon, municipalities were competing to create the coolest covers around, drawing inspiration from nature, classic folklore, and contemporary culture (including the pop icon Hello Kitty). *Manhoru* (adapted from the English *manhole*) mania has since inspired photography, rubbings, pins, stickers, even quilting pattern books based on the art and design of Japanese manhole covers.

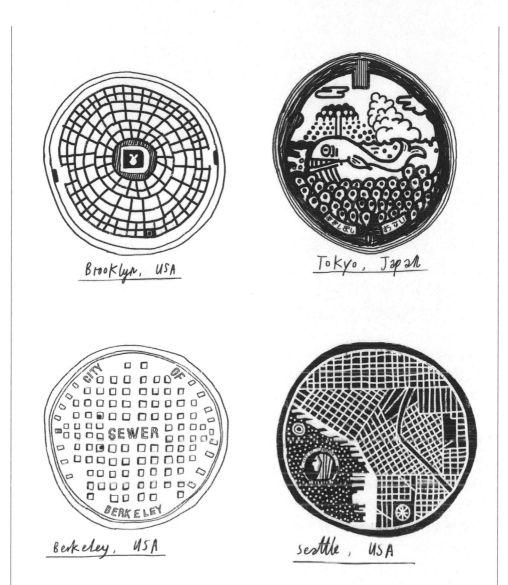

Brooklyn, USA

Tokyo, Japan

Berkeley, USA

seattle, USA

It's easy to see the influence of other Japanese art forms in these lid designs, but their appearance is meant to be more than just aesthetically appealing. The cross-hatching and other patterns with lines and curves running in different directions offer traction, helping to reduce wheel slippage in rainy or icy conditions. This strategy can be found around the world, even in countries where striking graphic designs are less common.

Many Japanese manhole covers have other less visible features designed with safety and quality of life in mind. Tapered designs, which angle inward from top to bottom (like a cork or stopper in a glass bottle), rattle less than conventional round covers when driven over, reducing noise pollution. For areas prone to flooding, special hinged lids have been engineered to flip over to one side when pushed up by water, then flop back into place when the pressure subsides. This hinge system helps prevent catastrophic lid launches that can result in immediate hazards and also leave behind potentially deadly empty holes in the street.

While some of these innovations are regional, many basic aspects of manhole cover design are relatively universal. Take the round geometry of most covers, for instance. A circle is an amazing shape! Circular sewage access lids can't fall into the holes they cap, whereas square or oval lids can be lifted up, turned sideways, and chucked into the very voids they were made to cover. Cylindrical sewage access tubes resist soil pressures evenly, and their uniformly round casings are easier to machine on a lathe. Heavy circular covers can be flipped sideways and rolled along roads as well. A round of applause for circles.

While Japan has become known for the aesthetics of its manhole covers, other places have distinctive designs with elements of regional significance or clever functionality. The triangular manhole covers of Nashua, New Hampshire, point in the direction of subsurface flows. In Seattle, a series of manhole covers feature embedded city maps—the raised city grid on these also functions as a multidirectional anti-slip element. In Berlin, rounded cityscapes and other creative city-specific covers have inspired at least one artist to roll on paint, then press shirts on relief patterns to create custom hand-printed casual wear. Even less overtly impressive designs can hint at bits of local history, like the old manhole covers in London embossed with T. CRAPPER, for the Thomas famously associated with modern flush toilets. Manhole covers are going to dot cities for practical reasons no matter what, but that doesn't mean they can't serve as canvases for creative expression or de facto plaques as well.

# UPWARDLY POTABLE

## *Drinking Fountains*

ONE SPRING DAY IN 1859, THOUSANDS OF LONDONERS GOT dressed up in their finest clothes and gathered to get a view of a new civic sensation: the city's first public drinking fountain. It might seem like a strange object of celebration, but this unveiling was a big deal for the city. Life in London at the time was nightmarish for working-class residents due in part to a lack of clean water. Many citizens drew their drinking water from the River Thames, a stinking cesspool polluted with human waste, dead animals, and nasty chemicals. Just one year before the fountain was constructed, the Great Stink (as the press came to call it) had overwhelmed London. At one point, Queen Victoria tried to take a cruise on the river but quickly called for the boat to return to shore due to the smell. A British journalist marveled that his was a nation that could "colonise the remotest ends of the Earth" but "cannot clean the River Thames."

Concern at the time over the filthy river wasn't so much about the stench as it was the deadly diseases associated with that awful scent. Cholera had killed tens of thousands of people in preceding years, and one theory held that the foul air was to blame for spreading such epidemics. But some people were skeptical of this explanation, including scientist John Snow. He believed infected drinking water was to blame—and he set about to prove it.

During one particularly bad outbreak, Snow went house to house knocking on doors, asking if anyone at home was sick, then he attempted to map out the infections based on their responses. He used this information to identify a water well at the center of the impacted area that he suspected was the source of the outbreak, so he removed the pump handle to prevent people from using the well. The epidemic died down shortly thereafter, which helped bolster Snow's credibility. Snow's rigorous, data-oriented approach to diseases was novel, and he has since become known as the father of modern epidemiology.

Shortly after Snow's discovery, the Metropolitan Free Drinking Fountain and Cattle Trough Association (because, well, animals need clean water to drink, too) set out to build drinking fountains across London. By 1879, the group had built hundreds. For fountain advocates, though, it wasn't just about the condition of the water. Many were also trying to get people, including kids, to drink less booze. Water was dirty, and boiled drinks like coffee and tea were expensive, so a lot of people had little choice but to drink alcoholic beverages to quench their thirst. So-called temperance fountains were constructed in public parks, near churches, and outside of bars to provide a less intoxicating alternative. Many of these were ornate and monumental affairs erected with inscriptions about abstinence or verses from the Bible. Drinking fountains didn't really solve the problem of alcoholism as some proponents had hoped, but they did help set a new precedent for making clean water available to all citizens.

Even as they became essential, though, early fountains still had some design issues to overcome. Around the turn of the twentieth century, many featured a spigot and a common cup, which was usually suspended from a chain for everyone to use. It took time for public health officials to fully embrace the germ theory of disease and usher in new approaches that would not require users to put their mouths on shared surfaces. In Portland, Oregon, for instance, businessman and philanthropist Simon Benson commissioned a series of architect-designed fountains in 1912 that came to be called Benson Bubblers. These now-iconic multi-spout fountains "bubbled" water up from below for a thirsty populace.

Despite all this innovation, there remained a problem: backwash would drip back down onto the tops of the somewhat ironically named sanitary fountains. In some cases, people even put their lips to the spouts. There were proposals to put cages around the spouts to prevent this, but designers ultimately settled on fountains that produced upwardly arced jets of water—the kind still typically associated with drinking fountains today. Water fountains alone couldn't solve all of the hygiene and odor problems common in growing cities like London, but they at least provided a way for urban residents to enjoy alcohol-free hydration in an age of pollution-riddled industrialization.

# REVERSING COURSE

## *Waste Management*

EVERY YEAR FOR MORE THAN FIFTY YEARS, THE CHICAGO River has glowed bright green in honor of St. Patrick's Day. To the uninitiated, this phenomenon resembles a terrible toxic spill rather than a celebratory effort, but it is a beloved local tradition. It all started in 1961 when, according to some accounts, a business manager for the Chicago plumbers' union named Stephen Bailey spotted a plumber with green stains on his white coveralls. The plumber had been using dye to trace wastewater outflows, which gave Bailey a grand idea. A first-generation Irish American, Bailey suggested to his friend, Mayor Richard J. Daley, that they dye the river in the heart of the city as part of the St. Patrick's Day celebration, thus sparking an annual custom. While observing the cartoonishly hued waters, onlookers could notice something unexpected if they watch closely: while most natural rivers flow *into* large bodies of water, the green dye can be seen flowing *away* from Lake Michigan.

This anomaly is the culmination of a series of interventions that started more than a century ago to tackle a problem faced by all large and expanding cities: excrement. Chicago is a relatively flat city, which is problematic for gravity-driven waste-removal systems. The stalled sewage issue grew worse over time as more and more people moved to the area. When a cholera epidemic brutally wiped out around 5% of Chicagoans in 1854, the problem became too big for officials to ignore. So, in classic nineteenth-century fashion, this big problem was addressed by a set of increasingly big, bold, and unprecedented engineering solutions.

Ellis S. Chesbrough was an engineer who had worked on water systems in Boston before moving to the Midwest, where he was appointed to Chicago's Board of Sewerage Commissioners in the 1850s. He came in with an ambitious plan: the city needed to be raised to help keep wastewater flowing. Over the course of the next several years, a number of buildings were lifted up to ten feet higher on mechanical jacks. It was a massive undertaking, with crews of workers cranking away in sync to raise up the local architecture building by building. This created quite a spectacle—people watched from the streets and even from the balconies of the occupied buildings being raised as huge multistory structures were lifted a fraction of an inch at a time while masons stacked up new foundations below. While this effort was underway, however, there was another pressing issue: drinking water. Raising the buildings would help move sewage out to the lake, but the lake was also where the city drew its fresh water, which presented a problem.

To deal with problem number two, Chesbrough proposed another unprecedented feat of modern engineering: workers would tunnel under Lake Michigan to create a two-mile intake line that would draw cleaner water from farther offshore. To speed things up, the tunnelers worked from both ends, burrowing sixty feet down, then excavating horizontally to meet in the middle. The work was constant—diggers dug by day and masons shored up the walls by night.

Even as this incredible project was underway, the city was expanding beyond its capacity and creating more waste. And it wasn't just human excrement—new slaughterhouses were cropping up in Chicago and dumping their waste in the so-called Chicago River, which is not so much a single waterway as it is an extensive network of natural and artificial rivers and canals. One particularly appalling section of the South Branch charmingly known as Bubbly Creek was actually named for the methane bubbles generated by rotting animal parts in the water. This stretch of water would even catch fire sometimes. Some of the city's detritus made its way out to the two-mile mark in Lake Michigan, then flowed back into the new water intake system. There was talk of pushing intakes out even farther, but ever longer intake tunnels would never be enough to keep up with the city's growth.

A bigger, bolder solution was needed, and so an even more ambitious idea was proposed: reverse the entire Chicago River. Instead of waste from the river flowing into Lake Michigan, clean water from the lake would flow into the city. This would, once and for all, solve the pollution problem by pushing it downstream to the Illinois River, then the Mississippi, and into the Gulf of Mexico—much to the consternation of other cities along the way. The project took years to complete and required thousands of workers, tons of dynamite, newly invented digging equipment, and year-round construction to carve out the deep canals. In January of

1900, the last dam was opened and the waterway finally began to reverse its course, flushing the waste downstream, which prompted this *New York Times* headline: "The Water in the Chicago River Now Resembles Liquid."

As this project was being executed, cities located downstream fought to keep this horrific flow of excrement from pouring into their backyards. St. Louis's legal cases against the reversal eventually made it all the way to the Supreme Court. In weighing the arguments, Justice Oliver Wendell Holmes questioned "whether the destiny of the great rivers is to be the sewers for the cities along their banks." The court's answer was, in effect, *yes*—St. Louis could not stop Chicago's grand redirection plan. It was to some extent already the norm for cities to dump waste into natural rivers as well as artificial waterways, and these court cases upheld that precedent. Cities would just have to create their own wastewater treatment plants to compensate for upstream pollution from other cities.

Reversing the flow of the Chicago River was an epic project spanning decades, so vast and impressive that it would later be dubbed a Monument of the Millennium by the American Society of Civil Engineers. Now, more than a century later, there is growing concern about the potential *re-reversal* of the river. With Lake Michigan water levels at record lows, there are already seasonal reversals in parts of the flow. Without further interventions, this could become a permanent change and threaten one of the largest freshwater supplies in the United States. Perhaps there is a moral here about human hubris in the face of nature, or maybe the problem calls for another groundbreaking engineering project even greater than the last one.

# CIRCLING BACK

## *Subsurface Cisterns*

A SERIES OF NEARLY TWO HUNDRED LARGE BRICK CIRCLES can be found embedded in certain San Francisco streets, some of them almost spanning the width of the pavement. In the middle of each one sits a round metal disk, which, at a glance, looks much like a manhole cover guarding the entry to a sewer system. Yet the water below these disks isn't wastewater. The bricks trace the edges of huge underground cisterns that are part of the city's Auxiliary Water Supply System, which also encompasses water reservoirs, pumping stations, and fireboats. These resources form a backup system in case primary water sources fail, which is a problem the city has faced before.

During and after the 1906 earthquake, fires sprang up around San Francisco. Thousands of people died, and the majority of the city was destroyed by the earthquake and subsequent fires, which burned for days. In the midst of this disaster, water mains broke across the city and roadway rubble blocked firefighters.

In the wake of this tragedy, the city's cistern network was expanded to make water more accessible if something like this were to ever happen again. Firefighters can tap into the water in these underground cisterns to battle the flames without worrying about water mains being connected to the municipal source. Framed in robust concrete and steel (in part to protect them from seismic events), the cisterns can hold tens to hundreds of thousands of gallons each. They are easy to spot by design: the brick rings help signal their locations while the metal lids in the middle are clearly labeled CISTERN against a checkered anti-slip grid.

In addition to these cisterns, there are also sets of fire hydrants topped in blue, red, and black, each tied to a different reservoir. The idea here is similar: if the main water systems go down, reservoirs located at Jones Street, Ashbury Street, and Twin Peaks can be tapped. If all else fails, there is yet another method available to firefighters, a backup to these backups: brackish water can be pumped directly from the San Francisco Bay. Two pumping stations on the Bay can push up to around ten thousand gallons per minute, and they are backed up by a pair of fireboats that can also supply salty water. There's no way to anticipate every disaster, but there is a lot of redundancy in this system. It draws on experience—and a wealth of water in the bay—to help make the city more future-proof, a visible testament to the fortitude of a metropolis that has burned down before but is determined to never burn down again.

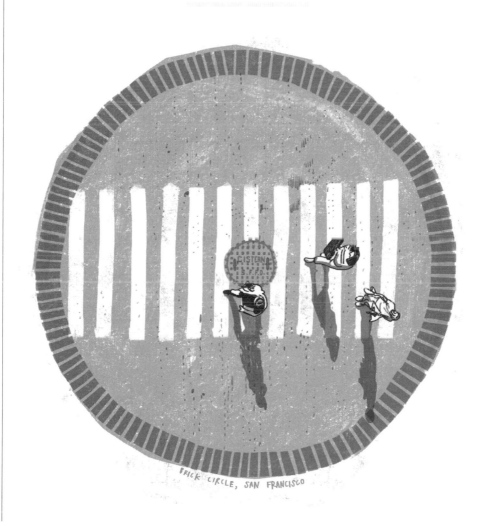

FRICK CIRCLE, SAN FRANCISCO

# APPLES TO OYSTERS

## *Flood Mitigation*

WHEN HURRICANE SANDY STRUCK IN 2012, STORM SURGES flooded buildings, streets, and tunnels in New York City. It was a devastating reminder of how fragile America's biggest metropolis could be, particularly in the face of rising sea levels and other effects of climate change. Some politicians and engineers called for modern solutions like floodgates or massive seawalls to combat these rising environmental threats. Others, though, began digging into the history of the city and wound up proposing ideas for the present based on precedents from the past, drawing inspiration from an era when giant oyster reefs surrounded Manhattan.

Before it was the Big Apple, New York was the Big Oyster. The city was built at the mouth of the Hudson River, a fertile estuary packed to the gills with marine life. Scientists and historians estimate that trillions of oysters once surrounded Manhattan, and these bivalves filtered out bacteria from the water and served as a food source for the human population. Beneath the waves, these reefs also provided a less obvious benefit: vital protection against storm surges and coastal erosion. Unlike many mollusks, oysters build up complex reef systems under-water, up to dozens of feet high. Such reefs used to span hundreds of thousands of acres along the Hudson River estuary. The rough texture of these structures helped break up large waves before they reached the shore and served as a natural buffer for the city.

Oysters may not be the first association one makes with the urban landscape of New York City, but back in the 1700s, they were everywhere. In the growing city, oysters were consumed by rich and poor alike. Huge mounds of shells piled up in the streets alongside oyster houses. Ground-up shells were even used as construction materials, burned for lime and ground up to make mortar. Pearl Street was reportedly one of the roads paved with these remnants, hence its name.

Oystermen began seeding the shallows of the harbor to produce hundreds of millions of oysters per year to meet popular demand. But as the city grew, so did its waste output, and as efficient as the oysters were at filtering out waste, they could not keep up with the byproducts of the growing population. In the early 1900s, public health officials traced a series of deadly disease outbreaks back to the oyster beds, which led to their closure. As the water quality worsened, the remaining oyster population continued to dwindle. By the time this pollution crisis was addressed by the Clean Water Act in 1972, the oysters were all but gone, and with them, the biodiversity and natural protection they had provided.

In recent years, there have been attempts to bring the oyster population back, but highly dredged and flat-bottomed waterways make it challenging to revive their ecosystem. The oysters need something to hold on to—something that raises them off the muddy riverbed and helps them get a grip. In 2010, Manhattan landscape architect Kate Orff pitched just such a solution. Presented first as a speculative project, her basic "oyster-tecture" design proposal was simple: elevate huge nets made out of textured marine rope just above the seafloor, then seed them with larvae to help create a semi-artificial oyster reef that would benefit the city. Since the project was first proposed, Orff's firm, SCAPE, has received government funding to try out their Living Breakwaters initiative—a variant of the original oyster-tecture concept that employs rocks rather than ropes. The resulting oyster reef should help reduce coastal erosion, build up beaches, and protect against storms. SCAPE has also teamed up with the Billion Oyster Project, which collects shells from restaurants around the city and turns them into substrate that new oysters can grow on.

Even if this project works, it won't entirely stop water from coming ashore during a massive surge. Seawalls have been considered by New York and other coastal cities, but these create a hard barrier that cuts people off from access and assumes a fixed maximum water level. Rather than trying to divide land from sea, plans to regrow oyster reefs offer a chance to mediate between built and natural environments. These reefs can be used to create a more nuanced buffer of cleaner, calmer waters along shorelines while also providing a framework for habitats. This kind of hybrid design is neither fully organic nor artificial—it is something new, part ecosystem and part infrastructure, and perhaps a step toward a better relationship between cities and the waters that surround them.

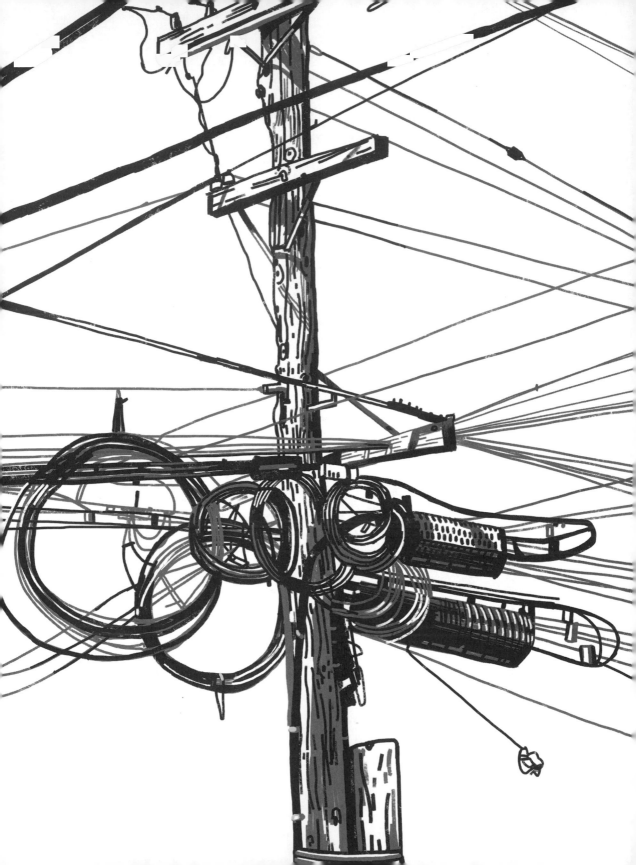

# TECHNOLOGY

WIRES CONNECT US. THE TWENTIETH century saw cities become covered in a haphazard layer of wires connecting people to electricity, light, information, and one another. Cities in the twenty-first century have seen many of these wires disappear, at least on the surface, but the networks of connection will always remain.

LEFT: *Utility pole supporting power grid and internet cables*

# FINE LINES

## *Utility Poles*

"THESE GIANTS ARE MORE CONSTANT THAN EVERGREENS," observed John Updike in his poem "Telephone Poles," an ode to America's vast network of wooden utility posts. "They have been with us a long time. They will outlast the elms." Indeed, these stalwart stakes are still around. They have been part of telecommunications systems ever since Samuel Morse was down to the wire on the first big test of his newfangled telegraph machine.

Before pivoting to pioneer an unprecedented form of telecommunication, Morse had been a painter for much of his life, well known in American halls of power for making portraits of former presidents and other famous figures. While working on a commission in 1825, he got a letter from home explaining that his wife was ill. The message arrived in Washington, DC, by horse carrier, but it came too late. By the time Morse got the news, she had already passed away. It is widely believed that this tragedy is what spurred him to put down his paintbrush and take up the cause of long-distance communication.

Slightly more than a decade later, Morse publicly debuted his first telegraph machine, but without anyone to send the signals to, it wasn't a very useful invention. So he set about using his political connections to lobby the government and secure funding for the creation of a telegraph network. In 1843, Congress finally gave Morse $30,000 to demonstrate his system's city-to-city capabilities. He and his team began laying out underground wires between the Capitol Building in Washington, DC, and a Baltimore train station, but the lines kept failing. Low on time and money, they decided to dig them back up and string wires across trees and poles instead. This revised strategy worked, and America's abundance of timber helped this aboveground approach spread across the nation.

By 1850, thousands of miles of telegraph lines were in place, mainly across the East Coast. A few years later, the first telegraph cables were stretched along the bottom of the Atlantic Ocean. Then, in 1861, East and West Coast networks in the United States were connected across the Great Plains to form a transcontinental telegraph. The transformative power of these networks was profound. It had taken eight days for news of Lincoln's election to reach the West Coast in 1860, but news of his assassination five years later was transmitted almost instantly.

The telegraph became a way to send messages over long distances, but it had local uses, too. In DC and around five hundred other US cities, telegraph-based emergency call boxes enabled people to contact police stations and fire departments. Before two-way radios, police officers would also use these boxes to check in along their patrol routes.

It would take time for Morse to get the pay and recognition he deserved, but in the end, he became rich and famous—his name embedded forever in the code used by telegraph operators. In 1871, employees of Western Union declared a Samuel Morse Day and organized an associated celebration timed to coincide with the dedication of a new statue of Morse in Central Park. At age eighty, Morse skipped some of the activities but attended a reception that evening in the city where he dictated a telegraph to a waiting operator who sent out a message of peace and thanks to telegraph operators around the world. Morse died less than a year later and probably never imagined how much utility poles would evolve in his wake.

By the early 1900s, what had started out as a few wires strung across simple post-and-crossbeam supports had become huge and tangled affairs, burdened with telephone and power lines running along higher and higher stacks of horizontal slats, some reaching dozens of feet into the sky. In rural places still on the fringes of connectivity, people even rigged up networks using barbed wire fences as transmission lines. Meanwhile, ever more lines zigzagged across city streets. Some purpose-built towers could support and route thousands of wires.

Today, these networks are more streamlined—bundles are neater and often supported by metal rather than wood structures or are run underground instead. But what we still call a telephone pole continues to do a lot of infrastructural heavy lifting. It may seem like we live in a wireless age, but utility poles are still there to facilitate voice and text communications, transmit electricity to and through cities, and connect people in ever-evolving ways.

# ALTERNATED CURRENTS

## *Power Grids*

IN THE LATE 1800S, POWER PLANTS WERE CHANGING THE landscape of the Los Angeles area. Regional demand for energy was largely driven by the need to provide refrigeration for the powerful citrus industry, but it also led to Los Angeles becoming an early adopter of electric street lighting. The city was a pioneer at a time when power plants were novel and best practices were still being sorted out, including frequency standards.

Most electricity comes in waves of alternating current, and the number of pulses per second defines the frequency of the current. At first, there were no national frequency standards for the electricity being sent down the wires—both 50 and 60 hertz were common frequencies. Within a certain range, any number will work fine for typical households or businesses. A bulb might noticeably flicker at a lower frequency (like 30 hertz), but there's not much visible difference between 50 and 60. In Southern California, an engineer working on a big new plant picked 50 hertz while the rest of the country was mostly using 60. California always seems to march to the beat of its own drummer—or electric pulse.

Over time, some compatibility problems emerged, including household appliances that had to be built differently for different regions. With clocks, there was a particularly visible (and frustrating) issue. Electric timepieces used the pulse cycle to keep time, so they were dependent on that consistent sixty pulses each second to know how long a second was. This meant a clock made in New York but powered by California's 50-hertz grid would lose about ten minutes per hour. As California started to get more and more power from places like the Hoover Dam, which pumped out electricity at 60 hertz, the power output required conversion, and the situation grew more expensive and difficult to manage.

So the City of Los Angeles made the switch to 60 hertz in 1936. Then the Southern California Edison company decided to switch everyone else in the region around the city (around a million customers) over to sixty-cycle current in 1946. This was a huge undertaking that impacted all kinds of specialized as well as everyday power-using equipment. Conversion crews were sent out to rebuild machines and appliances for bigger commercial and industrial clients as well as area residents. Clocks, meanwhile, could be taken by their owners to a special "clock depot" where technicians would rebuild these electric timepieces to work at 60 hertz.

By 1948, all of Southern California had switched over to the new frequency. In the process, around 475,000 clocks, 380,000 lighting fixtures, and 60,000 refrigerators were reworked to function on the new system. As big of an undertaking as that was at the time, the decision showed a lot of foresight— as Los Angeles continued to rapidly expand over the coming decades, addressing the problem would have only grown more difficult.

Frequencies still aren't standardized globally today; most of Europe is on a fifty-cycle system. In rare cases, two different systems are used within a single country, which can cause problems. In Japan, incompatible grids make it harder to transmit power from one city to another across the country. Systems converting power between 50 and 60 hertz get stressed in emergency situations. In the wake of the Fukushima Daiichi nuclear disaster, this resulted in blackouts. Despite such drawbacks, these disparate systems are unlikely to be reconciled anytime soon—it's just too big of a switch these days. For better or worse, there's a lot of inertia when it comes to both power structures and power infrastructure.

# Moonlight Towers

## *Street Lights*

For much of human history, the moon was the brightest source of light after nightfall. The city of Austin, Texas, changed this in 1894 with a series of thirty-one "moonlight towers" erected to illuminate the downtown streets. In contrast to the moon's soft glow, the light from these tow-

ers was intense—each of them supported six lights that together could brighten the city for blocks in all directions. While Wabash, Indiana, was the first US city to use arc lights, Austin was a relatively early and eager adopter of this technology. New York, Baltimore, Detroit, and other major metropolitan areas also developed similar arc lighting systems, which emerged and spread as modern power plants came online.

Some of the moonlight towers, including the ones in Austin, were thin, trussed metal affairs up to fifteen stories tall, held in place with networks of guy wires. Others featured wide bases that spanned entire city blocks, tapering upward like miniature Eiffel Towers. Shapes aside, they worked in similar ways: the carbon arc lights sitting at the tops of these towers created a continuous spark between two electrodes. The effect was around a thousand times brighter than gas lights. Consequently, arc lights were far too intense to be put down at street level, hence the looming towers that spread the illumination around. Even up high, they were so bright that people would take to the streets at night with umbrellas to reduce the glare.

These new lights transformed Austin. They turned night into day and enabled round-the-clock urban activities. Some critics found their brightness harsh and unflattering, casting every wrinkle and flaw into sharp relief. The lights were also loud and dirty. Burning exposed arcs of power gave off annoying buzzing sounds and dropped ash on the streets below. Others also worried about the effects of night lighting on human sleep, crop growth, and animal behavior. The biggest problem, though, was the maintenance—the electrodes had to be changed out about *once a day,* which meant that workers had to go up and down the tall towers regularly.

By the 1920s, most cities had abandoned or dismantled their arc lighting towers in favor of new incandescent bulbs on posts that were easier to maintain—but not Austin. The city had fallen on hard times in the early twentieth century, and lacking funds to dismantle and remove them, officials left the old tower structures in place even as newer, more conventional street lights went up around the city.

In the 1950s and '60s, there was talk of finally getting rid of the moonlight towers, but at this point, some saw them as local monuments worth saving. So the towers were added to the National Register of Historic Places in 1976, with all the rights, privileges, and annoyances that this entails. Maintaining the dozen or so towers that remain in Austin in a historically consistent way means making repairs with historically accurate parts, right down to custom-cast nuts and bolts. This is neither cheap nor easy.

Still, the price of maintaining the towers is one that locals seem happy to pay. As a lighting technology, moonlight towers may be an evolutionary dead end—one step along the way from candles to gas to incandescent bulbs and modern LED lighting—but to Austinites, they are cultural artifacts, immortalized by local bands and cocktail bars, not to mention Richard Linklater's *Dazed and Confused.* These structures have become more than just vintage infrastructure—the hope of a "party at the moontower" is now part of the cultural fabric of Austin.

# DIALED BACK

*Electricity Meters*

IN THE MID-1970S, STEVEN STRONG WAS HIRED TO ADD solar thermal panels onto an apartment building in New England in order to heat water. While he was at it, he also added a few solar photovoltaic panels to the roof— the kind that generate electricity. These were such a new technology at the time that Strong had to figure out for himself how to wire them up and what to do with the excess energy they generated. He decided to send unused power back into the grid, which, to his surprise, caused the meter on the building to run backward.

When Thomas Edison built his first power stations, there were no electricity meters in people's homes. Instead, he started billing people a monthly fee based on how many light bulbs their household had. It wasn't a very precise system, and meters followed soon after—ones not too different from those still in use today. Now, when electricity comes into houses, a little dial turns forward to show how much is used. It turns out that the little dial also rotates in the other direction when electricity leaves a home. This was a surprise to everyone, including the meter designers, who had never conceived of such a scenario.

For most people, power only flows one way, but there are exceptions—including people who use solar panels to generate their own energy, for instance. By default, excess electricity created using solar cells travels back out into the grid to be distributed elsewhere. In most states, people can even get paid for this extra output. The practice is called net metering (referring to the net amount of energy used), and while it started off as a relatively noncontroversial practice, there are now big political battles being fought over it.

Strong's choice, coupled with the way meters were (accidentally) designed to work, effectively set a precedent for the rate that people would be credited for the excess power they produced with solar panels. Baked into this precedent is the idea that electrons being produced by the solar panels are of equal worth to ones coming from the grid, which sounds obvious and intuitive at first but would later become a point of contention. Over the following decades, legislation was written in several states that put this concept into law. Homeowners would effectively be paid a retail rate for their contributions, which was a higher rate than utility companies paid when they bought electricity from large power plants.

At first, utility companies didn't really see this as a problem—solar panels were expensive to buy and install, and thus pretty rare. Heading into the 2000s, though, solar adoption grew as the technology got cheaper and better. So utility companies have grown increasingly concerned about buying back electricity at a retail rate that is higher than their wholesale one. They argue that this not only cuts into their profits but also hampers their ability to maintain infrastructure for consumers.

Politicians, engineers, and economists are examining different solutions, including redesigning the electric meter to better reflect the true economic value of electrons at a given moment. In the end, some balance may need to be struck between consumers and producers because homeowners will be less inspired to put up eco-friendly solar panels without incentives, but without profits, utility companies won't be able to maintain the existing grid. Solar energy is the focus for now, but the way our grids evolve will also have broader implications for wind, geothermal, and other sustainable energy production methods going forward.

# NETWORK EFFECTS

## *Internet Cables*

WITH THE MODERN INTERNET, WIRELESS DEVICES, AND all this talk of the "cloud," it's easy to forget the physical infrastructure that makes these technologies possible. There are the overhead and underground lines, of course, plus satellites, but perhaps the most important (and invisible) strands of the web are the underwater cables carrying around 99% of international data traffic. Running up to 25,000 feet deep, a few hundred slim fiber-optic tubes form the backbone of the global internet. In total, hundreds of thousands of miles of these lines wrap around the world.

Mapping out ideal paths for these cables can be a serious challenge. Surveyors have to identify the stablest and flattest routes, a process made more difficult by obstacles like coral reefs and shipwrecks. Once a route is established, burying the lines helps reduce damage in shallow waters. Digging machines are lowered and towed behind ships to create trenches for cables, which are then naturally covered up by sand and soil. The type of cable armor necessary to keep these lines intact varies depending on locations and expected hazards—sharp ridges, curious sharks, fisherfolk, and anchor-dropping ships have to be taken into account.

Even with all of this planning and engineering, lines are sometimes disrupted, and while gnawing sharks are more likely to make headlines, the most common culprits behind outages are of the less sensational human variety. On average, there are a few cable failures per week around the world. These are usually not enough to completely disrupt service, which can be rerouted through other cables temporarily. When issues arise, specialized ships are sent out to splice in replacement sections. These vessels are loaded with thousands of miles of cable and remote-controlled vehicles that dive down to lift damaged lengths from the ocean floor. Ironically, while workers on these ships are in some ways more connected to these cables than virtually anyone else, they have to use satellites to get online. It's remote work, not in the modern coworking-space-nomad sense but much more literally.

Given the cost, complexity, and risks of this system, one might wonder why satellites don't carry more of the load. In short, it's still cheaper and faster to run data under the sea. While some companies are testing out balloons and other aerial strategies, for now, the "cloud" is still a creature more of the oceans below than of the skies above.

# ROADWAYS

THE ROMANS FIGURED OUT SOME-thing critical when it came to maintaining an empire: if you want a bunch of disparate communities to function under one government, build roads. Roads are a staggering yet often overlooked technology. As the things that drive on them have gotten faster, traffic engineers have had to race to keep up, sometimes creating obstacles to slow us back down. Given how deceptively simple and ubiquitous roads are, it can be easy to miss how much their design and functions have shifted and adapted over time.

---

LEFT: *Residential roadway with centerline and various users*

# ACCELERATING CHANGE

## *Painting Centerlines*

EDWARD N. HINES WAS DRIVEN BY A PASSION FOR ROADS; he was a cyclist and activist who helped convince Michigan to pass road-related legislation, including a change to the state constitution that would generate more taxpayer funding for roads. When the Wayne County Road Commission was created in 1906, Hines took a spot on it alongside Henry Ford. Then he made his indelible mark on America's roadways in 1911. According to one version of this origin story, Hines was driving along a country road behind a milk truck when an idea came to him. As the vehicle leaked its liquid cargo onto the road, Hines was inspired to invent lane-dividing lines. The tale may seem a little far-fetched, but regardless of how it happened, Hines is broadly credited with the creation of the centerline. The first stripe of paint was laid down in Wayne County, which includes Detroit. From there, lines began to be drawn through curves and other danger zones, then eventually on all roads in the county and finally the entire state. Today, roadways across the country feature millions of miles of paint from coast to coast. But while centerlines are an integral part of everyday traffic infrastructure, most of us can hardly recall a typical one in a precise way.

For years, psychology researcher Dennis Shaffer would ask his students at Ohio State to estimate the length of dashed road stripes. The median answer was around two feet despite the fact that federal guidelines recommend ten feet with thirty feet in between. Some lines aren't actually that long, but many are, especially along major highways, and they are all much longer than two feet. In short: people's sense of line distance tends to be massively different from the reality of that distance.

Part of the misperception comes from the fact that people in cars are typically looking farther out at the road ahead, so the length of the lines seems shorter. But another key to understanding the difference lies in speed—the way people perceive the world when moving quickly through it. Long dividing lines, wide lanes, and clear vistas help reinforce the illusion that drivers are traveling at a reasonable pace along a highway, even if that velocity is incredibly high compared to the speeds at which humans historically moved through the world. Visual cues can not only make higher speeds feel normal, they can encourage drivers to speed up.

This phenomenon isn't only limited to lines—the presence or absence of objects alongside a road can change drivers' perceptions of time and distance and inform their sense of speed. Take sidewalks and street trees, for instance. In many prewar suburbs, roadside trees were arrayed along verges between car-filled streets and pedestrian sidewalks. In postwar suburbs, some planners were concerned about the collision risks posed by this roadside greenery and began to experiment with putting trees on the other side of the sidewalk. Clearing out objects that could cause damage in collisions seems sensible on the surface, but it can have certain unintended side effects, like creating the visual impression of a wider paved area for drivers. More open roads encourage faster travel thanks to reduced "edge friction" from peripheral objects. A reduced number of obstacles also exposes pedestrians to increased danger when speeding vehicles swerve off roads.

All of this points to a larger traffic engineering issue: people tend to use what's given to them. Presented with wide open spaces, drivers will go faster. Intentionally closing off space by adding trees and other landscaping along the side of the road may make a driver a little more anxious but also more cautious, which can in turn make roadways that much safer for everyone.

# SHIFTING RESPONSIBILITY

## *Blaming Jaywalkers*

IN THE EARLY 1900S, AMERICAN ROADS WERE MAINLY occupied by pedestrians strolling leisurely. As more and more automobiles hit the streets, though, collisions became a serious problem. Thousands of people were dying each year, many of whom were children. As historian Peter Norton recounts in his book *Fighting Traffic,* cars began to be viewed as harbingers of death. One newspaper cartoon of the era depicted a car as a toothed monster being worshiped on a pedestal, framing it as a modern Moloch—a polemical automotive-age resurrection of an ancient biblical deity associated with child sacrifice.

At the time, these deaths were treated as exceptional tragedies. Memorial parades were held and monuments were built. Speeding cars were naturally blamed for the mortality crisis and were even compared to high-tech weapons of war. An article in the *New York Times* likened the crisis to an armed conflict: "The horrors of war appear to be less appalling than the horrors of peace. The automobile looms up as a far more destructive piece of mechanism than the machine gun. The reckless motorist deals more death than the artilleryman. The man in the street seems less safe than the man in the trench. . . . The greatest single lethal factor is the automobile." It got to the point that Cincinnati had a referendum on the ballot in 1923 to require speed governors that would put a mechanical twenty-five-mile-per-hour speed limit on cars.

By the 1920s, there were a lot of carmakers, dealers, and motor clubs growing up around the fast-evolving automotive industry. Various interested parties (collectively known as motordom) banded together to push a pro-car agenda. They wanted to shift the blame away from vehicles and onto reckless people instead. It wasn't just drivers, they argued, but pedestrians, too, who were at fault. Either way, their logic was that cars didn't kill people—people killed people—a refrain still heard today from various American lobbying groups (see: the NRA).

Motordom even coined a new term: jaywalking. At the time, *jay* referred to a person from a rural area who walked around and gawked at the city, oblivious to other pedestrians and traffic around them. So *jaywalking* was a natural extension of this concept—a way to vilify pedestrians over vehicles and call out people who crossed the street at the wrong place or time. The strategy worked. People started to understand roads differently. Streets were increasingly becoming the territory of cars while consideration of pedestrians took a back seat.

Over the following decades, more and more design effort would go into helping cars not only take priority in cities but also get them into and out of and between cities faster and faster. Looking back, it's hard to say which came first—America's love for cars, which led to all of this infrastructure, or the proliferation of roads, which led to the inevitable dominance of these vehicles. Either way, the passion of motordom arguably took America down a long and perilous one way street.

# KEY INDICATORS

## *Crash Testing*

EARLY CAR ADS TENDED TO FOCUS ON AESTHETICS, luxury, and freedom over safety. One Chrysler safety director likened cars to women's hats and suggested that "they have to have special attractiveness, and sometimes they even compromise with function." Much as carmakers had sought to blame pedestrians for collisions in the early twentieth century, there was also a push to fault drivers for injuries caused by car wrecks rather than, say, the plate glass that would shatter and slice up passengers or a steering wheel that might impale a driver on impact.

The argument from manufacturers was essentially that a "safe" car wasn't possible, even as car crashes came to be the leading cause of death in the United

States. Public service announcements warned people to watch out for bad drivers, who were singled out and derided as the "nut[s] behind the wheel." The problem wasn't just that someone needed to design safer vehicles but that someone needed to recognize that such a thing was possible, which is where engineer Hugh DeHaven entered the picture.

DeHaven had been a pilot in training in the Canadian Royal Flying Corps during World War I until his plane crashed and left him with an array of devastating internal injuries. While recuperating, he realized that a knob on his safety belt had made his organ damage much worse than it might have been otherwise. He decided to work toward a better design. DeHaven began running crash tests with eggs and other delicate objects while also watching for news of survival stories that might hold clues to better aircraft safety designs. From his experiments and observations, he concluded that the key was spreading out impacts over time and space—in essence, "packaging" people to distribute the load during a crash.

DeHaven then turned his attention toward ground vehicle collisions, which were much more common, gathering data wherever he could. He would call up hospitals and morgues to get information on car wrecks, but it wasn't until he teamed up with the Indiana State Police for a yearlong study that he made breakthroughs about which parts of cars were the most dangerous in crash situations. He discovered that hard knobs and sharp edges caused a great deal of damage, as did steering columns, which would thrust into drivers on impact. In the decades since, collapsible columns have saved tens of thousands of lives according to government studies.

Still, car companies resisted DeHaven's conclusions. It would be years before they began to make things like collapsible steering columns standard in new vehicles. Concerned with potential negative impacts on car sales, the industry wanted to avoid discussing safety with the public. It would take concerned advocates like Joan Claybrook and Ralph Nader to publicize and champion car safety. Finally, President Lyndon Johnson gave an address in the Rose Garden in 1966 that framed the issue as a public health crisis—an epidemic more deadly than war. New legislation followed, which, among other things, created federal crash databases.

Basic safety technologies that were invented or mandated in that era are still around today and still saving lives, though a lot of incremental design innovations have helped, too, thanks in part to a wealth of data. Automotive death rates have declined substantially in the last fifty years, aided by detailed on-the-scene police documentation of crash causes. This data has been critical in helping designers make safer vehicles as well as safer roads to drive them on.

# CEMENTED DIVISIONS

## *Lane Separators*

A TREACHEROUS STRETCH OF CALIFORNIA HIGHWAY NEAR Lebec known as Dead Man's Curve was, true to its name, the site of a number of crashes back in the 1930s and '40s. The presence of a painted centerline clearly wasn't sufficient, so a central guardrail was added to reduce head-on collisions. Unfortunately, with its steep grade and more than four-thousand-foot elevation change, this section of the Ridge Route remained dangerous. It also didn't help that truck drivers had a tendency to run up against the rails intentionally, using friction to help slow them down on steep descents, which damaged the barriers. So the guardrail was eventually stripped out and replaced with a series of more robust parabolic concrete dividers in 1946.

The approach seemed to work, but it was slow to take off in California. New Jersey picked up on this basic design a few years later, however, and continued to iterate on it, developing barriers that curved outward toward the bottom to form a wide, flat base and curved inward as they tapered to a thin top. These are now primarily known as Jersey barriers. Over time, different heights, widths, and angles were tested to see which ones worked best in crash situations. They look simple, like a relatively obvious (if Brutalist) solution to divide roads, but there's more to them than that.

"The average motorist has no idea how sophisticated these barriers are," writes engineer Kelly A. Giblin in *Invention & Technology* magazine. "Their primary function is obviously to separate opposing flows of traffic. But their wedge design was developed to minimize the severity of accidents by restoring control of a vehicle on impact," Giblin explains. "In a shallow-angle collision—a sideswiping—the Jersey barrier lets the front tire ride up its lower angled face and gets the vehicle back on the roadway with minimal damage." In other words, the barrier not only reduces head-on collisions, but it also reduces crashes (and crash severity) on either side of the divider by keeping vehicles pointed forward.

The design eventually made its way back out West. In the late 1960s, the California Division of Highways did their own testing using remote-controlled vehicles that were driven into barriers at different angles and speeds. Their study concluded that "the New Jersey concrete median barrier is an effective, low-maintenance design," leading the state to roll the barriers out along more and more highways. By 1975, more than one thousand miles of Jersey barriers could be found winding through dangerous roads across more than a dozen different states.

Over time, the shape has improved, and more modular and flexible design options have been developed. Early versions commissioned by the New Jersey State Highway Department were mostly permanent cast-in-place solutions.  Today, mobile concrete- or water-filled plastic variants can be temporarily slotted into place during road construction projects. They often come with a pair of hoops on top for lifting with heavy machinery or gaps on the bottom so forklifts can slide in to easily pick them up and stack them. Some space-strapped routes like San Francisco's Golden Gate Bridge even use a "zipper" version that can be raised and dropped back down one lane over by a specialized truck in a smooth and continuous sequence. As this vehicle moves slowly across the bridge, it adds a lane in one direction while taking away one in the opposite direction, adjusting for traffic patterns that change over the course of the day.

It's hard to look at Jersey barriers and see much more than a lump of concrete formed into a commonsense shape, but everything about them is highly engineered. No single inventor made these dividers what they are today—they are a product of a lengthy and ongoing design process. In a lot of ways, they reflect roadway development more broadly, where intuitive starting points lead down winding paths to solutions that only seem obvious in hindsight.

# EXTRA TURNS

## *Safer Intersections*

SINCE THE 1970S, A LOGISTICS DIVISION OF THE UNITED
Parcel Service has instructed the company's delivery drivers to avoid making left
turns. This may sound like an extreme practice at first, but it's based on solid engineering research. Upon investigation, UPS concluded that taking more lefts leads
to more travel time, higher fuel costs, and an increased risk of collisions. In many
cases, taking left turns forces a vehicle to cross oncoming traffic lanes as well as
pedestrian crossings. UPS isn't alone in their conclusion—federal data has shown
that more than 50% of crossing-path incidents involve left turns while only around
5% involve right turns.

Other drivers could take a page out of UPS's book and only turn right, but traffic
engineers have come up with some more fundamental structural solutions, including the Michigan left. Also known as a Michigan loon, a boulevard turnaround, or
a ThrU-turn, this roadway design eliminates left turns at conventional four-way
intersections by combining a U-turn farther down the street with a right turn at
an intersection—drivers overshoot, turn around, come back, and turn again. To be
fair, it's a bit more complicated than a simple left, but studies suggest that it can
reduce collisions. It can even speed things up by shortening traffic light phases
because no time needs to be allotted for lefts during a cycle.

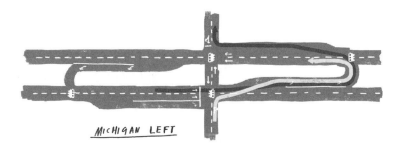

MICHIGAN LEFT

Similar solutions like the bowtie (so named for its shape) also involve overshooting, turning around, and coming back, but this variant utilizes roundabouts on either side of the intersection to facilitate the process. Then there is the jughandle (sometimes called a Jersey left), which perhaps counterintuitively shifts left turns to the right of intersections. Drivers still have to cross a lane to turn but do so at simpler junctures, which makes main intersections with crosswalks safer for pedestrians.

It should be noted that the term *Jersey left* is also at times applied to a technique that drivers use to speedily turn left at a conventional intersection in order to jump ahead of oncoming traffic as soon as they see a green light. This dangerous practice is not limited to New Jersey; people also call this (usually illegal) maneuver by other names such as the Boston left, the Pittsburgh left, or the Rhode Island left depending on where they hail from. Michigan lefts, bowties, and jughandles may take up more space and be more confusing for out-of-town visitors, but at least they are less dangerous than racing to turn in front of oncoming vehicles.

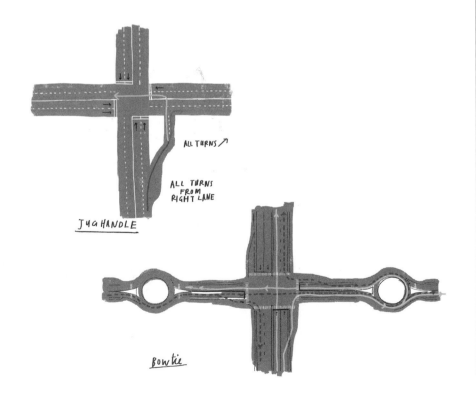

# CIRCULATING LOGIC

## *Rotary Junctions*

THE CITY OF CARMEL, INDIANA, BOASTS AN UNUSUAL claim to fame on its local government website: "Carmel now has more than 125 roundabouts, more than any other city in the United States." According to city data, replacing signaled intersections with roundabouts has saved the city money while also reducing collisions by 40% and crashes with injuries by 80%. Drivers also save money on gas. While some find roundabouts confusing at first, data suggests they are generally safer and more efficient at moving traffic than four-way stops and other kinds of intersections. While they have detractors, roundabouts, as it turns out, have big fans, too.

Across the Atlantic, where roundabouts are a bit more common, the irreverent UK Roundabout Appreciation Society extols the many virtues of "the roundabout ... truly an oasis on a sea of tarmac," which they view as far superior to "fascist, robotic traffic lights where we are told when to stop and go." And any discussion of British roundabouts must include the most magical of them all: the Magic Roundabout.

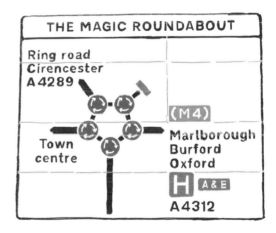

Located in Swindon, England, this uncanny ring junction was designed by engineer Frank Blackmore of the British Transport and Road Research Laboratory back in the 1970s. He tested out solitary roundabouts, then started trying double, triple, and quadruple variants. The final quintupled implementation in Swindon was originally called County Islands, but it was nicknamed the Magic Roundabout, a moniker that stuck and later became its official name. It really isn't one roundabout—it's five smaller roundabouts that run clockwise, arrayed around a larger one that runs counterclockwise. As impossible as it may seem at first glance, this configuration is actually very efficient and has since been adopted (and adapted) in other parts of Britain.

It works like this: each circle around the periphery allows cars to enter from feeder roads. Cars then rotate through the various circles to exit where they want. Experienced navigators can move through it fairly quickly and directly while less proficient ones can always go with the flow, working their way around the edge until they get where they need to go. Initially, traffic police officers were stationed all around to make sure drivers could understand the flow of traffic, but people soon got the hang of it.

If this all still seems crazy and complicated, consider the relative simplicity of each choice a driver has to make along the way. They only have to follow the lines and arrows, yield to others already in a given circle, and keep moving incrementally toward their destination. As a whole, it looks like a mess, but at each step, it's relatively straightforward. Plus, any complexity could also be spun as an advantage: increased awareness forces drivers to pay more attention to the road and their surroundings rather than relying on signs or signals.

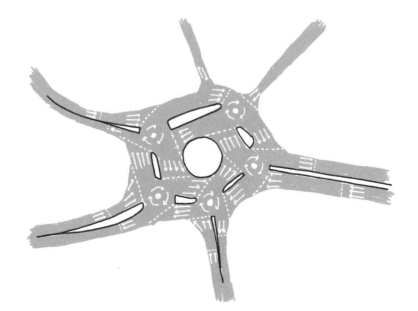

The Magic Roundabout still has its critics. It was voted the worst roundabout by a British insurance company, named one of the world's worst junctions by a motoring magazine, and ranked as one of the ten scariest intersections in a driver survey. Such intimidating reviews may help explain why roundabouts are less popular in other countries, including the United States.

Few American cities have embraced these alternative junctions with the same enthusiasm as Carmel, which for much of its history relied primarily on conventional intersections. It is only in recent decades that the momentum there has shifted. One roundabout led to the next and so on, and they have increasingly proven to be greener, faster, safer, and cheaper options. As reported in the *Indianapolis Star,* area resident Nathan Thomas appreciates these benefits but also jokes that he likes roundabouts "because it's enjoyable to weave back and forth and I feel like a race car driver," a somewhat ironic assessment for a design aimed to make driving safer.

# INCOMPLETE STOPS

## *Calming Traffic*

WHEN DRIVERS SEE SPEED BUMPS, THEY TEND TO SLOW down, which is precisely the idea behind a pilot program in London that uses a perceptual trick as a traffic-calming device. The apparent bump is just paint on a flat surface, but it creates an illusion based on perspective. Seen from the side, the effect breaks down, but from the front, the 2D paint looks like a 3D bump in the road. It may be an illusion, but if it works, it could represent a very real way to slow down drivers alongside physical bumps, humps, and lumps.

There isn't universal agreement on what to call the various forms of "umps" out there. For most people, a speed bump is what first comes to mind, which, by some accounts, is simply a taller and thus more severe version of a speed hump. Then again, the National Association of City Transportation Officials doesn't refer to speed bumps at all in its descriptions of "vertical speed control elements." In

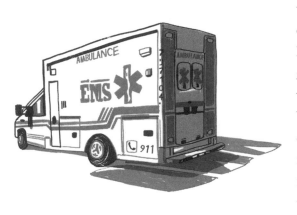

their list, though, is one clever variant that stands out from the rest: what they call "speed cushions" (others call them lumps), which have specially designed gaps positioned so the widely spaced wheels of emergency vehicles can go between a pair of bumps (or lumps or cushions or whatever) rather than having to slow down and go over them like normal cars. There are many variants of traffic-calming designs out there, including pinch points, chicanes, gateways, and various other kinds of raised pavements and curb extensions. Suffice it to say that urban designers have tried a lot of tricks to slow drivers down.

This wide array of physical barriers can be helpful, but some solutions can create problems of their own, including passenger discomfort as well as air and noise pollution as vehicles bounce up and down. In theory, solutions that are purely visual could help address these issues. Optical illusions are one option, but there are other tricks, too, like an odd street-spanning brick circle that appeared in Cambridge, England, in 2016. In this case, unfamiliarity was meant to confuse drivers into going slower. The confounding circle has been jokingly referred to as a "UFO landing pad," an "urban crop circle," and a "free doughnut zone."

Speaking with *BBC News* about the design, road safety analyst Richard Owen argued that "the behavioral science which sits behind it is quite good." From his perspective, "it's about making drivers feel much more uncertain about the road environment, and that's the way you slow cars down without using vertical humps." That said, in the very framing of that solution another problem becomes evident: once familiar with this phenomenon, drivers will presumably learn to overlook it, and its benefits will wane over time. The same is true of an illusory speed bump that doesn't deliver a jolt to those who speed over it. Even if they work in some exceptional cases, such illusions rely on a driver having experience with actual humps, bumps, or lumps. Put another way: replacing all physical umps with fakes would eventually prove self-defeating.

# REVERSING GEARS

## *Changing Lanes*

ON SEPTEMBER 3, 1967, THE HÖGERTRAFIKOMLÄGGNINGEN went into effect, and millions of Swedes went from driving on the left side of the road to driving on the right. Commonly shortened to Dagen H, or H Day, this turnaround was arguably the most massive and efficient overhaul of driving infrastructure that the world had ever seen. There is no right or wrong way to run opposing lanes of traffic, but as the Swedes had learned, there are compatibility issues.

Historically, the side of the road that people walk, drive, or ride on has varied and shifted. When horseback was a primary mode of transit, people usually rode on the left side so their right hand remained free to greet or attack oncoming riders, depending on what the situation called for. With the rise of horse-drawn carriages, conventions began to change. Drivers would often sit on the left rear horse, so their dominant right hands could better control the rest of the team that stood to the front and right of the driver. It then made sense for them to drive on the right side of roads so drivers would be positioned in the middle of the lane and be able to keep track of their surroundings more easily. Still, there was no universal convention, and as cars began to replace horses, everyone tended to follow local traditions.

Until Dagen H, Swedes drove on the left while neighboring countries like Denmark, Finland, and Norway all stuck to the right. Visitors who traveled back and forth were frequently involved in collisions due to their unfamiliarity with local traffic patterns. In addition to this danger, a lot of Swedes drove imported cars from countries like the United States. Even Swedish automotive companies made cars for export that were meant to be driven on the right. But some of these vehicles wound up being used in Sweden, which positioned drivers along the edge of the road and made it harder for them to see and navigate. To combat these issues, the Swedish government made the case for switching to the right and put the decision up for a public vote.

Public response to the idea of reversing lanes was overwhelmingly negative; 82.9% of voters wanted to stick with the familiar convention. In the end, the government overrode its outraged citizens and declared that a change had to be made. Officials began creating entire departments to help with the impending transition, addressing physical infrastructure as well as public awareness. They distributed pamphlets, made public service announcements, and designed signs and stickers featuring a new *H* logo, which was short for *höger,* or "right." A Swedish television station even held a contest to write the best song to help people remember the imminent switch. The winner, *"Håll Dej Till Höger, Svensson"* ("Stick to the Right, Svensson") by the Telstars, involved a bit of a double entendre. In Swedish, "keeping to the right" is shorthand for being faithful to your spouse while "going left" means having an affair.

In the hours leading up to the changeover, most cars were kept off the road as construction crews switched around road signs and performed final infrastructure tweaks. Then, at 4:50 in the morning, a horn blared and a loudspeaker announced the switch. Remarkably, H Day went very smoothly, thanks in part to drivers displaying excessive caution in the face of what was presumably a terrifying shift—there were even fewer accidents than normal.

The relative painlessness of this transition did not go unnoticed around the world. A year after Sweden switched sides of the road, Iceland also moved over to driving on the right. Then, in the 1970s, former British colonies including Ghana and Nigeria switched from left to right to align with their neighbors in West Africa. Today, the vast majority of the world drives on the right. In places like the United Kingdom that still stay left, critics occasionally argue for a switch to the right. There is, however, one notable exception to this overall trend.

In 2009, the island republic of Samoa did the reverse of what Sweden and so many others had done: they went from driving on the right, like most of the world, to driving on the left. Moving to the left was tactical, aligning Samoa with the country's three closest major economies (Australia, New Zealand, and Japan). Among other advantages, by making the switch, they could import used cars from Japan, which has one of the cheapest used car markets in the world. This right-to-left transition went smoothly, though that wasn't much of a surprise, as Samoa has only a few major roads.

These changeovers go to show that even when traffic patterns in countries have changed dramatically, drivers have proven themselves more than capable of adapting to new circumstances. These precedents should buttress any arguments in favor of making bold decisions when it comes to improving urban life by changing our relationship with roads. As it turns out, a shift that all but literally flips a driver's experience upside down can prove safe in the end, even one that defies 82.9% of the voting public.

# PUBLIC

A S POSTINDUSTRIAL HUMANS *NOT* encased in motorized steel vehicles got run off the road, they had to figure out new places to occupy in the leftover spaces. That hasn't always been easy. For decades, the needs of pedestrians and bicyclists have been sidelined, forcing them to scratch out an existence on the margins. But these constituencies have recently been fighting back, and the tense relationship between car-dominated routes and alternative modes of transportation is being renegotiated in a much more public way.

**LEFT:** *Interstitial space between street and sidewalk with grass and trees*

# ON VERGES

## *Interstitial Spaces*

THERE'S OFTEN A THIN LINE BETWEEN A STREET AND sidewalk. At times, this proverbial thin line widens out into a strip of land—sometimes called a verge—that can take various shapes and go by different names in different places. In New Zealand and some parts of the United States, these are called berms. In parts of Canada and the Upper Midwest, they are known as boulevards. In places along the East Coast and West Coast, they are sometimes referred to as curb strips. They can also be sidewalk lawns or sidewalk plots in the American South, swales in South Florida, devil strips in Northeastern Ohio, and the list goes on: besidewalk, grassplot, park strip, hellstrip, tree belt, planter zone (for obvious reasons), or furniture zone (since they provide space for benches, utility poles, fire hydrants, and other "street furniture").

Perhaps these stretches of land have evolved so many different monikers precisely because they can serve a correspondingly wide variety of functions. They open up space for greenery, street lights, and bus shelters, and act as barriers for pedestrians on sidewalks, protecting them from collisions as well as puddle splashes. They play ecological roles, too, helping manage runoff and mitigate water pollution while providing habitat zones.

For all their various uses, however, verges do come at a cost. In packed urban areas, they are sometimes seen as underutilized space. In many dense and picturesque old cities, verges are notably absent, and that absence shapes the experience of those places. Imagine an old cobbled road in an ancient city with no curbs, verges, or other things separating street from sidewalk; vintage architecture is piled up on both sides to frame a cozy scene. This could be many places in the world, from the narrow roads of Bayreuth, Germany, to the winding *hutongs* of Beijing, China.

Whether or not to employ verges comes down to local priorities regarding how land should be allocated for greenery, architecture, pedestrians, cyclists, and motorists, as well as how these allocations are best connected or separated, divided or shared. It would be easy to argue that more verges means more green space, which is a net good, but some truly wonderful cities rely on the absence of verges to foster density, walkability, and other more intangible aims.

# CROSSING OVER

## *Pedestrian Signals*

IN THE WAKE OF GERMAN REUNIFICATION, THERE WAS A concerted effort on both the former East and West sides to erase visual cues that the border had ever existed. In the midst of all this coming together and associated celebration, though, there were points of contention—often seemingly small things, like the Ampelmännchen. For decades, these "little traffic light men" had signaled to residents of East Germany when to (or not to) cross the street. Their role, though, grew beyond simply helping people navigate their city—by the time the Berlin Wall fell, they had become far more loaded with local significance than their creator had ever intended.

These little figures were designed in 1961 by traffic psychologist Karl Peglau. His big idea was to use not just color but also shape to create signals that would work for people with impaired vision or color blindness. Part of his solution was to make the "walk" and "don't walk" characters quite different. One thing the walking and standing figures had in common, though, was a whimsical straw hat. These hat-wearing Ampelmännchen would come to star in their own comic strips and play key parts in public service announcements regarding street-crossing safety. So when plans were announced to standardize signals across East and West, and potentially get rid of these iconic figures, some citizens protested. As a result, not only were some Ampelmännchen preserved in the East but others even started popping up in the West.

Today, these characters are arguably more popular than ever before. People spend millions of euros a year on Ampelmännchen memorabilia. The figure of the green walking man in particular has become a kind of standing ambassador for *ostalgie* (nostalgia for East Germany). As reported by *Deutsche Welle,* this figure "enjoys the privileged status of being one of the sole features of communist East Germany to have survived the end of the Iron Curtain with his popularity unscathed."

LONDON    PARIS    New York    Madrid

While these figures from the former GDR are particularly well known and much beloved, city-specific pedestrian icons are by no means unique to Germany. There are usually some basic commonalities across countries, like red and green for stop and go, and a relatively static pose paired with a more active one. Seen side by side, though, such characters show a surprising amount of variety in their shape and movements as they stride, amble, jog, or even dance to the loud chirping of street-crossing signals. Individually, they are easy to overlook, but taken together with other visual cues, these icons play their bit parts in making different cities distinctive, recognizable, and memorable as they help people cross streets.

# SHARROWED ROUTES

## *Cycling Lanes*

THE SHARED LANE MARKINGS ON STREETS FOR CYCLISTS
that eventually evolved into what we call sharrows were a compromise from the very
beginning. An early version of this lane-share marking was developed by traffic engineer James Mackay for Denver in 1993. At the time, the city was reluctant to spend a
lot of money or give over a lot of space to bike-friendly
design solutions like dedicated lanes. Mackay's cheap
and simple solution could be painted in existing lanes
to point cyclists in the direction of traffic and serve
as a visual reminder that drivers should share the
road. The design depicted an abstracted cyclist inside
an arrow. This shared-use-lane pavement marking
became informally known as the bike in the house.

A more recent and widespread dual-chevron variant was first called a sharrow (a portmanteau of share
and arrow) by Oliver Gajda of the City and County of
San Francisco Bicycle Program. Subsequent success
in California, perhaps aided by its catchy new name,
led to these icons being deployed around the country.
Though they have mostly appeared on residential
and other urban streets, they've even shown up on
fast-moving highways. Their usage has proved divi-
sive at times, but they have a lot of supporters.

Sharrows seem to work well by some metrics according to studies commissioned by the Federal Highway Administration. The markings can help
shift cyclists outside of the dangerous "door zone" alongside parked cars and
reduce wrong-way cycling on roads. In theory, these symbols also raise drivers'

awareness of bikers sharing their lane. In practice, though, some studies have come back with ambiguous or even negative results—it's not entirely clear how effective sharrows are. Regardless, "shared lane markings should not be considered a substitute for bike lanes, cycle tracks, or other separation treatments where these types of facilities are otherwise warranted or space permits," according to the *Urban Bikeway Design Guide* put out by the National Association of City Transportation Officials.

In a perfect world, bikes would presumably get their own dedicated lanes, but that's not always feasible, so sharrows continue to be a middle-of-the-road option in many places struggling with spatial and budgetary limitations. Some cities are still iterating on this relatively new urban design innovation. Boston, for instance, has tested out what one reporter dubbed "sharrows on steroids," which are basically sharrows reinforced with dotted lines within a wider vehicular lane. In Oakland, solid green paint has been deployed along stretches of road to indicate shared lanes, adding more visibility than periodic sharrow markings. Perhaps these enhanced sharrow solutions will prove more effective or at least serve as a stopgap in cities where making space for cyclists has been particularly difficult. For now, though, sharrows are still too often used as an excuse to do less rather than more for urban cyclists.

# CONGESTION COSTS

## *Easing Gridlock*

A FEW YEARS BACK, PARIS BEGAN EXPERIMENTING WITH a "day without cars," during which vehicular traffic is all but eliminated in central parts of the city. It's part of a larger project of rethinking urban space and redesigning to prioritize pedestrians and cyclists. This push is not unique to France. In London, a hefty congestion charge applied to most vehicles during high-traffic times on weekdays discourages excessive downtown car traffic. In Barcelona, effectively car-free superblocks are being created by combining sets of nine blocks and forcing vehicles to move around their exterior. In China, where urban megaprojects abound, there has even been talk of designing brand-new car-free cities from scratch.

This drive to eliminate cars may be picking up speed, but it's not exactly new. As far back as the 1970s, places like Manhattan had people championing a car-free future. Cars had been slowly taking over New York City for decades. Tolls had been rolled back on bridges between boroughs while streetcar lines had been pulled up to make more room for cars. Back then, Sam Schwartz—known as Gridlock Sam for coining the now-ubiquitous traffic term—was a young traffic department employee who wanted to push back against urban automobiles. He and his colleagues advocated ambitious solutions like a complete ban on private vehicles in Midtown Manhattan during the week from ten a.m. to four p.m. The city got as far as printing signs before this car-free red zone idea was officially scrapped. In the aftermath, Schwartz and other activists pitched all kinds of approaches to help clear up the streets, including mandates that would allow only cars with two or more people to drive in Manhattan.

Predictably, politicians and businessmen pushed back against these and other efforts to reduce car traffic and balked at the idea of turning roads into bike lanes and public plazas. Some worried that creating more public space would boost already high urban crime rates. Industry lobbyists claimed that cutting off cars would also hurt shopping and hotels. In the wake of all of this, *gridlock* came to mean not just literal traffic jams but also the bureaucratic congestion encountered in urban politics and politics in general.

In recent years, New York City has slowly made progress toward the reduced-traffic world Gridlock Sam envisioned decades ago. Pedestrian-only plazas, protected bike lanes, congestion pricing, and tolls are all back on the table. Even Times Square has been freed of cars. The city has experimented with other car-free areas, too, which may seem like a radical vision of the future, but actually reflects a return to a time before cars pushed everyone else out of the way.

# EXTRAVEHICULAR ACTIVITIES

## *Naked Streets*

SOME CITY PLANNERS, RESEARCHERS, AND ANALYSTS have begun to question whether certain staples of street design like signals, signs, curbs, and barriers that are explicitly intended to keep us safe actually make us safer. Towns all over Europe have started to experiment with streets where cars, buses, bikes, and pedestrians can travel more freely in the same space, challenging a dominant paradigm of modern urban design. This trend is sometimes called the "naked streets" movement. A British Department for Transport guide describes such "shared spaces" as places remade to "improve pedestrian movement and comfort by reducing the dominance of motor vehicles," thus "enabling all users to share the space rather than follow the clearly defined rules implied by more conventional designs"—rules that divide users and dedicate more space to automobiles. One Dutch champion of this novel trajectory has taken to walking backward across streets with his eyes closed in order to demonstrate how safe it can be.

In Poynton, England, there used to be a mess of signs and lights with a few small sidewalks and some haphazard guardrails to keep pedestrians safe. Then, a few years back, all of these traditional traffic signifiers were removed. The town spent four million pounds to expand sidewalk space and strip the city center of conventional demarcations. Now, the only marker left is a little sign that says, POYNTON SHARED SPACE VILLAGE.

The idea is that without clearly demarcated zones, everyone will be more cautious—commuters will slow down, make eye contact, and visually negotiate with others. Meanwhile, cars won't spend time waiting at traffic lights, allowing drivers to move more quickly through intersections. In theory, shared spaces work well for pedestrians, who can walk wherever they want more freely. In practice, people often still walk where they would expect to see crosswalks, and when asked, many report preferring things the way they were before.

By the numbers, some of these experiments seem to be working, with data pointing to a reduction of collisions and near misses after shared spaces are installed. According to some estimates, shared spaces can also reduce travel times and delays by 50% or more. Still, that doesn't mean these designs can work for everyone. From the beginning, shared space strategies have taken heat for providing insufficient protections for disabled pedestrians, especially the visually impaired. In Britain, there have been political battles over whether to keep or remove shared spaces or study them further before pushing forward.

Preliminary designs by groups like the Danish Building Research Institute hint at more balanced approaches that might work better than either extreme. Their concept includes both the mixed traffic of shared spaces but also some traditional urban design elements like raised street textures and button-activated crosswalks for pedestrians with disabilities. Any such new strategy will require further research and testing as well as public education, engagement, and feedback. If this trajectory ultimately leads to a paradigm shift, it may mean once again rewriting the rules of what a city can and should look like.

*Chapter 4*

# ARCHITECTURE

**W**HEN PEOPLE THINK OF CITIES, they often think of big buildings. That's fair. Grand and imposing structures are often used to represent the pinnacle of human achievement. The architect usually gets the credit, but no building is a pure creation that springs perfectly formed out of a single person's mind. Buildings are a surprising hodgepodge of constraints, regulations, mistakes, fashion, history, compromises, and inelegant workarounds. Yet that makes them all the more beautiful and intriguing. As you walk on a city street lined with buildings, be sure to look up but also be sure to look deeper. Pay attention to how the doors move. Consider what materials were used in construction. What parts are old? What's been replaced? These choices all have stories behind them that are often more interesting than the official narrative.

---

PREVIOUS: *Stabilized ruins along the Mississippi River in Minneapolis*

# LIMINAL

THE TRANSITION POINT BETWEEN shared public space and private interior space is both the first and the last place you interact with a building. You push. You pull. You push when you're supposed to pull. You fumble with a lock. If you're lucky, all these interactions happen smoothly on the ground floor. If you're unlucky, and there's an emergency, you may be forced to discover whether a window opens or a thin metal fire escape can hold your weight. If a building fails at these transition points, it fails as a building.

LEFT: *Revolving and swing doors for public ingress and emergency egress*

# IMPERFECT
# SECURITY

## *Locked Entries*

IN THE LONG HISTORY OF DOORS AND LOCKS, THERE WAS only a brief stretch of time when people could feel a justified sense of perfect security. It lasted for about seventy years, starting in the late 1700s, with a highly secure mechanical lock that no one was able to breach. Before this period, locks were easy to break. Designers relied on predictable and beatable forms of trickery like false keyholes made to throw off would-be thieves and trespassers. Anyone hoping to keep something safe found they mostly had to rely on the goodwill of people inclined to conform to the norms of society. All of this changed when an English inventor named Joseph Bramah made a breakthrough in security design.

Bramah's design is now widely considered the first high-security lock. In simplified terms, the device added layers of complexity between the key and the bolt mechanism, making it harder to pick. Remarkably, the lock's inventor made no effort to hide its inner workings. Instead, he openly published plans and invited lockpickers to defeat his creation. He was so confident in his design that he crafted a stand-alone padlock version to put in his London storefront. Painted in gold letters on a sign next to it was a message: "The artist who can make an instrument that will pick or open this lock shall receive 200 guineas the moment it is produced," a sum that would amount to tens of thousands of dollars today. For decades, people tried and failed to hack it.

In the wake of Bramah's lock, more sophisticated locks with additional security features were developed, including Jeremiah Chubb's "detector lock." A regulator mechanism inside would freeze up the lock entirely if a tumbler was pushed too far. This not only worked to prevent intrusions, but it also alerted owners to the fact that someone had tried and failed to break in. One cheeky advertisement for the lock read, "My name is Chubb, that makes the patent locks. Look on my works, ye burglars, and despair." This new lock drew the attention of consumers as well as the government. To test whether it was really unbreakable, the state offered a jailed burglar an official pardon if he could crack this device; Chubb sweetened the pot for the crook by adding one hundred British pounds as a bonus reward. Despite being an expert lockpick, the convict tried for months and ultimately failed.

The golden age of perfect security ushered in by these and other seemingly uncrackable designs lasted well into the 1800s until the American locksmith Alfred Charles Hobbs crossed the Atlantic to visit the Great Exhibition of 1851 in London. For many, the steel-and-glass Crystal Palace—which foreshadowed the essential elements of future skyscrapers—was the big draw, but not for Hobbs. For him, it was a set of supposedly unbreakable locks at the exhibition that would test the lock-breaking skills he had honed during his time in the security industry. Hobbs had built a profitable business out of going around to various banks across the United States, subverting their existing security systems, and then offering them an upgrade.

The exhibition locks would prove challenging for Hobbs, but not unbeatable. In the end, he picked the Chubb detector lock and bypassed its regulator by using the mechanism against itself. He methodically tripped each part of the lock into its fail-safe position, then reworked it into a normal locked position, thereby learning a piece of the puzzle with each intentional overreach. After unlocking the detector lock multiple times, he moved on to Bramah's "safety lock," which was developed more than a half century before but still hadn't been picked. Hobbs spent more than fifty hours spread across two weeks on the problem and slowly cracked this supposedly unbeatable device. His solution wasn't elegant—it took a lot of time and would be hard to replicate—but it shattered the idea of perfect security.

In the wake of these breakthroughs, locksmiths continued to develop new and more sophisticated locks. Without a unifying idea of perfect security, though, approaches to lock design soon diverged. While high-security needs were met with ever-more impenetrable devices, most homes and offices wound up becoming easier to break into than they would have been with a Bramah lock. The pin-and-tumbler lock is ubiquitous not because it works especially well but because it is cheap and easy to install. Chains and bolts and bars and alarm systems abound, but these technologies also aren't failproof. Modern competitive locksport is less about whether a lock can be beaten than about how fast the task can be done. When it comes down to it, the trust that people put in the security of most entryways is now once again less about the lock itself and more about faith in a broader social order that respects the division between public space and private property.

# OPEN AND SHUT

## *Revolving Doors*

IN THE LATE 1800S, THEOPHILUS VAN KANNEL BROUGHT a novel German innovation to the Big Apple, installing a revolving door as the entrance to a restaurant on Times Square. His company advertised that their doors "Cannot Be Left Open, Blown Open, or Slammed. Are Always Closed, Yet Allowing the Passage of Persons"—or, put less bombastically, they could be open and closed at the same time. After millennia of people having to swing or slide doors open and shut, the revolving door was a big turning point. This new type of door proved to be useful not just for avoiding awkward social door-holding interactions but also for keeping out dust, noise, rain, and snow. The "always closed" aspect of such openings served another function, too, which a group of MIT students set out to quantify in 2006.

As part of a study about the effects of door choices, the group found that revolving doors exchange eight times less air than typical swinging doors, which results in a lighter load for building heating and cooling systems. Each pull (or push) of a hinged door draws air with it and forces HVAC machines to compensate. Over time, this passage in and out can add up to thousands of dollars in wasted energy and associated environmental costs per year for a heavily trafficked building. These downsides are compounded by the fact that most people confronted with the choice skip over revolving doors in favor of adjacent swinging ones. For some users, a revolving door compartment can feel cramped and awkward. For others, including people with disabilities or anyone pushing a stroller or carrying bags, these spaces can be physically difficult to navigate.

Some designers have tried using signage to direct more people toward revolving doors, but there are other ways to guide users to a preferred entry or exit. Revolving doors are more often selected when their compartments are spacious and allow those passing through to feel safer. At hotels with more prominent revolving doors, it also helps when staff members don't actively encourage people to take swinging alternatives by automatically opening them for guests. People follow paths of least resistance and go with the flow as long as their routes remain obvious and unobstructed.

Revolving doors can work well when they work, but when they fail, the results can be catastrophic, as in the case of Boston's Cocoanut Grove nightclub, which caught fire in 1942. The blaze killed 492 people, many of whom were trapped inside when the primary revolving-door entrance became packed with fleeing patrons. Other exits had been boarded up, bolted shut, or tucked out of the way. Ones that could have worked in theory became jammed in practice because they swung inward rather than outward. All of these design flaws complicated the chaotic scene and made it more difficult for people to escape. The next year, Massachusetts began passing safety laws that, among other things, required revolving doors to be flanked by outward-swinging alternatives with "panic bars" to make exiting safer and easier. There was a sobering design lesson embedded in this tragedy: as important as doors are for letting people in, they are even more important for letting people out.

# Improved Egress

## *Emergency Exits*

FIRE HAS LONG BEEN ONE OF THE GREATEST EXISTENTIAL threats to buildings and their occupants, but it hasn't always received a proportional amount of design consideration. Back in the 1700s, fire escapes were not the built-in features we imagine today but rather mobile ladders on carts hauled to blazes by firemen. By the mid-1800s, major cities like New York were experiencing a huge influx of citizens, and these old-school ladders were increasingly not up to the challenge. Cheaply built with narrow staircases, highly flammable tenements towered ever higher, so the city began requiring these to have an on-site means of egress. Landlords predictably opted for the most inexpensive solutions they could find, like ropes and baskets that could be used to lower people down the sides of structures. Other innovators came up with even wilder ideas, like parachute hats, which looked delightful but proved rather ineffective in execution. One engineer actually suggested that archers on the ground could shoot arrows with ropes attached to them up to high floors for fleeing residents to shimmy down.

Most of these solutions were wisely left by the wayside as iron fire escapes began to be attached to buildings. While these were often scary to navigate, having something stable and permanent attached to a facade was at least a few steps up from amateur archery. Of course, building owners were not particularly excited about the added costs of these more robust options. Many went out of their way to minimize compliance, executing the bare minimum allowed by law and using loopholes whenever possible.

New York's ten-story Asch Building was supposed to have three staircases, but the architect believed two would be sufficient because an exterior fire escape ladder would offer a third means of emergency egress. The top three floors of the Asch Building were rented to the Triangle Shirtwaist Company, which had approximately six hundred workers crammed inside when a fire broke out in 1911. The blaze spread quickly, and employees scrambled to find a way out. Some workers on the tenth floor made it to the roof and survived by using an older "scuttle" skylight escape to exit upward, while most workers on the eighth floor made their way down the stairs to the street. Many on the ninth floor, though, were trapped due to locked doors and overcrowded staircases, forcing them to use the metal fire escape, which collapsed under their weight. In total, 146 people died. This horrific incident became a rallying point for workers' rights advocates and led to a lot of publicity, activism, and reform. But strangely enough, the building fared much better than its occupants. It had been well designed to withstand a large fire but not to help people escape from one. The deadly disaster illustrated that fireproofing wasn't enough—a good system of egress was essential, too.

After the Triangle Shirtwaist Factory Fire, the National Fire Protection Association started collecting data and studying effective egress. Exterior metal fire escapes, they determined, were too infrequently used and thus tended to fall into disrepair. Their metal attachments were also prone to erosion from being exposed to the elements. They were also challenging for children, people with disabilities, and women who were hamstrung by long skirts and other fashion norms of the times. The NFPA also noted that people don't naturally run toward fire escapes when panicked—they go down familiar routes like the primary staircases they use regularly. All of these observations and conclusions helped shape new approaches to escape routes.

In modern high-occupancy buildings, the flow of people during an emergency has become a top consideration from the outset of the design process. A typical system of egress involves smoke detectors and signage, but it also includes more structurally integrated features, with entire staircases, corridors, and evacuation routes baked right into architecture. Most fire escapes have essentially been swallowed up by buildings, evolving into fortified fire stairs. Inside contemporary structures, fire stairs often double as ordinary staircases used on a daily basis. The difference now is that these otherwise-ordinary stairs are given extra protections and features to make them safer routes of escape during fires, earthquakes, or other disasters. Some metal fire escapes have been grandfathered in, but for the most part, they are simply a vestigial reminder of how much a long-standing and well-justified fear of fires has shaped urban environments.

# MATERIALS

FROM STONES IN SCOTLAND TO bamboo in China, buildings are shaped by local materials, needs, and traditions. As buildings got bigger and safer, building materials have done much of the heavy lifting. In many places where fires ravaged neighborhoods and even entire cities, bricks were selected to replace wood; concrete later proved a cheaper and faster alternative to brick, albeit with its own downsides. New methods of making wood stronger, more durable, and fire-resistant have many advocates pushing for this ancient building material to be a primary choice for future architecture. Despite these shifts, one thing remains constant: no single material will stay in fashion forever.

LEFT: *Homes in St. Louis partially demolished by brick thieves*

# STOLEN FACADES

## *Recycling Brick*

FOR MUCH OF ARCHITECTURAL HISTORY, AIR-DRIED bricks were the only kind of bricks. They were used in many of the earliest known cities along the great river valleys of northern Africa and southern Asia, where mud and water were readily available. These simple bricks worked well in warmer climates. Fired bricks came along a few thousand years later and proved to be a much more robust and adaptable option. They were a natural choice for the Roman Empire as it spread across a wide range of climates. Techniques for firing largely flickered out in many of its fractured territories as the empire faded, but with the Industrial Revolution, mass-produced bricks once again proved a popular, efficient, and economical choice. They have become so ubiquitous in modern times that when people say "brick" everyone reasonably assumes they mean fired brick.

A black market for fired bricks may sound improbable at first—bricks are heavy and not terribly expensive per unit—but in some places, there comes a time when the building blocks of structures are worth more than the buildings themselves. St. Louis reached just such a tipping point toward the end of the twentieth century, after a long history of making and using bricks across much of the city.

When hundreds of wooden buildings in St. Louis were ravaged by fire back in 1849, the city had passed legislation requiring new buildings to be constructed from fireproof materials. Around the country, other massive fires caused various municipal governments to rethink wood as a primary building material, too, but St. Louis had something of a built-in advantage: the Midwestern city was home to a large amount of high-quality red clay. The region also had a lot of coal to fire local clay into brick. It was "a perfect storm of materials, labor, and industrial innovation," explains Andrew Weil of the Landmarks Association of St. Louis, "that combined to make St. Louis into a brick producing powerhouse." By 1890, St. Louis boasted the world's largest brick-manufacturing company, and other cities were seeing the value in the region's especially durable all-weather bricks. Millions of bricks were exported across the United States. Bricks were so cheap and plentiful in St. Louis that even working-class homeowners could afford to have one-of-a-kind brickwork laid out in complex and ornate arrangements along domestic facades.

As the brick industry boomed, however, the foundations of white flight were being laid. Following World War II, the GI Bill enabled military veterans to get home loans and move out to white-picket-fenced suburban houses. Many people ended up leaving cities and vacating urban homes, even ones built out of high-quality bricks that could stand for hundreds of years. Particularly in under-resourced neighborhoods, people began to demolish homes for their constituent materials. Lots of legally or illicitly recycled St. Louis bricks ended up in other parts of the country, particularly the American South, where the mild climate allows even weather-sensitive interior bricks to be used on the outside of buildings.

By the early 2000s, brick theft was rampant and dozens of houses in North St. Louis were being partially or entirely destroyed each month for their building materials. Some brick thieves would loop cables into one window and back out of another to pull down entire walls. Others took things a step further, setting buildings on fire to burn out anything flammable in the structure. When firefighters showed up, their high-pressure hoses would knock down the bricks, conveniently cleaning off attached mortar in the process. Once the smoke cleared, the freshly toppled bricks were easy for the arsonists to pick up and resell to brick suppliers. Unlike their ancient air-dried predecessors, high-quality fired bricks are portable and valuable on the secondary market.

In St. Louis, it's still common to see bricks on the facades of new buildings, but they are often just that: a facade. Over time, newer masonry veneers have grown thinner and thinner, and these slimmer facades rely more on hidden wood, metal, and concrete supports. Creating more traditional, brick-heavy homes is challenging and cost-prohibitive, so a thin veneer of clip-on bricks is often used instead. In other words, bricks, which started out as load-bearing elements, have evolved to become mostly decoration. Modern building construction may be less regionally varied and more homogenized, but standardized, cheaper, mass-produced materials can help make housing affordable, which in turn makes cities more equitable and better places for everyone to live.

# AGGREGATE EFFECTS

## *Cracking Concrete*

EVEN BEFORE THE NEW BOSTON CITY HALL BUILDING WAS completed in 1968, critics were calling for it to be demolished. City dwellers of the mid-1900s had become used to the bulging geometries and stark rectilinearity of Modernism and Brutalism, but many still expected more traditional gold domes and Greek columns for municipal buildings. The design of Boston City Hall was intentionally bold, with a series of cantilevered floors jutting out over an adjacent plaza and thick concrete supports framing dark little windows. Its large spans and daunting overhangs were meant to show off the potential of concrete as an architectural material, the hope being that this modern approach would spur a new era of urban revitalization.

Boston City Hall has received awards and been praised by architects, but it has also made numerous worst-buildings lists since its construction. For some, it falls into what architecture critic Ada Louise Huxtable called the "architectural gap, or abyss, as it exists between those who design and those who use the twentieth century's buildings." Criticism that this municipal structure was cold and alienating played into local political battles. It became a talking point of mayors and city council members as they vied for public support with promises to tear it down. Love it or hate it, though, the building was meant not only to be grand but also to serve as an example of how an incredible material once used by the vaunted Roman Empire could reshape modern built environments.

Ancient Romans left behind marvelous aqueducts, durable paved roads, sophisticated sewer systems, and other remarkable works of design. Out of their era came the Pantheon, which still holds the record as the largest unsupported concrete dome in the world, standing tall and wide without the metal reinforcement used extensively in concrete buildings today. The potential of concrete was lost for more than a millennium before it was rediscovered and iterated on by engineers over the last few centuries. By the early 1900s, this material had made its way back into city infrastructure and began to be lauded as a material of the future. Water, cement, and aggregate (often sand or stone) were cheap and easy to obtain, and with iron or steel reinforcement, concrete could also span long horizontal distances. It thus became the go-to building material for roads, bridges, tunnels, sidewalks, and finally buildings, though its architectural applications have been met with mixed feedback.

The phrase *concrete jungle* is sometimes used to depict urban landscapes as artificial and unpleasant. It can conjure images of a certain bland commonality across cities, but concrete is a product of place, too, and so its composition often varies across environs. Concrete is at once global and local. One of the reasons Roman concrete persisted for so long was because it included regional ingredients like the volcanic dust that strengthened their admixtures. Contemporary concrete buildings also vary in color and texture depending on local earth, stone, structural needs, and building traditions.

Modern concrete, however, is not the miracle material many imagined it would be. Structures built with it today often start to decay in mere decades. In some cases, poor ingredients are to blame, but even with higher quality materials, that same steel reinforcement that helps provide tensile support also hastens the demise of the structures it supports. As rebar rusts, it stops helping and starts hurting. The steel expands, cracking the surrounding concrete. Often invisible on the surface, this damage compromises structural integrity and can lead to costly repairs if not outright demolition.

Some engineers are seeking to learn from long-lasting ancient Roman examples in order to develop admixtures that can remain stable or even become more durable over time. Other researchers are working on projects like self-healing concrete in which embedded materials are activated when exposed to water or moist air and then expand and spread to fill cracks as they develop. Even if these kinds of solutions materialize, concrete comes with other baggage, including serious environmental impacts that have grown in proportion to its popularity.

Second only to water, concrete has become one of the most consumed products in the world. Unfortunately, concrete takes a ton of energy to make and is composed of materials that may seem abundant but are actually limited. Demand for sand has skyrocketed in recent years, particularly the rough sand that is useful as concrete aggregate. Billions of tons of sand are mined each year just for construction purposes. The increasing scarcity of sand and the growing recognition of concrete's role in climate change has led designers to consider other materials both old and new.

# HYBRID SOLUTIONS

## *Amassing Timber*

WHEN IT WAS COMPLETED IN 2017, THE BROCK COMMONS Tallwood House in Vancouver, British Columbia, became the world's tallest timber-framed building, topping out at more than 170 feet. On its exterior, facades dominated by wood-grained panels serve to highlight the tower's primary structural material. Inside, wood-to-wood connections limit the need for metal and relegate steel-reinforced concrete mainly to the base and the elevator core. It may seem surprising, but after a century of concrete, glass, and steel dominating urban landscapes, wood is making a comeback thanks to new mass timber building technologies, fire safety innovations, and a growing interest in eco-friendly design.

As a material, wood is presumably as old as human architecture, used to frame ancient temporary dwellings by our distant ancestors. Throwing together sticks led to tents and shacks and simple timber construction, but wood's potential has evolved a great deal more in recent years. In the Brock Commons Tallwood House, prefabricated cross-laminated timber floor panels are supported by glue-laminated timber (or "glulam") columns. These engineered wood columns are much stronger than ordinary cut lumber and can be made into large structural elements without cutting down large old growth trees. Wood has other advantages, too. It is much lighter than concrete or steel, requires less energy to move, and has a fraction of the environmental cost. Its main ingredient is also renewable and international— trees can be planted, harvested, and cut locally in many places and farmed like a fruit or vegetable.

"Wood is one of nature's most innovative building materials," writes Becky Quintal for *ArchDaily*. "The production has no waste products and it binds $CO_2$. Wood has low weight," she notes, but it also offers "a very strong load-bearing structure compared to its lightness." Fire is still a problem, but not as much as one might imagine, as wood actually performs well under heat stress. It can be "more fire resistant than both steel and concrete," notes Quintal, in part because wood contains water, the evaporation of which can delay a blaze. In a fire, wood chars on the outside, which protects the wood on the inside. While steel heats up quickly and buckles, wood first drops water weight and then burns slowly from the outside in. Many municipalities around the globe are catching on to these advantages, adapting building codes around new fire-tested timber products and building techniques. The material once abandoned by many cities in the wake of devastating historical fires may now play a key role in remaking cities in the years to come.

# REGULATIONS

T HE FORM THAT ARCHITECTURE takes is in part a function of available materials, local climates, and building technologies, but these are only the most tangible factors. In addition, there is a layer of rules, regulations, and taxes that play a significant (and often surprising) role in shaping buildings, from the sizes of individual bricks to the shapes of entire skylines.

LEFT: *Canal houses in Amsterdam reflecting municipal tax strategies*

# SECULAR ORDERS

## *Taxable Units*

TAXATION CHANGES FROM ONE GOVERNMENT TO THE next, but in many cases, the impacts of old taxes can linger for centuries, subtly embedded in built environments. In the wake of the American Revolutionary War, Britain faced a mountain of debt due to extensive overseas military expenditures, so King George III introduced a British brick tax in 1784 to raise revenue. The rule was straightforward, as was the initial workaround: each individual brick was taxed, which led manufacturers to start making bigger bricks. The Crown fought back by increasing the per-brick tax and doubling taxes on bricks over a certain size. Some manufacturers went out of business, unable to sell their old stock without paying hefty taxes, while others kept calm and carried on. Meanwhile, some builders avoided the fray entirely by shifting to timber and other building materials. Still, many buildings were built out of the newer oversized bricks, making it easier for historians to date such structures.

This wasn't the first or the last time that taxes would reshape architectural design in the United Kingdom. In 1684, a baker trying to bypass a hearth tax, which was used as a proxy for taxing family units, tapped into a neighbor's chimney rather than building her own. Her hack, however, led to a fire that destroyed twenty homes and killed multiple neighbors. The hearth tax was subsequently criticized, which may have contributed to King William III's introduction of a less incendiary window tax in 1696. The logic behind this tax was simple: the more windows a building had, the more people paid. In response, citizens ended up boarding or bricking up a lot of windows in rooms deemed less important. Some remain that way to this day despite the eventual repeal of the tax.

These kinds of taxes even made their way from exteriors to the interiors of British homes. In 1712, a British tax on patterned, printed, and painted wallpaper led to a trend of people buying plain paper and stenciling designs on it themselves.

In 1746, a weight-based tax on glass sparked a shift in design strategies, prompting glassmakers to craft smaller, more delicate, and often hollow-stemmed glassware that became known as "excise glass."

The United Kingdom wasn't the only country in which taxes shaped design. Dutch canal houses are at the heart of Amsterdam's contemporary character, but they weren't designed that way for aesthetic reasons. Taxed on their frontage rather than their height or depth, many Dutch buildings were built thin, tall, and long to minimize tax obligations for their owners. In turn, this typology necessitated narrower staircases, which led to exterior hoist systems for moving furniture and goods into and out of upper floors. These old hooks and hoist wheels still hang off the front of many structures to this day. Narrow buildings packed together along the cobblestone streets of this picturesque place were not part of some vision to make a cozy urban experience for modern tourists but rather the product of creative tax planning.

The shapes and sizes of bricks, windows, glassware, and even the dimensions of facades may seem like minor aesthetic details, but layers of taxation and other municipal regulations have cumulative effects. Over time, these elements add up to form the architecture that we now see as quintessential and integral to the character of historic neighborhoods and cities.

# FORMATIVE SETBACKS

## *Mansard Roofs*

THE MANSARD ROOF (SOMETIMES CALLED A FRENCH ROOF) is an iconic design often associated with Georges-Eugène Haussmann's grand and sweeping vision of Paris. Commissioned by Emperor Napoléon III in the mid-1800s, Haussmann's infamous urban renovation reshaped large swaths of the urban landscape. With it came much of the city's now-classic look and feel—its wide streets and its mixed-use structures with their consistently thick stone walls, repeating details, and aligned heights. Along the tops of these cream-colored, limestone-veneered structures sit rows of dark, steeply sloped mansard roofs punctured by dormer windows. These iconic mansard roofs, though, actually pre-dated Haussmann. Their widespread adoption was spurred in large part by something much more mundane than one visionary's sweeping master plan—humdrum municipal height limitations.

In 1783, Paris implemented a twenty-meter (roughly sixty-five feet) restriction on building heights, but with it came a crucial caveat: this limit was based on measuring up to the cornice line, not the roof zone above. Historically, Parisian buildings were tall, narrow, and deep, and typically featured a shop on the ground floor, a shopkeeper's residence above that, and family residences above that. The top floor was often used for storage, but population pressures made that real estate too valuable. Property owners seeking to optimize their habitable space responded by building mansard-type roofs, effectively creating an additional rentable floor above and beyond what would otherwise be allowed. Later, window-based taxes offset some of the financial incentive behind this design strategy, but they didn't put an end to this style.

Similar restrictions in other places helped the mansard roof spread beyond Paris. A 1916 zoning resolution in New York City called for setbacks on tall buildings. Mansard roofs represented an elegant way to comply with this rule.

While some developers stepped their buildings back in jagged increments to deal with setback requirements, other designers tilted the tops of buildings back from the street by creating huge multistory mansard roofs. Today, mansard roofs can be found around the world, some built to work with (or around) legislation, and others simply because they look good.

# HEAVEN TO HELL

## *Property Limits*

AS FAR BACK AS THE THIRTEENTH CENTURY, A POWERFUL principle has informed the legal notion of property ownership—*cuius est solum, eius est usque ad coelum et ad inferos.* Or in English: he who owns the soil owns everything above and below, from heaven to hell. The idea is intuitive but potent, asserting that landowners not only own their land but also an infinite vertical column of space above and below the surface. Before subway systems and air travel and tall buildings, this approach worked well enough, but the rise of cities and new technologies complicated things. The heaven-to-hell principle (often abbreviated to *ad coelum*) has been chipped away at in the centuries since it was coined.

Around the time the first hot air balloon took to the skies in 1783, people began to realize that, under laws based on *ad coelum,* trivial trespass violations could occur when an airborne traveler passed over someone's land. As plane travel began to take off in the United States, *ad coelum* was curbed by the government through legislation like the Contract Air Mail Act of 1925 and Air Commerce Act of 1926, which carved out rights for aircrafts.

Over the next few decades, the idea of airspace as a public highway began to take hold. Then, in 1946, *United States v. Causby* helped put a definitive end to the idea of unlimited aerial ownership. Thomas Lee Causby was a farmer with a problem: his chickens were literally being scared to death by low-flying military planes. So he sued the government. The Supreme Court concluded that the government can't claim airspace rights below a certain height, but their ruling also stated clearly that *ad coelum* "has no place in the modern world." Causby won compensation for flights that had passed over his property below the public airspace altitude of 365 feet.

Back down on (and under) the ground, the *ad infernos* aspect of *ad coelum* has been similarly challenged, with the principle holding less sway the lower one goes.

Various laws and rulings have established that sufficiently deep sewers, subways, drainage tunnels, and particle colliders do not deprive surface owners of their land rights. Mineral and water rights further complicate the concept of *ad infernos:*

> **MINERAL** rights can apply to fuel sources (coal, gas, and oil), precious and industrial metals (gold, silver, copper, iron), and other resources (salt, limestone, gravel, and so on). In many places, these can be bought and sold independently of surface rights.

> **LITTORAL** rights can extend outward for properties adjacent to bodies of water, like an ocean, bay, delta, sea, or lake. In most places, there are allowances for usage tied to low or high waterlines that inform private use and public access rights.

> **RIPARIAN** rights deal with water that flows through properties, like rivers and streams. Small bodies are generally limited to "reasonable use" with various exceptions and restrictions (to protect watersheds, for instance). Larger ones are usually treated much like public highways. The details get complex fast because interest in these moving waterways is shared by so many parties beyond a given property owner, including cities, states, and other owners with their own rights. Even rain falling on private property can be problematic—some municipalities restrict rain barrel usage on the grounds that retaining water denies rights to potential water usage for people who live downstream.

Land, air, water, and subsurface rights may go unnoticed by many property owners, but restrictions around them have fundamentally shaped urban environments in highly visible ways. Cities like New York are heavily informed by such rights, with building setback rules shaping tall towers.

The Big Apple also permits the sale of air rights in certain cases to developers who want to build higher structures than would otherwise be allowed. This process can help owners of smaller historic buildings justify and fund preservation efforts rather than demolishing and building taller and more lucrative structures. In simplified terms, the owner of a historic ten-story theater with permission to build fifty stories might sell their remaining forty stories' worth of air rights to the developer of a nearby skyscraper faced with a similar fifty-floor cap but who wants to build a ninety-floor tower. While the specifics can get a bit more complex, this kind of transfer has helped save a number of old NYC theaters. Today, it would be just as hard to imagine a Manhattan without its classic low-rise Broadway venues as it would be to imagine the same city without its tall skyline-defining high-rises.

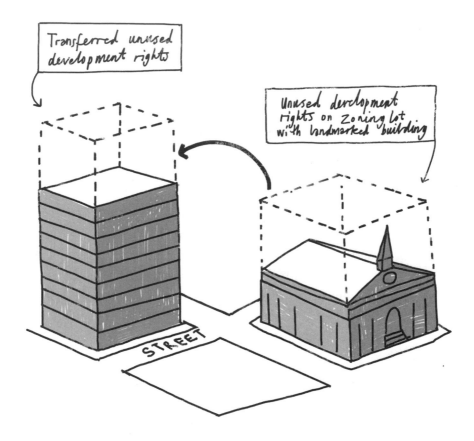

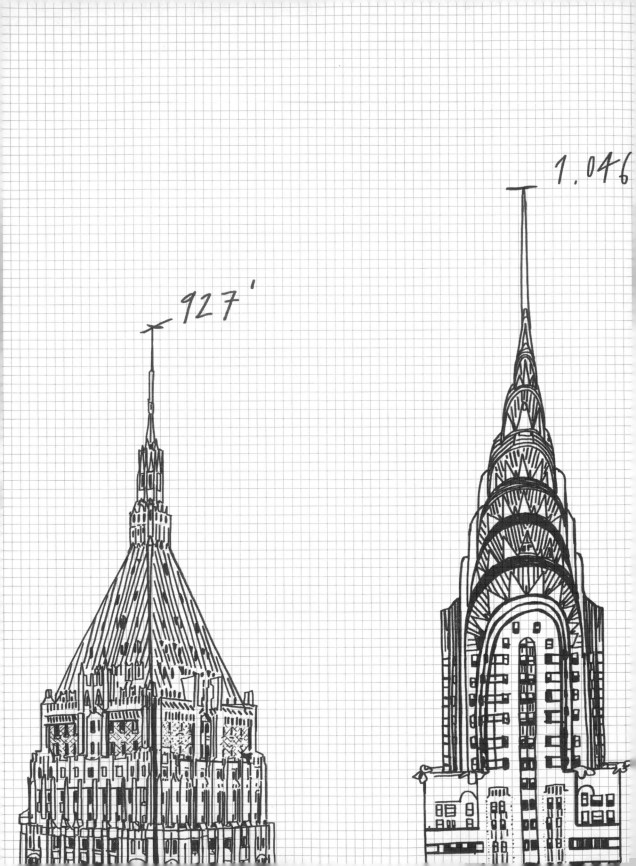

927'

1.046

# TOWERS

A SKYSCRAPER IS A MACHINE THAT IS designed to turn land into money. In dense cities with expensive real estate, building story on top of story of rentable space is the logical result, but it took a few key developments to make tall buildings possible, most notably the self-braking elevator and steel-frame construction. Once those innovations were introduced, cities began to grow upward at a dizzying pace, though attaining new heights also led engineers to encounter new and unprecedented challenges along the way.

LEFT: *Two New York City skyscrapers competing for height records*

# BRAKING GOOD

## *Modern Elevators*

ELISHA OTIS DIDN'T INVENT THE ELEVATOR—LIFTING boxes and platforms up and down using ropes, pulleys, and other machinery goes back thousands of years. Like many designers and inventors, he simply saw a problem and came up with a solution. In this particular case, Otis was working with a crew lifting and installing machinery at a furniture factory in the early 1800s when a rope snapped and sent a two-story service elevator platform crashing down. Having witnessed the impact of this failure firsthand, he developed a braking system for the company and earned himself a promotion.

By 1854, Otis had taken his idea further, replicating the falling elevator situation on a larger scale in a public setting. Standing on a forty-foot-high platform at the New York Crystal Palace, he gestured to an assistant to cut a support rope to simulate a snapped elevator cable. Otis fell just a few inches before his automatic brake kicked in and brought the platform to a halt, eliciting cheers from the audience. While Otis didn't dream up the idea of a vertical lift system, he made it safer and showed off its safety in style.

The success of the brake dovetailed nicely with other engineering innovations of the era. Before the elevator took off, conventional architecture more than a few stories tall was rare; most tall buildings were niche structures like churches or lighthouses. As technological innovations enabled progressively taller buildings, stairs were increasingly a limiting factor for the humans who had to walk up them. Otis saw the potential for elevators to change the world and began to market them as solutions to this growing staircase problem. He sold his first order for a passenger elevator for use in a five-story retail building in New York City in 1857.

Following Otis's death in 1861, his sons iterated on their father's invention and began marketing it more aggressively to the public. They targeted hotels, convincing them that with a fancy elevator in place, rich guests could quickly ascend to the top floors and escape the noise and bustle on the first level. Historically, the ground floor was the most accessible and thus the most desirable, but it didn't have to be, they argued. As elevators spread, buildings grew higher, and the penthouse level eventually became the most luxurious floor.

Over the century that followed, various companies would continue to improve on elevator designs, making them speedier and smoother to keep up with the rise of ever-taller towers. Completed in 2009, the Burj Khalifa tower rises a dizzying 2,717 feet above the flat desert landscape of Dubai. Among its other selling points, the building was outfitted with the world's fastest double-decker elevator made by none other than the Otis Elevator Company. This lift travels thirty feet per second, taking passengers up 124 floors in about one minute, and it is just one of more than seventy Otis elevators in the building. It took a lot of impressive engineering to make this tower possible, but it seems safe to say that without elevators such tall structures would never get built at all.

# CLADDING SKELETONS

## *Curtain Walls*

FOR MOST OF ARCHITECTURAL HISTORY, BUILDING heights were limited by the physics of stacking heavy blocks on top of one another. Greek and Roman temples worked largely because they sat close to the ground, with thick support columns. Egyptian pyramids reached higher, but those verticals were made possible by wide bases. Gothic cathedrals relied on buttresses to reach toward the heavens, but even their heights were limited. Up through the nineteenth century, ten-story urban buildings were mostly rare marvels, and those that existed came with significant downsides. Their masonry walls had to be thicker at the bottom, which meant less floor space on lower levels. A classic example of this conundrum is the Monadnock Building in Chicago, built in 1891. At sixteen stories, the building was exceedingly tall for its time, but to achieve that height, the walls at the base had to be six feet thick.

Such limitations posed a serious dilemma for John Noble Stearns, a silk importer who purchased a plot of New York City land at a prime location along Broadway in the late 1800s. Various architects told him that it would be impossible to build a structure more than ten stories tall on this twenty-two-foot-wide site without sacrificing around half of the interior space on the first floor. An architect named Bradford Lee Gilbert, however, claimed that he could do what others had deemed impossible and create a tall tower with walls no more than a foot thick.

While other architects looked toward traditional materials, Gilbert had his eye on technologies of the Industrial Age—in particular, steel bridges that could support trains with tons of cargo passing over them. He posited that the same structural principles and materials could be turned from a horizontal application to a vertical orientation. Using structural steel in a building wasn't an entirely new idea, but designs like Gilbert's took things a step further. In his Tower Building, the masonry, which normally supported a structure, would form a thin "curtain wall" and would provide no structural support—the bricks would be entirely supported by the steel skeleton instead. This "frame and cladding" approach would become the universal method for making tall buildings.

At the time, innovative approaches like Gilbert's were met with a healthy amount of skepticism. In response to such critics, Gilbert offered to place his own offices on the top floor of the Tower Building to demonstrate his confidence in its capacity. During the construction process, he reportedly even scaled the building's framework as eighty-mile-per-hour winds swept through it. From above, he dropped a plumb line to show the stability of the steel frame.

Upon the building's completion in 1889, Gilbert was good to his word and moved into the penthouse. For years, he could sit at his desk and watch other towers sprout up around the city using the same structural approach he had helped pioneer. The Tower Building would stand only for a few decades before being demolished, but it would go down in history as one of the first buildings of a new era, heralding the rise of ever-taller skyscrapers.

# TOPPING OUT

## *Skyscraper Races*

THE ENGINEERING CAPACITY TO BUILD HIGHER AND higher buildings heading into the twentieth century launched a perpetual race to the top. Around the world, the title of world's tallest building has been given out over and over again even though designers, engineers, developers, and clients know their structure will hold this record for only a short while. In recent years, the skyscraper race has become an international phenomenon, albeit a relatively repetitive and increasingly vapid one, as a new tower in Dubai challenges one in China, or Saudi Arabia pulls ahead of South Korea in the race. Back in the 1920s, though, this kind of vertical rivalry was more novel. Things got especially tense when two skyscrapers in the same city were each slated to become the tallest, a competition made all the more intriguing because the lead architects were bitter rivals.

William Van Alen embodied the architect-as-artist stereotype, more devoted to the creative process than to things like schedules or budgets. His former partner, H. Craig Severance, meanwhile, was a rational, by-the-book type who was more interested in the business side of the enterprise and maximizing profits. When the two had a falling-out and went their separate ways, Severance's business savvy helped him find a lot of lucrative work in New York City during the Roaring Twenties. Van Alen had a tougher time until automobile magnate Walter Chrysler came along. Chrysler wanted a tower that would be tall, magnificent, and original, and he thought Van Alen could realize this vision. Severance, meanwhile, was investing with a financial partner in a big new building located at 40 Wall Street that would be profitable, ordered, and efficient. Each team set out to make their tower the tallest in the world.

The first announcement came from the Chrysler Building team: their structure would be 820 feet high, taller than the then-highest Woolworth Building, which clocked in at 792 feet. Severance's team came out a few months later with their own announcement: 40 Wall Street would be 840 feet. New height announcements flew back and forth even as construction was underway. Higher and higher targets were set. Magazines and newspapers covered the competition, keeping a curious public up to speed.

Chrysler and Van Alen worked on ways to adapt their expressive design to ever-increasing heights, even stretching out the building's iconic Art Deco dome to gain altitude. Severance, meanwhile, added more floors to stack the deck in a simple, methodical countermove. But the ultimate victory wouldn't be due to either of these strategies; it came down to a hidden surprise instead.

As both towers went up, Van Alen had a team working on a secret weapon inside the Chrysler Building. Bits and pieces of metal were hoisted up within the center framework of the building and then assembled to create the vertex. This 185-foot-long triangular spire destined to top the Chrysler Building was hidden inside until the other building reached its final height. At that point, the vertex was lifted up to the top of the Chrysler building. The result was a 1,046-foot structure, the tallest in the world.

With its steel-clad arches, sunburst triangular windows, hood ornament–style eagles, and hubcap-esque friezes, the Chrysler Building got a mixed reception from architects and the public. Regardless, it eventually became a highly recognizable icon of the city while few people can picture 40 Wall Street (later renamed the Trump Building). Less than a year later, the Empire State Building would eclipse both buildings, setting a new height record. The Chrysler Building's brief time as the world's tallest tower no doubt fueled some of its initial fame, but these days what makes it still stand out in a sea of taller towers is its distinctive aesthetic.

# UNANTICIPATED LOADS

## *Managing Crises*

BY THE TIME THE FIFTY-NINE-STORY CITICORP CENTER skyscraper was built in 1967, New Yorkers were getting used to seeing improbable steel-and-glass towers rise up around them. Still, it was one of the tallest buildings in the world, and its unusual steeply sloped roof helped it stand out even in the increasingly crowded Midtown Manhattan skyline. But while most eyes were focused above, it was easy to miss something unusual going on down below. A set of four stilt-like supports lifted the main structure high off the ground—not at the corners, as one might expect, but in the middle of each side. This design decision was born out of the need to satisfy a requirement of the church that occupied one corner of the block. The whole block had belonged to this church, so when they sold it, they did so on the condition that any new structure had to accommodate a new church building in the same corner location. This presented a challenge.

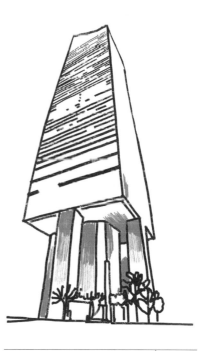

Architect Hugh Stubbins led the project, but most of the credit for the design solution goes to its chief structural engineer, William LeMessurier. His idea was to raise the building up over the church by situating supports along each side and then brace the building with a series of steel chevrons. These V-shaped supports would channel loads down to the stilts centered on each of the tower's four facades. A tuned mass damper—essentially a huge chunk of concrete resting on pressurized ball bearings—would help stabilize the building and keep it from swaying in the wind. It all seemed to work out fine until LeMessurier's office got a phone call in 1978.

Diane Hartley was an undergraduate architecture student who had been study-ing the building for a thesis project. In the midst of her research, she had calculated that the structure was specifically vulnerable to quartering winds blowing in from the corners. She wanted to verify her calculations with LeMessurier's engineering reports but couldn't find his data to confirm. When she contacted his office to ask about their math concerning this particular vulnerability, the firm started to worry that something might indeed be amiss and that Citicorp Center's structural supports could buckle, which could cause the entire building to blow over in the wind. In most buildings, side winds are of greater concern, and corners are quite stable, but the side-stilt approach of this one changed the equation. Making mat-ters worse, a cost-saving decision to use bolts rather than welds at key joints had rendered the structure especially vulnerable.

LeMessurier checked the math and concluded that something had to be done. He compared the velocity of winds the building could withstand with weather data and found that a storm strong enough to topple Citicorp Center hits New York City every fifty-five years on average—and that was only if the tuned mass damper keeping the building stable was working to counterbalance the movements of the structure around it. In a blackout, he realized, the device might lose power, leaving the tower vulnerable even in a less extreme storm scenario. For each year the CitiCorp Center stood, LeMessurier figured, it had about a one in sixteen chance of collapsing. It was a catastrophic disaster waiting to happen right in the heart of Manhattan.

LeMessurier and his team reached out to Citicorp to coordinate emergency repairs on the building. With the help of the New York Police Department, they worked out an evacuation plan spanning a ten-block radius. Three different weather services were tasked with keeping an eye on potential windstorms. With Hurricane Ella drawing near, the city had 2,500 Red Cross volunteers on standby as construction workers went into action. Retrofit crews welded throughout the night in secret and quit at daybreak when the building occupants returned to work. The storm, meanwhile, never made landfall, and the people who worked inside the building were never notified.

By sheer coincidence, New York City newspapers were on strike at the time, so the media missed out on the scoop and the whole affair flew under the radar. Years later in 1995, writer Joe Morgenstern overheard a retelling of the events at a party. He interviewed LeMessurier and broke the story in *The New Yorker*—Diane Hartley, the architecture student who first called attention to the oversight, was unnamed at the time and only later learned of the chain of events her call had set in motion. In the end, a building that was never quite a contender to be the world's tallest found another way into the spotlight and history books—albeit not in the way its designers ever would have wanted.

# PERSPECTIVE MATTERS

## *Redefining Skylines*

MODERNISM WAS ON THE RISE IN THE MID-1900S, BORN out of aesthetic ideals as well as material necessity. The typical minimalist steel-and-glass look of mid-century skyscrapers was championed as clean, functional, and structurally honest, and most architects fell in line with this design aesthetic. So when plans were unveiled in the late 1960s for a Postmodernist pyramid-shaped tower to sit in the heart of San Francisco, there was a lot of pushback, especially from the architectural community.

The Transamerica Pyramid, which came to serve as both the headquarters and the logo for the Transamerica Corporation, would redefine the skyline, dwarfing surrounding buildings and becoming the tallest structure in the city. Some saw it as an affront to good zoning and smart urban planning; others attacked its unusual form as a marketing gimmick. The local chapter of the American Institute of Architects spoke out against its construction as well. The two hundred feet of unused space at the top of the building that completed the pyramid shape was a particular affront to the functionalist sensibilities of the Modernist-leaning architects at the time. Protestors took to the street wearing pyramid-shaped dunce caps. Neighbors sued to halt construction. A ballot initiative to limit building heights was introduced. The

design was reviled as an "inhumane creation" and "second-class . . . Space Needle." But the designer and client ignored the pushback and outcry and moved forward with construction.

In the decades since the tower was built, however, some critics have had a change of heart. The passage of time has played a role in this, but experiencing the building as part of the city has also helped put it in perspective. The Transamerica Pyramid sits at a very peculiar intersection in San Francisco's downtown financial district. The block it occupies is surrounded on four sides by ordinary gridded city streets, but it also sits at the terminus of Columbus Avenue, which comes in at a forty-five-degree angle. Views from this street reveal an entirely different side of the structure—or edge, as it were. Perhaps the original designers could have gotten more people on board had they publicized illustrations of this perspective in advance, assuming, of course, that the effect was by design.

There are other inelegant things about the building that architects love to hate, like the awkward way it meets the ground below or the strange window shapes, which are byproducts of the overall form. Still, if critics had their way back in the late 1960s, the San Francisco skyline would be a lot less distinctive today. The Transamerica Pyramid is no longer the tallest building in the city, but it still stands out from the rest of the fairly conventional steel-and-glass towers in the skyline that came before and after.

# BEYOND ABOVE

## *Engineering Icons*

THE SKYSCRAPER RACE OF THE TWENTIETH CENTURY started out as a show of corporate power with buildings like the Sears Tower, the Chrysler Building, and the Transamerica Pyramid being developed in parallel with the rise of the United States as a political and economic power. In recent years, there has been a shift toward naming projects after places rather than companies, with structures like the Shanghai Tower and the Makkah Royal Clock Tower becoming icons of their respective cities. Taipei 101 is one such place-named building and it isn't just tall, it's *supertall,* a designation given to any building more than three hundred meters tall. At 508 meters (1,667 feet), this tower easily earns that designation.

Upon completion, Taipei 101 was the world's tallest building, which is no small feat given the obstacles it had to overcome in terms of its urban environs as well as the geology and weather of the region. Earthquakes and typhoons had to be factored into the engineering of Taipei 101, and local flights needed to be rerouted around it. But above all, tenants and visitors had to be convinced that the massive building would be safe and comfortable to occupy. To help foster this sense of security, architect C. Y. Lee modeled the exterior on an elongated pagoda and adorned it with gold coins, lucky dragons, and other auspicious design elements that played a part in selling this building to the public. Inside, project designers went even further to reinforce a sense of safety and comfort.

A key strategy for keeping this structure stable is a tuned mass damper, which is essentially a counterweight against the winds, but unlike most dampers, this one also serves as a core aspect of the building's identity. In some towers, the tuned mass damper is a weight on rollers; in others, it is a block of concrete suspended in a pool of liquid. In Taipei 101, it is a gigantic pendulum that slows the sway of the structure. A number of tall thin skyscrapers have dampers of some sort, but they are usually hidden behind closed doors on locked upper floors. In Taipei 101, the enormous damper is the star attraction of the building.

Located toward the top of the tower, a massive gold-painted orb is suspended by four bundles of thick cables. This sphere is made up of forty-one stacks of solid steel and weighs as much as 132 elephants. The result is a highly visible display of the building's safety, but the developers didn't stop there. They also hired the Sanrio Company, famous for marketing Hello Kitty, to brand this creation. The company came up with Damper Babies, little cartoon figures with the body of a tuned mass damper, a big head, and little arms and legs. These adorably rotund figures come in black, red, yellow, silver, and green, each with their own personality. With vertical lines for eyes and circular mouths, their faces subtly spell out the number 101. These colorful characters adorn the hallways leading to and from the damper in Taipei 101. The Damper Babies also narrate animated videos and appear on all kinds of products and as toys in the tower's gift shops.

Taipei 101 lost the title of world's tallest building to the Burj Khalifa in Dubai in 2010. Supertall structures, once rare, are now sprouting up in other locations as well, pushing Taipei 101 ever farther down the list. Still, Taipei 101's golden damper has helped keep international attention on the building, which has become a symbol of the city. Given their proliferation, supertall buildings cannot depend on their height alone to achieve notability. This is why Taipei 101 leaned into things like Damper Babies while also racking up all the superlatives it could, including biggest wind damper in the world, fastest elevators in the world, and the tallest LEED-certified green building in the world. Many other savvy skyscraper developers are catching on, too, adding unique features like giant clock towers, glass observation decks, or external sky slides. These days, the focus is increasingly on offerings that educate, entertain, and generate interest to make structures memorable beyond the fleeting accolades that accompany short-lived numerical records.

# GROUPED DYNAMICS

## *Street Canyons*

SEEN FROM AFAR, SKYLINES CAN APPEAR TO BE DOMI-nated by singular structures like space needles or jagged shards. On the street, all kinds of buildings play roles in our experience of a city. Road-flanking architecture can impact not only on-the-ground aesthetics and daylight access but also heat and wind conditions. Sometimes these aggregate effects are hard to predict or simply not taken into account by designers. In extreme cases, even a single unassuming building can have unexpected effects that are unpleasant or downright dangerous.

As Beetham Tower in Manchester was completed in 2006, an aesthetic glass "blade" sticking out above the main structure was found to make an uncanny noise when wind passed over it, likened by one listener to a "middle C on the piano." Various fixes have been attempted, including sound-dampening foam and wind-redirecting aluminum additions, but the structure has continued to wail during storms. The building's architect has apologized for the noise. He is the owner of the penthouse unit, so the sound is something that he's very familiar with.

But passing breezes can be more than just an acoustic nuisance. Bridgewater Place in Leeds, sometimes called the Dalek, has faced even more serious wind-related issues. Due to its shape, prevailing winds hitting the tower were channeled down its side, which resulted in ground-level wind speeds of up to eighty miles per hour. In 2011, a truck was lifted and flipped over by these winds, tragically crushing a pedestrian in the process. People walking down the sidewalk have been knocked down and injured as well. Various attempts to curb the problem have been implemented over time, culminating in giant wind baffles arrayed around the base of the structure. The building owners have even had to reimburse the city to the tune of more than a million dollars for associated municipal expenses like the cost of rerouting traffic on windy days.

A building nicknamed the Walkie-Talkie Tower at 20 Fenchurch Street in London has also had issues with wind, but it was the tower's relationship with the sun that has earned it other nicknames like the Walkie-Scorchie and the Fryscraper. During construction, it was discovered that the building's concave facade could reflect and channel sunlight, raising temperatures on the streets below. The skyscraper managed to melt the plastic components of a parked vehicle, and it even lit a rug on fire in a neighboring building. One reporter demonstrated its power by frying an egg on the street below in the sun's reflected glow. The problem has since been mitigated with a layer of shading.

One could hope that these kinds of problems would get engineered out of a tall building before it gets built. At the city level, though, the cumulative effects of groups of tall buildings can be even harder to control. So-called street canyons in dense cities can create microclimates. Arrayed along rectilinear city grids, sets of skyscrapers can effectively increase wind speeds. Depending on their geometries, clusters can also raise temperatures by capturing solar energy or trapping warm air, thereby exacerbating existing urban heat island effects. In some cases, street canyons channel aerial pollutants up and out of the way—arguably a net benefit to the citizens below—but in other places, tall towers can collectively trap and recirculate smog in undesirable holding patterns.

Some street canyons also have more surprising secondary impacts. Arrays of tall buildings can produce entrancing effects like the so-called Manhattan Solstice. This seasonal convergence aligns sunrises and sunsets with the narrow spaces framed by tall buildings on either side of city streets. While this phenomenon is not unique to New York, the picturesque impact can be particularly potent in flatter places like the Big Apple, which has largely unobstructed views out to the horizon (give or take a bit of New Jersey). Astrophysicist Neil deGrasse Tyson has dubbed the phenomenon Manhattanhenge. Tyson has wondered whether future archeologists might think Manhattan's gridded streets and avenues were built to honor seasonal solar alignments. Since this "rare and beautiful sight . . . happens to correspond with Memorial Day and Baseball's All Star break," he mused, "future anthropologists might conclude that . . . the people who called themselves Americans worshiped War and Baseball," which wouldn't be wildly inaccurate except the dates of these events move around from year to year.

Cities are complex systems, but work is being done to better understand them. Scientists, engineers, and urban designers study larger interactions, while many architecture firms also model the effects of individual buildings in context on a case-by-case basis. Like a forest full of trees, the whole of a city is more than the sum of its individual towers, no matter how tall or iconoclastic they may be.

# FOUNDATIONS

W HILE SKYSCRAPERS DEFINE CITY skylines, most of us mere mortals experience the city primarily in and around the first few stories of its buildings. Storefronts, residences, and museums are where our sense of place is established. A shopkeeper or a commercial tenant in a strip mall can have as much impact as a world-famous architect when it comes to shaping the character and our day-to-day experience of a familiar neighborhood.

LEFT: *Contrasting addition to the Royal Ontario Museum in Toronto*

# Vernacular Enclaves

## *International Districts*

Whether in San Francisco, New York, Los Angeles, or Las Vegas, the pagoda roofs, dragon gates, and other chinoiserie of Chinatowns make them easy to spot amid neighborhoods with more conventionally Western vernacular. For those just arriving from China, though, the aesthetic of these places can seem more foreign than familiar, full of styles that are out-of-date and design elements remixed in haphazard ways.

San Francisco's Chinatown originally looked quite similar to the rest of the city, with brick homes and Victorian Italianate facades. Chinese immigrants banded together in the area not for any particular love of its architecture but out of political, social, and economic necessity. Nineteenth-century San Francisco was not very welcoming or accommodating to this population. At the time, Chinatown had a reputation as a slum filled with drugs and prostitution, an image reinforced by tour guides seeking to play up this exotic enclave. "The Orient in America— A Stroll Through Chinatown by Day and by Night—Habits of the Heathen Chinese" was far from the most offensively titled *San Francisco Chronicle* article written about the place.

When the devastating 1906 earthquake and the resulting fires leveled much of San Francisco, residents of Chinatown were largely unaided by their neighbors during and after the crisis. The fire department focused available resources on the wealthy residents in places like nearby Nob Hill and even dynamited some buildings in Chinatown in an attempt to stop the flames from spreading.

Some local authorities saw this tragedy as an opportunity to wipe the slate clean. Before the dust had settled and the smoke had cleared, strategies were already being proposed to relocate Chinatown permanently to Hunters Point to make way for white-owned businesses to occupy this central neighborhood's prime real estate. The city's mayor commissioned architect and urban designer Daniel Burnham to draw up plans aligned with the City Beautiful movement, a fraught vision of clean white cities that was popular at the time. Chinese residents fought back, leveraging their economic influence and threatening to leave town entirely and take their business enterprises with them. The city capitulated.

This left open questions, however, about how to rebuild a Chinatown from scratch. A local businessman named Look Tin Eli hired architect T. Paterson Ross and engineer A. W. Burgren to design some new structures for the Chinese community even though neither man had been to China. They instead relied on centuries-old images, primarily of religious vernacular, to develop a new look for the new Chinatown. The resulting architectural collages were drawn from various Chinese traditions as well as questionable American ideas of what China looked like. Their approach was picked up by others in the neighborhood and became the basis for a fresh aesthetic that would come to shape Chinatowns around the world.

The hybrid look launched by San Francisco's Chinatown may seem convoluted, but the idea was quite straightforward: community leaders knew the area would be a tourist attraction and played to that crowd. It was vaguely exotic but safe enough for middle-class white America. The visitors and their cash began to flow into Chinatown, and Chinatowns around the country soon followed suit. Such Western-friendly remakes helped improve the public image of Chinese immigrants in various cities—but they also perpetuated stereotypes and misunderstandings about Chinese culture. Ultimately, these places are neither Chinese nor American, neither historically accurate nor fully fanciful, but something in between: unique cultural and architectural hybrids of Chinese American history.

# REALITY CHECKS

## *Service Centers*

A TYPICAL CHECK CASHING STORE MAY NOT INSPIRE PASS-ersby to marvel at its architecture, but the designs of these places make it very clear how these businesses work. Though they function in the financial sector, these stores bear little resemblance to banks, which often feature columns, ferns, plush carpets, and quiet interiors to connote wealth. At a bank, a customer may be greeted at the door by someone in a suit or at least a row of smiling tellers but be unsure whether they should take a seat and wait for a banker or walk up to a service counter. And to someone with little experience in similar institutions, it could be hard to tell what services they offer without reading through promotional pamphlets or submitting to a sales session with a smooth-talking agent. The average check cashing store could hardly look and feel more different than a typical bank.

In 2008, the owner of the largest chain of check cashing stores, Tom Nix, explained key aspects of their interior design to Doug McGray for a *New York Times* article. Nix emphasized that the decor was very deliberate, as was the absence of decorative flourishes. The places were intentionally modeled after corner grocery stores, neighborhood places where everyone is welcome. There are no carpets either—Nix's stores all feature linoleum flooring. This choice is meant to ensure that construction workers and other laborers with dirty boots feel comfortable coming in off the street.

Check cashing stores are intuitive to navigate, often featuring big signs with lists of services and prices. The financial transactions that happen inside can be predatory and extremely bad for the working poor, but for the most part, the fees are at least clearly on display. A bank may offer customers five different checking accounts, a variety of investment options, and other financial instruments that have complicated rates laid out in dense pamphlets; check cashing stores, meanwhile, present fewer options that are easier to grasp.

Check cashing and payday lending places take a lot of heat for manipulative practices and exorbitant fees, but for better or worse, their linoleum floors see a lot of foot traffic. For people who don't need to use them, they may be easy to overlook—just another storefront in a sea of retail—but even though they may not radiate fanciness, they are highly designed places. Some modern banks have begun taking notice of some key elements of these designs and are abandoning the ferns and filigree in favor of branches that mimic other retail spaces or even incorporate coffee shops to make their spaces seem more casual, friendly, and accessible.

# APPROACHABLE DUCKS

## *Commercial Signifiers*

JUST UNDER TWENTY YEARS AFTER IT WAS COMPLETED, a seven-story office building shaped and painted to look like a giant picnic basket was put on the market. At its peak, the offices inside housed five hundred Long-aberger Company workers in this audacious structure modeled after one of the company's iconic handmade products. It served as a giant advertisement for their medium market basket and is a classic example of what Postmodernist architects Robert Venturi and Denise Scott Brown have dubbed a "duck."

Ducks are buildings that explicitly represent their function through their shape and construction. This peculiar designation traces back to one very specific building: the Big Duck located on Long Island in New York built to house a shop selling ducks and duck eggs. The form of the building explicitly showed passersby what they will find inside, signaling its purpose in a different way than the much more common "decorated shed" type of building. Decorated sheds are generic structures with added signs and decor that denote their purpose, such as big-box stores or restaurants with huge signage.

Venturi and Scott Brown developed the distinction between ducks and decorated sheds while studying the Las Vegas Strip in the late 1960s and early 1970s. At the time, the idea of architects studying such a commercialized place designed for the masses was unusual if not outright scandalous. Where other Modernist professionals saw Sin City as a wasteland of kitsch and pseudohistorical architecture and ornamentation, Venturi and Scott Brown found rich layers of meaning in the symbolism applied to otherwise boring buildings.

Robert Venturi, Denise Scott Brown, and Steven Izenour published their findings and opinions in the controversial *Learning from Las Vegas.* The book made waves in the architecture world and galvanized other contemporary architects to stake out sides in the ensuing battle between Modernism and what would eventually come to be seen as Postmodernism. Venturi, Scott Brown & Associates took the lessons of their trip to heart, sampling and remixing historical architectural styles and adding playful signs and symbols to their buildings that became hallmarks of the Postmodernist movement.

Whether they view historical decor as cool or kitschy, designers today still struggle with whether and how to use ornamentation in contemporary architecture. Many people have criticized the work of Postmodernist architects, and some critics have also attacked the designations of ducks and decorated sheds as subjective or arbitrary, but the influence of this thinking persists. If nothing else, it is a fun way to divide the buildings of the world. A duck building is a rare bird, and when you come across one in the wild, it can be delightful.

# COMPETITIVE STARCHITECTURE

## *Contrasting Additions*

AFTER YEARS OF RENOVATION AND REMODELING, THE Royal Ontario Museum in Toronto opened a controversial, context-defying addition in 2007 dubbed the Crystal. This 100,000-square-foot extension was designed by internationally renowned starchitect Daniel Libeskind. It is a complex geometric composition of interlocking glass, aluminum, and steel that wraps partially around the traditional-looking original brick museum building. The angular addition is about as different from the Italianate Neo-Romanesque original as any architect could possibly envision; imagine a historic train station jammed up against Superman's Fortress of Solitude. In reference to this strange juxtaposition of old and new, ordered and chaotic, one critic (writing as if they were the client) quipped, "That's the last time we hire TWO architects." Overall, this building does a good job of signaling its importance, but visual hierarchy can begin to break down when disjunctive approaches start dominating the urban landscape.

Anyone familiar with Libeskind's work, or that of other Deconstructivist architects like Frank Gehry, knows that their approaches often result in bold and quite complicated buildings with or without regard to the landscapes or structures around them. In some cases, an explicit break from the fabric of the city and its historical context makes good sense in light of a building's purpose, program, and importance. A museum might reasonably be expected to stand apart from its surroundings. Shape and style can signal the cultural or civic significance of a building, which presumably was the intent of both the impressive original museum in Toronto as well as Libeskind's bold addition. But when applied to less civic buildings, like the Westside Shopping and Leisure Centre in Bern, Switzerland, that same architect's angular contortionism is arguably a bit much. Whatever one's opinion may be, both of these examples show that it's hard to judge a building in isolation; physical, social, and cultural contexts are important as well. For better or worse, history is replete with examples of architecture that stands out, including many buildings that were criticized for doing so at the outset.

Paris is full of prominent examples, the Eiffel Tower perhaps being the most famous case. This exposed-metal structure was widely ridiculed as an eyesore when it was erected, and many onlookers were only mollified upon learning that the plan at the time was for it to be temporary. But the tower wound up becoming a permanent fixture of the skyline and has since become the most famous structure in Paris. Similarly, the Centre Pompidou, designed by an all-star architecture team that included Renzo Piano and Richard Rogers, was declared a "monster" when it was unveiled. Its inside-out approach puts circulation and mechanical systems on the outside, leaving open-plan space within for galleries. It has since come to be seen as groundbreaking, at least by some. Designed by I. M. Pei, the glass-and-steel Louvre Pyramid was also panned by many when it was added to the Parisian landscape. The pyramid shape was seen as both anachronistic and inconsistent, seeming to randomly reference ancient Egypt while using modern materials that clashed with the historic French Renaissance style of the museum building. Today, it's a landmark structure.

Each of these examples visibly signals a structure's importance relative to its surroundings either directly through their architecture or indirectly in how they respond (or don't) to their various contexts. These buildings make bold pleas for attention and generally succeed in getting it. There are risks, though, in taking intentional exceptionalism too far or applying it indiscriminately. It's fine when everyday buildings like houses, banks, and shopping malls blend in a bit more. Not every structure can or should be outstanding. In a world full of buildings made to stand out, none actually would.

# HERITAGE

T HE CHOICES WE MAKE WHEN WE build reflect cultural priorities and values, as do our decisions about whether and how to maintain and preserve historic structures erected before our time. Forward-thinking development and backward-looking preservation can often come into conflict as cities evolve. How and what we choose to keep, restore, rebuild, stabilize, or simply allow to decay has an incredible impact on the character of our cities.

LEFT: *Imprints of old demolished building interiors left on adjacent structure*

# Heathen's Gate

## *Overlapping Narratives*

THE REMAINS OF CARNUNTUM, AN ANCIENT ROMAN CITY and military fort complex, sprawl along the edge of the Danube River in Austria near Vienna. Visitors travel from around the world to explore this large open-air museum and learn from pieces of the past. Remnants at the site are in various states of disrepair and reconstruction. Some of the buildings lie in ruins, while others have been stabilized or even rebuilt using historical techniques and materials.

Among these various built artifacts sits a huge triumphal monument believed to have been erected by Emperor Constantius II, who commissioned it to commemorate his military victories. In the Middle Ages, this massive quadrifrons memorial was thought to be the four-faced tomb of a pagan giant, which led to it to be called Heidentor, or Heathen's Gate. (Ironically, Constantius II was an Arian Christian and rather infamous for persecuting pagans.)

This arched monument has partially collapsed over time. It has not been physically reconstructed, but its historic form has been brought back to life for visitors in a simple yet compelling way. Near it sits a transparent panel mounted on a pair of metal supports—like a see-through plaque—and on the panel is a line drawing. When viewers line up the illustration with the structure, they can see the outline of the monument's original shape overlaid on the crumbling ruin. In essence, viewers can observe the past and present at once by mentally reconciling the ruin and the panel outline. It's a low-cost, low-tech trick but an effective one.

These types of heritage sites attract all kinds of attention from archeological to aesthetic, but competing interests can complicate decisions about preservation, stabilization, and reconstruction. Most can agree that ancient historical sites should be preserved in some form if possible, but the process of deciding where and how to intervene can be contentious. A single-period restoration approach can collapse the complex history of a place into one moment in time that cannot possibly represent the entire story of a building. Navigating nuanced questions about what to maintain or change is an ongoing cultural, political, and economic challenge for those interested in preserving historical buildings now and for future generations.

# LANDMARK RULING

## *Historic Preservation*

NEW YORKERS LOVE TO HATE PENN STATION. COMPLETED in 1968, it is a drab, dark, crowded space—quite different from its predecessor that went by the same name. Designed by McKim, Mead & White and completed in 1910, the original structure was majestic, a Beaux Arts marvel rising up out of the urban landscape. Massive Doric columns welcomed visitors, who then descended down a vast staircase into a huge open space with natural light pouring in through arched glass ceilings.

The grand architecture of the first Penn Station married historical building elements and modern industrial aesthetics, drawing inspiration from ancient sources and contemporary technologies. It was so impressive it helped shame the Vanderbilts, America's wealthiest family, into tearing down and rebuilding their own Grand Central Station, making it the landmark building it is today.

Over the decades, though, the original Pennsylvania Station began to show signs of wear. Passenger train travel began to wind down in the postwar Jet Age, and with the advent of the interstate highway system, revenue to maintain the expansive property was drying up. Pigeon droppings accumulated faster than they could be cleaned up, particularly in high, hard-to-reach places. Windows were broken faster than they could be fixed.

Penn Station's owners needed the place to make more money, and in dense, land-starved cities like Manhattan, air rights are always valuable. If the building wouldn't pay for itself, the owners figured they could at least cash out on the ability to build above it. There were proposals to construct a huge parking garage, office tower, or amphitheater, but it was the multipurpose Madison Square Garden arena that won out in the end. The tracks below would remain in place, but the building above had to be demolished to make room for the new tenants overhead. Due in part to the state of the structure at the time, there weren't a lot of vocal opponents to the demolition.

There was just one march to try to save the original station in the early 1960s, led by architects and organized by the Action Group for Better Architecture in New York. Giving themselves the oh-so-catchy acronym AGBANY, they shouted slogans like "Polish, don't demolish!" (It's fair to say they didn't have a lot of activism experience.) But there was no stopping the deconstruction to come. In 1963, the building started to come down. Granite and travertine details were stripped and dumped into a New Jersey swamp.

The new station design was dismally unpopular. In 1968, architectural historian Vincent Scully famously lamented that in the past "one entered the city like a god; one scuttles in now like a rat." It became increasingly clear to citizens and officials that a mistake had been made. In the aftermath, Mayor Robert F. Wagner created the first Landmarks Preservation Commission and new laws were introduced to help save old architecture. Still, many iconic buildings were lost in the years that followed, in part because the commission was slow to review and award landmark status to structures submitted for consideration.

In 1968, Grand Central also wound up on the chopping block. This station was on the same track Penn had traveled, losing money but with a plan in the works to develop something vertical that would generate more revenue. But in this case, citing new landmark laws, the officials stepped in and put a stop to the plan. A lawsuit between the building owners and the city followed and the case dragged on. With Jacqueline Kennedy Onassis lending her public support to the preservationists' cause, the uncertain fate of Grand Central went from being a local to a national story. The court case also went national, moving all the way to the Supreme Court, which ruled in favor of the landmark laws in 1978 and allowed NYC to save the historic station from destruction.

It's hard to say exactly how much of a role the loss of the old Penn Station played in saving Grand Central, but there's a case to be made that the demolition of the former helped prevent the destruction of the latter—as well as other buildings in and beyond New York City. Today, there remains a spot of sooty grime on the vaulted interior ceiling of Grand Central that has been left intentionally uncleaned to remind travelers and commuters of a time when this place was in ragged shape and facing demolition yet ultimately deemed worth saving.

# RECROWNED JEWEL

## *Complex Restoration*

WHEN IT COMES TO BELOVED BUILDINGS, IT'S NOT USU- ally hard to sell the public on returning a structure to a polished and familiar state. For older buildings, though, the process of creating a rehabilitation plan can be complex. Greek and Roman statues and architecture were originally painted with bright, bold colors, but any rehabilitation efforts that would return them to their original vibrancy, though historically accurate, would be controversial. Even some more contemporary structures, like the Statue of Liberty, are more familiar in an altered form—the figure's copper coating was originally as shiny as a new penny before it oxidized into the green it is today. When the statue went through an extensive renovation in the 1980s, many structural aspects were restored to their original glory, but no one seriously considered buffing away that coating to return the monument to its original bronze color. Then there is the case of Stirling Castle's Great Hall in central Scotland, a building that for generations featured a faded stone facade before a dramatic restoration rendered it yellow.

People tend to think of castles as grand stone structures with bold defensive turrets. In reality, many are complex and convoluted, constructed piecemeal over many years, decades, even centuries. Stirling Castle is such an amalgamation, featuring a palace, chapel, inner close, outer close, great hall, and other additions and renovations that reflect centuries of use. There has been some form of castle on this prominent hill since the twelfth century or earlier, but the current buildings mostly date back to the 1400s and 1500s. In the middle of this array, standing out from the rest, is a huge hall painted in a light buttery golden hue.

The Great Hall was of critical importance to Stirling Castle—completed in 1503, it was a place where kings and nobles would meet and feast and celebrate and make new laws. Historic Scotland, an organization tasked with public education and safeguarding national historic treasures, began to work on the structure's renovation in 1991. When the group took it over, the place was in very poor shape. For more than a century, the building was controlled by the War Office and treated as a utilitarian military structure. Windows, doors, floors, and ceilings had all been changed to make the place into a functioning barracks. The military had left behind a gutted shell that dimly reflected the building's former glory.

It was up to Historic Scotland, which was generally charged with maintaining the current states of structures, to decide whether to leave the hall as it was, restore it to the military occupation period, or return it to its appearance during some other prominent historical era. Considering its strategic, trade, and cultural significance starting in the 1500s, they opted to restore the building to match its sixteenth- and seventeenth-century heyday.

This choice came with some significant questions about what the building had originally looked like and how it had been constructed. The restoration team dug into historical records, looking at etchings for clues, though not all of these were consistent with one another. Different illustrations showed different heights, numbers, and locations of elements like walls, chimneys, and ridge beasts (grand creature statues perched on the roof). As the restorers learned more, they began to solve various interconnected puzzles as best they could. The probable ridge beast locations were ultimately determined by the strong points of the trussed hammerbeam roof-support structure below (itself re-created based on a survey illustration from 1719). Each discovery helped with the next, making the reconstruction increasingly accurate.

When the restoration was unveiled, locals loved some aspects like the roof and its supporting lattice of wood beams, but a simple and fundamental change to the building's exterior caught many off guard and generated significant controversy: the lime wash finish (rich with yellow ochre) on the exterior. As Historic Scotland had searched for clues about the building's past, some of the historical finish was found still clinging to the sides of the structure that had been covered over by an old addition. This discovery provided direct insight into the building's previously colorful facade. At a time when much of the built environment was boring gray and brown, the Great Hall had, as it turned out, been dazzling yellow, highlighting its importance to the city and the region.

The renovation of the Great Hall took years, and for much of that time, the building was shrouded in scaffolding and plastic. So when it came time to reveal the work to the public, many were shocked by the bright yellow finish and had no reservations about expressing their disapproval. In hindsight, perhaps there could have been more communication with the community about the plan. In the end, the work is as accurate as Historic Scotland could make it, and it paints a clearer (if much brighter) picture of the past than a muted gray facade ever could. For some local residents, it can still be jarring, as any major change to the built environment can be. For visitors, it's stunning—not at all what one would expect—and quite educational, too, as it shows people how colorful history can be.

Going forward, this kind of intensive physical restoration may become less and less common thanks to digital modeling tools. These days, history-minded organizations can re-create various (known or speculative) states of a structure in 3D renderings rather than remodeling actual buildings. In this way, people can experience buildings as they evolved (or decayed) over the years or decades or even centuries, learning about the various states they passed through during their existence.

# ARCHITECTURAL LICENSE

## *Faithless Reconstruction*

EVEN NOW, DECADES AFTER THE FALL OF THE BERLIN Wall, the built environments of Central and Eastern Europe still show the marks of Soviet influence. Big boxy buildings of that era can be found in cities like Prague, Budapest, and Bucharest. Much of Warsaw is dominated by wide blocks of large and largely colorless Communist-era architecture, but there are exceptions. Districts like Old Town in Poland's capital are a familiar sight to European travelers, complete with tourist shops, carriage rides, and the beautiful historic-looking architecture visitors would expect to find in a major city. Looks can be deceiving, however, and in this case, that deception runs deep: these historic-looking structures were actually built after World War II.

Warsaw was decimated during the war to the point where there was talk of not rebuilding it at all or at least designating some other place as the capital of Poland. In the end, though, the government decided to build it back up, mostly in Soviet style: fast, cheap, and big. But along the old Royal Route, a historically important thoroughfare, they made a big show of involving architects, archeologists, and other specialists to rebuild the area that is now known as Old Town. They even made special kilns to turn old rubble into new building blocks as part of a publicized effort to preserve a sense of material continuity.

The project was seen as a success story in the face of destruction, an exemplary tale of rebirth in the wake of catastrophic devastation. Over time, though, locals started to notice that some things were a bit *off* about this marvelous remake. For starters, many of the buildings had historical facades but modern interiors. There were other inconsistencies, too—ones that were visible from the outside.

It was true that Old Town had civic landmarks like a grand theater and a castle before the war, but the area wasn't exactly touristy—it had been largely neglected and dilapidated. The rebuilt version, however, had been cleaned up and infused with nostalgia, drawing on history but also going well beyond any actual precedent. Buildings along the main thoroughfare were simplified in obvious ways—where rows of structures had once stood at different heights, new three-story replacements lined up neatly. Some have suggested that this decision to standardize rather than re-create reflected a kind of communist egalitarian ethos, with choices like sticking to a uniform number of floors serving as an object lesson in equality.

As planners began the restoration process, they drew inspiration from many different historical periods. For some architecture, they referenced the works of an Italian painter who had come to Warsaw back in the 1700s, an era well before the neighborhood's ruin in World War II. Bernardo Bellotto specialized in realistic, documentary-style painting, and while his works are very precise and highly detailed, he was known to take artistic license in his representations. Reconstruction efforts drew on these more idealized versions to create many of the buildings that now reside in Old Town.

It's not as if re-creating Old Town more accurately was impossible—students and architects had documented the city extensively with photographs and drawings shortly before it was devastated in the war. But for the Soviets, creating a fantasy replacement for Old Town served a dual purpose; it allowed them to bring the area back to a time before modern capitalism and demonstrate to the world that the city would be even better under their rule.

Today, replicas of various Warsaw paintings by Bellotto can be seen around the city set side by side with matching streetscapes to highlight the "success" of the reconstruction insofar as the places match the images. And in its way, it is a success—just not in terms of strict historical accuracy. Old Town also isn't unique in its more subjective approach even if it represents an extreme example. Around the world, attempts to mine history for the sake of nostalgia have resulted in similar kinds of neighborhoods that locals avoid and tourists love, places that are out of sync with the present and sometimes out of step with the past as well.

# Unnatural Selection

## *Subjective Stabilization*

Just east of the Roman Forum in Italy's capital sits the Colosseum, one of the most famous ruins in the world. Even for those who haven't visited, its markedly rotund form, multistory rows of stacked arches, crumbling curves, and general state of decay are familiar images thanks to modern media. But for centuries, the reddish-brown remnants of the Colosseum were also covered in another color: green. Until quite recently, there were trees, grasses, vines, and shrubs growing over what remained of the building and thriving in the varied microclimates of the structure, which range from damp and cool (in the shade on lower levels) to dry and hot (on the more exposed upper floors). This lush greenery inspired a number of historical artists and authors who visited Rome to write about their experience. Among these was Charles Dickens, who marveled at the "walls and arches overrun with green." Many historical paintings also depict the abundant life sprouting from the remnants of this ancient structure.

Impressed by the sheer variety of species inhabiting the ruins in the 1850s, a British botanist named Richard Deakin decided to do a botanical survey of this unique environment. He cataloged more than four hundred different species, some of which were quite rare (or completely absent, as far as he knew), in the rest of Europe. Puzzling over how these diverse plants could all wind up in one place, Deakin formulated a theory: the burrs and other seeds of these rare plants might have been carried in the fur and stomachs of the lions, giraffes, and other exotic foreign species that had been brought to fight in the arena by ancient Romans. It's impossible to be sure of this hypothesis, but it would help to explain the array of non-native species Deakin found.

For better or worse, archeology (aided by politics) eventually trumped botany, and this one-of-a-kind ecosystem was ripped out around a century and a half ago. In 1870, Italy was unified under a secular democratic government, which wrested control of the city of Rome from the papacy. Those newly in power supported a different kind of rational, scientific, modern Italian identity rooted in ancient Roman history. To support their vision, the green ruins of the Colosseum were cleared of what were seen as invasive species in order to make it more aesthetically pleasing as well as to help stabilize and preserve what remained of the building. While it is true that the plants were slowly destroying the ruin, they were also arguably a vital part of its living history. Architecture is more than just the building materials that make up a structure—the flora (or fauna) that inhabit buildings can also tell specific histories, or at least provide fertile ground for fascinating theories of lions and tigers and burrs, oh my!

# FADED ATTRACTION

## *Alluring Abandonments*

FROM MASSIVE AND MYSTERIOUS ANCIENT STRUCTURES to ordinary deserted homes, people are drawn to abandoned places and their time-spanning aesthetics. Of course, in young countries (like the United States) and young states (like California) with young cities (like San Francisco), ancient architectural ruins of Western civilization are not really a thing—but that hasn't stopped Bay Area locals from trying!

Located alongside the Pacific Ocean near the Golden Gate Bridge, the ruins of the Sutro Baths abut a seawall. There's a cave nearby as well as the remains of some old bathhouses. At first glance, these may look like some strange, ancient, long-lost Roman ruins, but this swimming pool and amusement park complex was constructed only slightly more than a century ago. The endeavor was a pet project of German engineer Adolph Sutro, who struck it rich in the mining industry. Like a West Coast version of John D. Rockefeller, Sutro poured a lot of money into San Francisco, including this elaborate project.

Sutro originally planned to build a huge outdoor aquarium that would be refilled by the tides of the Pacific Ocean. His plans kept expanding and evolving, though, in part because he employed an engineer initially and only brought an architect on board after much of the foundation work had already been completed. The place wound up not only with a network of swimming pools, connecting canals, and hundreds of changing rooms but also with a museum of oddities and other assorted ends. Much of the complex was enclosed by a huge glass shell, resulting in a kind of Crystal-Palace-meets-Coney-Island for the Bay Area.

Despite all of its wonders and attractions, the place lost money from the day it opened, due in part to its inconvenient location on the edge of the city. Hoping to draw more visitors, Sutro began pouring money into electric rail lines leading to the baths. But even after he was elected mayor in 1894, his beloved baths were still not profitable. When Sutro passed away a few years later, his family tried to unload the property but wound up operating it for another half century.

The family initially attempted to renovate Sutro's folly in order to attract more people. At one point, the lower pool was drained and filled with sand to create a kind of tropical indoor beach. If you've ever spent time on the cold shores of Ocean Beach, the idea of creating an indoor beach despite there being a natural beach right on the other side of the glass was slightly less crazy than it sounds. But alas, it's still not a great idea. The old indoor pool was later turned into an ice rink. More and more ideas were tried, but nothing that was added to the mix seemed to work.

Just as the site was poised for redevelopment in 1966, a fire broke out and reduced the buildings to rubble. The land was sold to the National Park Service in 1980. Today, it is part of the Golden Gate Recreation Area. While the place was never successful when it was active, it has actually become popular in recent years as a sort of admission-free modern ruin. And just like any built environment, it's still changing. Over the years, bits and pieces have continued to degrade and fall into the sea. Plants are creeping in as nature begins to reclaim the site and slowly turn it into a wetland. Birds stop by regularly and otters have been spotted in the big flooded pool. So now it serves a variety of functions despite (or because of) its decaying form, including inspiring awe in its curious visitors, especially ones who might initially assume it to be an ancient ruin.

# RUNED LANDSCAPES

## *Peripheral Traces*

IN THE SUMMER OF 2018, NORTHERN EUROPE SIMMERED through an exceptional heat wave that melted roads, roasted moors, and parched plants across the British Isles. At the time, researcher and ruin enthusiast Paul

Cooper wrote about a surprising effect of the drought in an article for the *New York Times*. "In the fields of England, Wales and Ireland," he explained, one could begin to see the reemergence of "lost lines of houses and settlements, barrows and henges, the street plans of ancient towns from Roman times to the Paleolithic and the Middle Ages—everywhere the past is returning, written on the landscape." Hints of vanished architecture began to resurface, ghostly blueprints made legible amid natural surface landscapes. Differences in soil quality, density, and porosity were impacting plant life on the ground and rendering the outlines and imprints of subsurface remains visible against either more or less healthy surrounding greenery.

Journalist Anthony Murphy was taking drone photography when he spotted a series of dark crop marks arrayed in a large ring on an Irish field. It was later determined by archeologists that a henge erected millennia ago had once stood in this location. The site would have gone unnoticed were it not for the unusual dry spell in this famously green country. The henge had been built of wood, which had long ago collapsed and rotted away, but the depressions left behind by these posts had a lasting impact on plant growth patterns. Crops growing in the deeper soil where the ancient monument had been erected stand out as greener and healthier than their neighbors, which enhances their visibility particularly in an extreme drought.

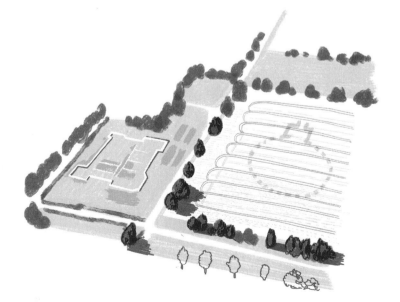

Across England, old gardens and structures were also revealed in places like the Chatsworth House in Derbyshire thanks to parch marks. In this case, the shape of an old seventeenth-century garden was similarly outlined by differential growth but in reverse: old paths and planters below the surface displaced soil and water, which resulted in sparser and unhealthier vegetation compared to the surrounding greenery. In nearby Nottinghamshire, less healthy plants highlighted the footprint of the elaborate eighteenth-century Clumber House mansion that was demolished after a series of fires; the outlines of rooms and hallways became expressed on the surface, like a giant one-to-one-scale blueprint (or brownprint) against the lusher green areas on all sides.

Crop marks and parch marks are just some of the organic signals that archeologists use to reverse engineer history. Frost marks can aid in finding old remains through differential freezing and thawing rates that reflect different soil types and water depths. Shadows cast by higher mounds of land can help people locate things like large earthworks with subtle grade changes or the overgrown foundations of old elevated forts and castles.

Some of these phenomena can best be observed via aircraft or drone videography, though infrared photography and thermal imaging can help, too. It's also worth noting that this kind of approach predates modern aircraft and other high-tech tools. As far back as 1789, naturalist Gilbert White observed how locals used surface moisture differences to locate buried bog oak (used for fuel) and wondered, "Might not such observations be reduced to domestic use, by promoting the discovery of old obliterated drains and wells about houses; and in Roman stations and camps lead to the finding of pavements, baths and graves, and other hidden relics of curious antiquity?" Indeed, Gilbert, they could.

In the centuries since, these kinds of marks have helped unearth archeological sites in Scotland and England as well as places like the ancient Roman city of Altinum, a precursor to Venice located in northern Italy. The markings aren't always easy to read, and they rarely tell the full story on their own—in most cases, they are a starting point signaling that something interesting may lie just below the surface. These ghostly impressions left on the archaeosphere outline how human history gets written into the surface of the earth. Whether old buildings are preserved, restored, or left to waste away, their remains can create lasting impressions.

# UNBUILDING CODES

## *Premeditated Deconstruction*

EVERY TWENTY YEARS, THE ISE GRAND SHRINE IN JAPAN is torn down and painstakingly reconstructed as part of a cyclical tradition dating back more than a millennium. This process speaks to Shinto beliefs about death and renewal, but it is also considered a form of historic preservation, with great care taken to carry forward every detail from each iteration to the next. This rhythm of regular demolition and reconstruction is not unique to Japanese spiritual architecture—the country has a long history of rebuilding more conventional structures, too.

In Japan, a dark familiarity with devastating natural disasters has contributed to an expectation that buildings will have limited life spans. Newer buildings are considered safer in part because structures subjected to the stresses of multiple earthquakes or floods can become compromised over time. Building codes have evolved over the years as well, leading people to have more faith in newer construction. Thanks in part to these factors, older structures face a general cultural wariness bolstered by government warnings. Whereas home values in other countries are usually expected to increase over time, the opposite trend can be seen in Japan. This devaluation of older buildings drives both new construction and a great deal of deconstruction. So in crowded cities where conventional methods of demolition can be disruptive or dangerous, creative methods for tearing buildings down have emerged.

Rather than blasting a building with dynamite or toppling it piece by piece with loud machinery, some innovative deconstruction companies carefully "unbuild" multistory structures one level at a time. Viewed from the exterior, tall buildings can appear to shrink and ultimately vanish entirely over the course of days, weeks, and months. Compared to typical techniques, which usually involve knocking things down quite suddenly and loudly, this approach reduces noise and air pollution while also making it easier to recycle building materials.

One such method of deconstruction involves starting at the top of a structure and working down. The Taisei Ecological Reproduction System begins with enclosing the uppermost floors of a building in an architectural shell that provides shelter as well as soundproofing for the duration of the deconstruction. A ceiling crane system is then suspended from the top of this cap to help facilitate the process. After a set of levels is disassembled, the cap is lowered. The process is then repeated floor by floor all the way down. Each step is carefully considered. Even the kinetic energy generated by lowering materials can be harnessed in the process; when a batch of components is lowered, a connected motor generates electricity, which is then stored in batteries and used to power lighting and equipment for crews working on-site.

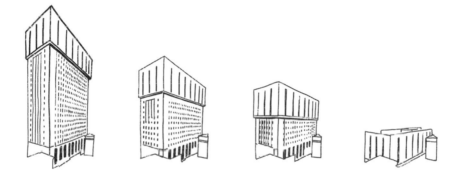

Top-down approaches may seem like the obvious (if not the only) way to go about a floor-by-floor deconstruction, but there are bottom-up ways to unbuild, too. The Cut and Take Down Method pioneered by the Kajima Corporation involves dismantling buildings at ground level by slowly taking each floor apart, then carefully lowering the next, and repeating the process. Working from the bottom floor can reduce demolition time in part by making it easier to separate out materials for recycling on-site without having to batch them up, lower them down, and unpack them below.

In Japan, there is an awareness that architectural short-termism can be wasteful, and efforts to avoid bad building decisions and make structures more durable have been around for a long time. Generations-old "tsunami stone" monuments along coasts feature etched warnings to deter people from building homes below historic high-water marks. On safer sites up higher, traditional wood joinery techniques have long helped Japanese architecture stand up to earthquakes. More recently, huge multistory test buildings have been erected on giant hydraulic "shake tables" to see how they break under simulated earthquake conditions; lessons from these stress-testing experiments have been used to shape better design strategies and building codes for new construction and for retrofitting older structures.

In parallel with improved building technologies, novel deconstruction methods offer lessons applicable both on and beyond the islands of Japan. These techniques may have been born in part out of regional circumstances, but (like the shrine in Ise) they embody a simple but fundamental truth about the nature of human constructions the world over: no building lasts forever. There is a lot to criticize about the global culture of planned obsolescence, but even well-built things eventually become obsolete. In that light, employing more deliberate, considerate, and sustainable deconstruction methods can offer old architecture a more graceful way to permanently exit the built environment.

*Chapter 5*

# GEOGRAPHY

W HEN YOU'RE A KID, YOU ALWAYS want the window seat on the plane. Then, you get older, your heart dies, and you opt for the convenience of the aisle seat. We want you to stay in that window seat and enjoy this vantage point—metaphorically, at least. The city's shape, its borders, its proximity to nature, and the use of its green space are especially observable from this great height. As we float in our imagination above the landscape, we can see the design choices that are too big for our earthbound bodies to take in.

PREVIOUS: *Patchwork plans, coordinated layouts, and landscapes of Los Angeles*

# DELINEATIONS

T HE SHORTEST DISTANCE BETWEEN two points may be a straight line, but in the real world, things are rarely that simple. First, we have to agree on where to start. When it comes to cities, this is not a trivial exercise. Urban centers and boundaries change, and the routes between them shift as well. The increasing speed of transportation in the nineteenth and twentieth centuries collapsed time and space and brought us closer together. This required a kind of coordination, planning, and level of standardization that had never existed before.

LEFT: *Zero markers both ancient and modern from cities around the world*

# Points of Origin

## *Zero Markers*

A FEW YEARS BACK, THERE WAS AN EFFORT TO FIND AND erect a plaque at the geographical center of San Francisco. When asked if such a marker was necessary, Public Works Director Mohammed Nuru explained to a *San Francisco Chronicle* reporter that "it's important to know where the center of the city is." When he was pressed to explain why it was important, though, Nuru said that "he didn't really know." The article continues: "After thinking it over, he suggested that once you know where the center is, you can tell how far some other place is from it, although he added that he didn't know what that was good for, either." The fact of the matter is, the endeavor to find a geographic center is generally less about functionality and more about establishing a symbolic point of origin.

Retroactively determining the exact middle of a city is not a straightforward proposition. Some may even call it futile. In a city surrounded by water, one has to make decisions about whether to include adjacent islands with the mainland and whether edges are established at high or low tide. In the end, the geographical center of San Francisco was determined to be in some shrubs near Twin Peaks. Since a marker would never be seen there, a brass disk was installed in a nearby sidewalk instead. It was stolen within a day. Presumably, the official center point of San Francisco is on some resident's shelf somewhere. This wasn't the first attempt to pin down this position either.

In 1887, Adolph Sutro, who would go on to become the mayor of the city, erected a statue at an artificially designated central point that was definitely not the actual center of San Francisco. It was called the *Triumph of Light* and it stood at the top of Mount Olympus in Ashbury Heights. It was subsequently neglected and slowly crumbled away for decades. By the 1950s, the city declared it beyond repair and the armless goddess was taken down. Only her raised plinth remains. This drive to find (or make) a center is not specific to modern cities like San Francisco.

In the prime of the Roman Empire, the dictum "all roads lead to Rome" wasn't strictly true, but it had a basis in reality. A vast network of main roads led toward a very specific point within the city: the Milliarium Aureum, also known as the Golden Milestone. This monument was erected in 20 BCE by the Emperor Augustus in the ancient Roman Forum. It was the place from which all distances in the empire were measured. The monument has been lost to history, but the idea of creating a physical centerpoint has persisted through the ages. The Byzantine Empire took up the tradition, for instance—fragments of their Milion of Constantinople were found in the 1960s.

Many modern cities including Tokyo, Sydney, Moscow, and Madrid have some form of "zero stone," sometimes referred to as a zero marker or point zero or kilometer zero. England has its mysterious London Stone, which dates back to the 1100s and may be of Roman origin, though historians still debate its original function. In more recent centuries, London has used a roundabout and statue at Charing Cross as a central point of reference to measure certain distances. Metropolitan police initially served only neighborhoods within a radius of twelve miles from Charing Cross, and hansom cab drivers were obliged to take fares only up to a fixed distance from that central point. Today, London cab drivers are still tested on their knowledge of an area six miles in any direction from Charing Cross. Aside from a small plaque, though, it would be hard to know this roundabout-encircled monument was such a key reference point.

In many other countries, zero markers are made to stand out in grander and more explicit ways. Some centerpoints are inscribed plaques set into the pavement while others are integrated into sculptures and obelisks. Often located in capitals, these objects have served as both cultural touchstones and practical reference points used to measure distances and establish mile markers within (and, in some cases, beyond) a city. Some zero stones are quite large and literal, like the one in Budapest, which is shaped like a huge zero with the letters *KM* (for kilometer) embossed on its base. Others are more ornate, like an elaborate marker in Havana, which originally contained a 25-carat diamond (this jewel was stolen in the 1940s, after which the city installed a replica). Some feature cultural references and icons, like the monolith in Buenos Aires featuring an image of Our Lady of Luján, the patron saint of the national road network. In Paris, the zero plaque in front of Notre-Dame Cathedral has long been a popular spot to take selfies; it's also the location from which distances are measured along France's national highway system.

Each of these markers follows its own logic and has its own aesthetic, but some trace their roots explicitly back to Rome. The architect of the Zero Milestone erected in Washington, DC, cited the Golden Milestone as his inspiration. This prominent marker sits just south of the White House in President's Park. Despite its inscribed intent as the "point of measurement for the distances from Washington on highways of the United States," roads outside of the District of Columbia do not actually reference this monument. Indeed, most US mile marker and distance systems reset from state to state, and signs for intercity travelers follow no single national convention. Like many of its kind, this zero stone is mostly symbolic.

# EDGE CASES

## *Boundary Stones*

"THE OLDEST SET OF FEDERALLY PLACED MONUMENTS IN the United States," according to Tim St. Onge of the Library of Congress, "are strewn along busy streets, hidden in dense forests, lying unassumingly in residential front yards and church parking lots. Lining the current and former boundaries of Washington, DC, these are the boundary stones of our nation's capital." All cities have borders, but in most cases, they are largely invisible. In DC, this set of stones has become a tangible foil for understanding the origin and evolution of a metropolis.

The boundary stones in DC trace back to the Residence Act of 1790, which called for the creation of a new capital city for the United States. There was disagreement about where to establish this federal city, but the Constitution gave the president the authority to make the decision. So, at President George Washington's behest, Secretary of State Thomas Jefferson hired an experienced colonial surveyor named Andrew Ellicott for the job based on his previous work mapping out the boundaries of various states.

Ellicott and his team cut through the semi-wild landscapes of Maryland and Virginia to map out a diamond-shaped city spanning ten miles on each side, putting up one stone per mile. These boundary stones were more than just geographic markers—they were also meant to act as a statement about the persistence of a still-young nation and a means to signal the permanence of its new capital. Each stone originally featured the inscription JURISDICTION OF THE UNITED STATES on one side and MARYLAND or VIRGINIA on the other (depending on which state a given stone bordered) as well as the year of their placement. A ceremonial stone from 1794 still sits along the Potomac at Jones Point right where President Washington (who was himself an experienced surveyor) laid out his plan to delineate the new capital's edges. Today, this stone is tucked into the seawall of a lighthouse and locked behind a metal gate in a concrete box.

More than a century after they were first installed, the vast majority of the original markers were still in place when a man named Fred Woodward set out to photograph and map them in 1905. He found many to be in disrepair and recommended that metal cages be installed around them for preservation purposes. Woodward lamented that "important as these ancient boundary stones are to the historian or antiquary, they are singularly unprotected and should at once be safeguarded against further injury or damage other than the necessary exposure to the elements." Following his advice, the Daughters of the American Revolution began wrapping the stones in barred iron enclosures for protection. Despite this treatment, some of the stones continued to be repositioned, removed, buried, or destroyed as the city expanded and changed over the twentieth century. Remarkably, the majority of them still exist in some form to this day. Whether integrated into the built environment, ignored, weathered, or missing entirely, each one tells its own site-specific story of urban development.

Southeast Boundary Stone 8 illustrates some of the travails these markers have faced. It was lost and replaced in the mid-1900s, then its replacement was buried under layers of landfill during a construction project. This replacement stone was found in the 1990s eight feet down in its mangled iron cage thanks to diligent historical research. It was left below ground for years for its own protection, and a surface-level replica was eventually erected in 2016—a replacement of a replacement, as it were. Nearby, Southeast 6 was actually well preserved by comparison until it was run over by a car in the early 2000s. Its cage was smashed and it was knocked off its base, though it has since been put back into place. The cage of Northeast 3 suffered some damage in recent years as well, but this already half-sunken stone remained largely intact. In some cases, stones have also been disfigured by well-meaning amateur historians who have affixed plaques directly to these monuments.

Since the 1990s, all thirty-six of the remaining original boundary stones have been included in the National Register of Historic Places, putting them on the radar of local and federal government agencies. The boundaries of DC have shifted over time, however, leaving some stones in adjacent states and further complicating their preservation. Some are now on private property, and it's hard to tell residents what to do with a stone sitting in their own backyard. "Like everything in America, there's a story to the stones," writes William Vitka of WTOP-FM, "and, like everything in DC, it's a precarious, convoluted mess of politics, money and geography."

For now, DC has focused its efforts on the stones still on or inside the city's borders. And while the markers have become ever more obsolete given the changes in DC's boundaries and the availability of online maps, the digital age has increasingly raised awareness of them, too. These days, urban history buffs can pull out a phone and track down the stones, connecting the dots of the city's history.

# DEFINING MOMENTS

## *Standardized Time*

A CHART OF TIMETABLES PUBLISHED IN 1857 LISTS A dizzying array of more than one hundred different local times across the United States, many just a few minutes apart from one another. For most people, time was a local phenomenon, and they saw no need for it to be otherwise. So when railroads banded together in the late 1800s to form the General Time Convention and pitch standardized times, the public was slow to get on board.

Before railroads, time differences weren't much of an issue—individual towns would set their clocks based on high noon (when the sun was at its highest), and travelers adjusted their watches as they walked or rode relatively slowly between towns and cities. Trains, however, collapsed both space and time, often carrying passengers through multiple time zones in mere hours. Early railroad station operators found themselves having to mark departures and arrivals differently depending on the origin and end points of a journey. When a miscalculation was made or a clock was off, the results could (and sometimes did) prove fatal when mistimed trains collided.

As the idea of standardized time zones spread, delegates to the International Meridian Conference in 1884 proposed a globe-spanning system that would involve twenty-four zones an hour apart. It seems like a fairly obvious solution now, but none of this was inevitable—time had worked just fine for thousands of years before it was sliced up into a twenty-four-piece spherical pie with a few rough edges and exceptions. The entire system was a subjective imposition on reality that reflected an unprecedented and permanent shift toward global interconnection.

It wasn't until 1918 that the US Congress officially adopted a version of the railroad time system. Other countries also took a while to fall into line. France stuck to Paris Mean Time for years even though it was only slightly under ten minutes off from Greenwich Mean Time—possibly the product of some cultural rivalry.

Up until just a few years ago, Russia's entire national train network remained on Moscow Time for uniformity and simplicity despite reaching across a number of time zones. One could argue that this had something to do with the ideals of Soviet egalitarianism, or perhaps it was due to Russian authoritarianism. For the most part, though, countries and their citizens adapted to the changing times relatively quickly. Standardized time ultimately became a defining characteristic of industrialization that put workers "on the clock" and ushered in an era of obsession with systematization and speed.

# ROAD BOOSTERS

## *National Highways*

IN THE EARLY DAYS OF THE AUTOMOBILE, THE UNITED States government didn't see much point in involving itself in a national system of roads. Horses, buggies, and streetcars served local transit purposes in cities while railroads provided comfortable intercity transportation options. The development and naming of roads was largely left to private regional and national auto associations. Typically, a group of enthusiasts would band together to connect existing trails into a longer route and give the new routes names like Lincoln Highway, Evergreen Highway, and National Old Trails Road. Signs were attached to telephone poles or trees or put up on buildings to mark the way, and dues were collected from individual members and businesses along the routes to help maintain them. It was a simple if somewhat haphazard, ad hoc system.

As cars grew more popular, cracks in this informal approach started to show. Routes were often not terribly efficient as they were designed to pass through dues-paying towns rather than take drivers more directly to their destination. Inconsistent signage led to confusion; in many places, multiple routes used the same stretches of road, which resulted in differing sets of markers. Then there was the motivation of the road boosters—some were just in it for the money, promoting their routes with little concern for making them safe, comfortable, or easy to navigate. The *Reno Evening Gazette* had scathing words for highway associations, observing that "with all their clamor, controversy, recriminations and meddlesome interference" these groups built "mighty few highways." The article directly attacked "clever boomers who are not interested in building roads but in obtaining salaries at the expense of an easily beguiled public."

In Wisconsin, State Highway Engineer Arthur R. Hirst had his own low opinion of big-talking road boosters, observing that "the ordinary trail promoter has seemingly considered that plenty of wind and a few barrels of paint are all that is required to build and maintain a two-thousand-mile trail." In 1918, his state rolled out their solution: standardized sets of numbered route signs that could be posted on utility poles, fences, trees, walls, or whatever else was handy. Hirst sought "to be rather profuse with these road markers" to help drivers navigate as easily as possible. Other states began to follow suit, and the federal government started to take notice.

Within a decade, standards were being established for many key aspects of national road infrastructure. Representatives of different state highway departments began coming up with ways to make things more uniform, like using different shapes for different types of signage in order to help drivers distinguish between them at a distance. This was the same era that gave rise to ideas like octagonal stop signs and sequential green, yellow, and red lights for traffic signals at intersections.

When it came to standardizing highway numbers, though, there was some pushback. One editorial at the time asked: "Can an edict from Washington wipe out the name Lincoln Highway and henceforth require that Americans shall know this great and famous artery of transportation as No. 64 or No. 13?" Indeed, it could. Perhaps unified number systems made roads seem a little more impersonal, but they certainly didn't get in the way of Route 66 becoming iconic despite its numerical designation.

All of this development and debate was happening at a time of massive automotive expansion. Between 1910 and 1930, the number of registered cars on American roads leaped from around 500,000 to more than 25,000,000. Named roads just weren't going to cut it. So in 1926, the US Numbered Highway System prevailed, with route numbers and locations to be coordinated by the American Association of State Highway Officials. There was much debate about the details, but the new rules of the road map came together as follows:

Hɪɢʜᴡᴀʏs ʀᴜɴɴɪɴɢ ɴᴏʀᴛʜ-sᴏᴜᴛʜ were generally assigned odd numbers that get higher from east to west.

Hɪɢʜᴡᴀʏs ʀᴜɴɴɪɴɢ ᴇᴀsᴛ-ᴡᴇsᴛ were generally assigned even numbers that get higher from north to south.

Mᴀᴊᴏʀ ʀᴏᴜᴛᴇ ɴᴜᴍʙᴇʀs were generally ended with a 1 or 0 while three-digit numbers typically denoted secondary or spur highways.

In the years that followed, tolls were levied in some places to pay for highways while "free roads" (later called freeways) were also introduced and funded by taxes (so not really free). But auto enthusiasts and industry executives dreamed even bigger, with proposals like Futurama, which General Motors debuted at the 1939 World's Fair in New York. This acre-spanning diorama envisioned a car-centric future of wide roads and ramps. Progress on this vision was slow during World War II, but in the wake of the conflict, the idea found a sympathetic leader whose military experience over the previous decades shaped his vision of America's future.

In 1919, a young lieutenant colonel in the US Army named Dwight D. Eisenhower had traveled in a military convoy from the White House to San Francisco along the Lincoln Highway. The trip was fun but difficult and tiring, Eisenhower would later recall. American roads at the time were nothing like the German autobahn system he would later encounter during World War II as Supreme Commander of the Allied Expeditionary Force in Europe. "The old convoy had started me thinking about good, two-lane highways," he explained, "but Germany had made me see the wisdom of broader ribbons across the land." As president, these observations would drive him to call for a federal highway system that would be later renamed the Dwight D. Eisenhower National System of Interstate and Defense Highways. Launched in 1956, this vast network took decades and more than one hundred billion dollars to build out. Today, it spans around fifty thousand miles and supports about 25% of US vehicular traffic.

Like the US highway system, north-south interstate routes were given odd numbers while east-west routes were given even ones. The ordering, however, was reversed—like mile markers, which start at the southern and western edges of states, interstate numbers get bigger from the south and west toward the north and east across the nation. In rare cases, interstates were split into two with an added letter as with 35W (west) and 35E (east) in Minnesota and Texas. Auxiliary interstate highways were designed to be circumferential or radial routes to serve urban areas. These looping highways have been given three-digit numbers, with a single digit added before the two-digit number of its parent route—I-10 and I-110 in California, for example.

While bridging cities and crossing state boundaries seemed like an ideal way to connect a country, this massive undertaking had side effects. In many cities, people were concerned about issues like neighborhood destruction, increased traffic, and environmental impacts, worries that proved to be well

founded. Protests in some places curbed interstate development. New York City narrowly missed having I-78 rip through sections of Lower Manhattan. Greenwich Village, Little Italy, Chinatown, and SoHo were spared in part due to the efforts of urban scholar and activist Jane Jacobs. Still, many freeways were built at the expense of poor and marginalized communities. Rural towns and suburbs may have benefited from this new network, but it came at a cost for many urban centers and created divisions that still remain.

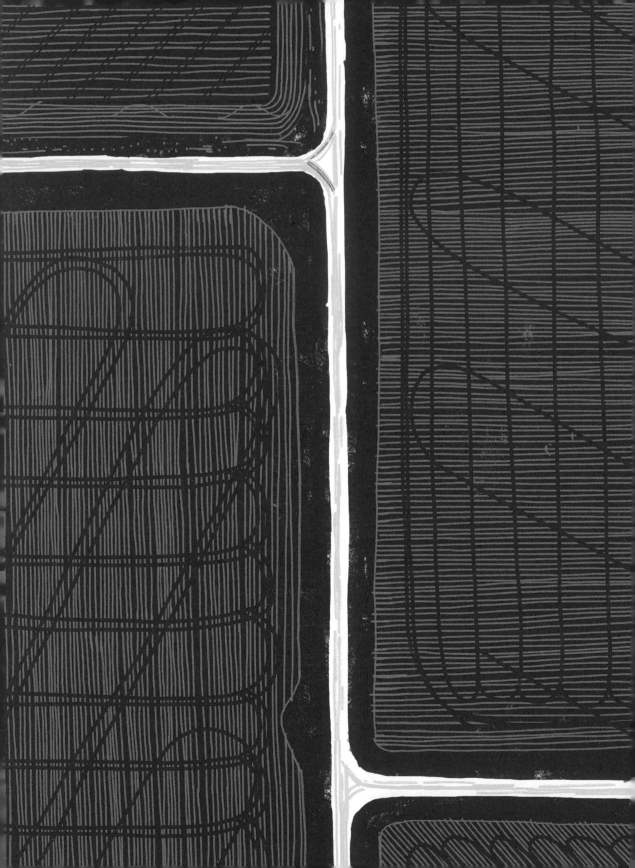

# CONFIGURATIONS

U RBAN PLANNERS HAVE A DIFFICULT task when it comes to imposing human order on a complex world. Even applying simple rectilinear grids to a round planet can be hard to do. But letting cities grow more organically can lead to a whole mess of problems and conflicts, so as difficult as it is, some planning is usually necessary. In the end, though, most cities are the product of various layers of planning that get imposed across generations; and their layouts often need to adapt and change as the needs of a city evolve.

LEFT: *Grid correction resulting from rectilinear plans applied to curved planet*

# ROUNDING ERRORS

## *Jeffersonian Grids*

IN THE AFTERMATH OF THE AMERICAN REVOLUTIONARY War, the United States had significant debts to pay, but it also had a lot of new territory to subdivide, allocate, and occupy. Founding father Thomas Jefferson came up with a solution to both problems by proposing to quickly sell land not yet developed by American colonists and use the proceeds to pay off creditors. The basic plan was simple: a series of thirty-six-mile-square townships would be established and subdivided into equal-size individual properties. These could be sold rapidly to buyers who would know that they were getting a standard plot and could feel confident purchasing it sight unseen. This egalitarian approach also fit Jefferson's larger vision of America as a nation of family farmers working the land that they owned and reaping the rewards. Parceling out uniform plots in this way seems logical, but applying grids on this scale was unprecedented. Grids had been used in ancient Egypt, Greece, and Rome as well as in modern cities like Philadelphia, but they were typically limited to small urban areas.

In the Thirteen Colonies, a lot of local land ownership had been modeled on traditional British "metes and bounds" systems. Plots were described in common language that used distances and directions and referred to physical features in the environment, like the corners of buildings and natural landmarks like rivers and trees. Of course, this system had its issues, like buildings being demolished, rivers shifting, and trees dying, but it had more or less worked. With the Land Ordinance of 1785, America engaged in a grand experiment to divvy up a huge swath of the continent in a much more organized and rigorous manner. There was one catch, but it was a big one: the plan was predicated on straight lines, but the Earth is round. It's not actually possible to impose a large grid of equal-size squares onto a spherical planet.

Some modifications had to be made to account for this incompatibility. Large visible jogs in roads, sometimes called grid corrections, were used to make townships and plots as equal as possible. If you've ever been driving down a long country road and suddenly encountered a T-shaped intersection, you may have driven into a grid correction. Absent historical context, these shifts might seem like a byproduct of local real estate shifting boundaries over time rather than Jefferson's expansive vision to grid a nation.

If you fly over the central United States today, you can see the effects of the Public Land Survey System. A patchwork quilt of squares dominates the landscape, particularly in less developed rural areas. Overall, the impression is one of regularity and order imposed on the natural world. If you look closely, though, you can see the places where a lofty theory met an unbending reality—small glitches in an otherwise grand grid.

# Unassigned Lands

## *Patchwork Plans*

BEGINNING IN THE 1800S, THE US GOVERNMENT BEGAN to force indigenous peoples into an area called Indian Territory in order to make room for American settlers. Later, tribes were again forced to relocate, clearing nearly two million acres and creating the so-called Unassigned Lands in what is now Oklahoma. While much of the country was being gridded for land sales, this area remained in flux and largely undeveloped.

Starting in the 1870s, white Americans from surrounding territories started petitioning to be allowed to stake claims in this area. Some even began a series of illegal raids, sneaking through Indian Territory into the Unassigned Lands at night. The leader of these raiders, later known as Boomers, was a man named David Payne. He would ride around Kansas shouting speeches to struggling farmers about how they should have the right to claim what he thought of as underutilized space. His orations managed to convince many people to buy into his vision of Oklahoma, and eventually the US government relented.

In the lead-up to the resulting Oklahoma Land Rush of 1889, it was announced that anyone who wanted a piece of this land could have one as long as they followed certain rules about staking claims. Would-be land grabbers were told to line up at the border at noon on April 22nd and await a signal. They could then rush in and hammer stakes down to claim plots up to 160 acres in rural areas or smaller lots in spots designated as locations for towns.

When the day arrived, tens of thousands of people from across the country and as far away as Liverpool and Hamburg showed up at the border to make a run for it. When the signal went off, people began running and riding horses as fast as they could to stake claims. There were people "shooting guns to speed up their horses and accidentally shooting each other," says Sam Anderson, author of *Boom Town*. There were riders falling off steeds and horses dying of exhaustion—it was "just about the wildest scene you can imagine."

Making things even more chaotic was the fact that not everyone had played by the rules and waited for the signal. Some grabbers ran in early or emerged ahead of others from hiding places in the forest. This faction of gun-jumping settlers became known as Sooners. This contingent quickly began laying out streets and lots according to plans they had made months in advance.

For the most part, Oklahoma's settlers were not urban planners, however, and most of them didn't give much thought to how a working metropolis needed to function as a whole—they were mainly interested in plotting out their own land for their own private use. By the end of the Land Rush, around ten thousand settlers had claimed basically every single square inch of the land that would become Oklahoma City, which left little room for anything else. In most places, "it was just tent flap to tent flap," explains Anderson, "and you didn't have any of the negative space that you really need for a city to work. You didn't have streets. You didn't have alleys."

As the next day dawned on the newly created city, two factions emerged. There were the Sooners, who had schemed things out in advance, and the rest of the settlers, who had waited for the official start of the land rush. Chaos reigned in the latter group, which was packed into ad hoc lots established on the fly, until they united to elect a citizens committee that would systematically survey the urban landscape and adjudicate disputes. In some cases, settlers would have to be displaced to make room for streets and alleys.

When this group got to the edge of Sooner territory, however, they were confronted with armed defenders who refused to give ground and participate in this reorganization plan. A compromise was eventually reached, but it required some creatively engineered diplomacy. The two main sections of the city had been laid out at slightly different angles that couldn't feasibly be stitched back together, and a series of diagonal jogs had to be employed to reconcile these disparate grids. The leader of the citizens committee, Angelo Scott, referred to these instances where the city doesn't quite line up as the "scars of a bloodless conflict." To this day, the romance surrounding the outlaw gang of cheaters who claimed land before the rule-abiding settlers even had a chance is so deeply rooted in Oklahoma's founding mythology that the University of Oklahoma football team bears the name Sooners.

# RECTILINEAR REVELATIONS

## *Coordinated Layouts*

THE URBAN GRID OF SALT LAKE CITY IS CENTERED AROUND a zero stone marker located at Temple Square, an important holy site for Mormons. City addresses read like coordinates for locations relative to this point—100 South, 200 East, for instance, is one block south and two blocks east of the square. Visitors navigating this system for the first time may find it unusual, but what is really jarring is the sheer size of the city's major blocks, which are 660 feet on each side. For context, nine downtown Portland, Oregon, city blocks could fit into one Salt Lake City block.

Salt Lake City was meant to be a different type of city, and not just in terms of its grid. From its inception, it was envisioned as a spiritual utopia for members of the

Mormon faith. Joseph Smith, founder of the Church of Jesus Christ of Latter-day Saints, was not an urban planner, but he tried his hand at it with the Plat of Zion, an idealized layout that could be applied to any Mormon city in any location. The plan was fairly simple: large blocks of equal size set into a rectilinear grid and centered around twenty-four temples. In theory, giving residents large lots would create a kind of rural city where homeowners could grow food in gardens and run family businesses downtown on their own properties. These residents would benefit from extra-large plots of land in the city's extra-large blocks. Alas, Smith never got to experience his utopian community—he was killed by an angry anti-Mormon mob in 1844. Leadership of the church fell to Brigham Young, who led his followers to the Salt Lake Valley, where they founded their new city in 1847.

Once there, Young dutifully drew inspiration from the Plat of Zion but tempered some of its more ambitious mandates with pragmatic modifications. Twenty-four temples seemed a bit much, so he decided to start with one. He also realized that the city would need business and industrial districts to thrive as a modern metropolis. But he left some of the biggest, most fundamental ideas of the Plat of Zion intact, including its huge city blocks.

City planners today know from observation that big blocks can be boring and provide fewer potential points of interaction and choice for pedestrians. New York City's short blocks are more active than its long ones, and Portland, Oregon, with its extremely small blocks, is famous for its walkability. The length of the blocks isn't the only issue either. Salt Lake City's 132-foot-wide streets can be problematic as well because they force pedestrians to walk farther to cross intersections. In some areas of Salt Lake, little buckets with bright flags have been placed at street corners so people crossing can carry something to make them more visible—a cheap and quick fix for a bigger issue.

To be fair to Salt Lake City and the hundreds of other towns modeled on the same basic plan, none of these shortcomings could have easily been imagined. At the time of the city's construction, vehicular traffic consisted of horse and ox carts, not speeding cars. Some people also argue that Young knew the larger blocks would have to be broken down as the city urbanized, suggesting that it was later officials who failed to adapt the city in ways its original planners had imagined they would.

Regardless, the city is dominated by cars today. This is a problem not just for pedestrians and cyclists but also for the health of area residents. Salt Lake City is surrounded by natural beauty, but the city itself has some of the worst air pollution in the nation. While the tall mountains around it attract outdoorsy people, like skiers and hikers, they also help trap smog. Coming down out of the bright, clear mountains, one arrives in a surprisingly hazy metropolis. This problem will only get worse if the city's population nearly doubles by 2050 as projected.

While some of Salt Lake City's issues can be traced back to the Plat of Zion, the reliance on a single unchanging plan has also caused problems. In the Church of Jesus Christ of Latter-day Saints, there is a principle called continuous revelation—a belief that new divine inspiration will come over time and shake loose old habits and dogma. Perhaps what cities like this one need is a form of continuous revelation—an openness to adapting old grids, Mormon or otherwise, to changing needs and times.

# Good Eixamples

## *Reconfigured Superblocks*

Nineteenth-century Barcelona is a good example of how bad cities could get in the Industrial Age. At one point, nearly 200,000 people were hemmed in by the city's historic medieval walls, and the population density reached twice that of Paris while life expectancy dropped to as low as twenty-three years old for the city's poor (and just thirty-six for the wealthy). Epidemics would sweep through the cramped metropolis and kill thousands of residents. New housing was crammed in wherever possible. One space-maximizing approach of jutting higher floors over the roads below, called jettying, was eventually banned because it blocked air and light on the roads below. In some places, buildings pushing out farther and farther with each added floor reached so far across the street that they nearly touched at their top levels. Needless to say, when it came time to finally build out some breathing room and expand this overly dense city, there was a great deal an aspiring planner could learn from Barcelona's unhealthy state.

Ildefons Cerdà was a little-known engineer when Barcelona's leaders decided to tear down the walls and expand with him at the helm of the project. In designing the Eixample (Catalan for "extension") district, Cerdà employed scientific methods to analyze what went wrong so he could create a healthier and more functional city. He concluded that narrower streets led to higher rates of disease. He also calculated the volume of air needed for populations to breathe and ran analyses of daylight access based on geometries and orientations of streets and buildings. Throughout his design process, he also considered how citizens would travel through a city and what kinds of businesses and institutions they would need to access regularly.

In the end, the Eixample would be massive, more than five hundred blocks of new construction that connected the old city with a series of outlying neighborhoods. In many ways, it was designed to be the opposite of Barcelona—huge and wide-open, with broad streets and plenty of access to light and air. Cerdà's vision was also utopian and egalitarian—blocks of equal size were set on a grid with open courtyards that would serve the rich and poor alike. To maximize light access throughout the day on all sides, the blocks were chamfered (their corners were cropped) and oriented diagonally with respect to the cardinal directions.

Though accessibility and equality sound like noble goals, grids don't always produce such idealized results. As historian and urbanist Lewis Mumford later exclaimed: "With a T-square and a triangle, finally, the municipal engineer could, without the slightest training as either an architect or a sociologist, 'plan'

a metropolis, with its standard lots, its standard blocks, its standard street widths."
In his opinion, many of "the new gridiron plans were spectacular in their ineffi-
ciency and waste." Supposedly egalitarian urban layouts, he argued, had limitations. "By usually failing to discriminate sufficiently between main arteries and
residential streets, the first were not made wide enough while the second were
usually too wide for purely neighborhood functions." In the case of the Eixample,
inequalities and side effects manifested over time after well-intentioned plans
were put into action.

Inevitably, Cerdà's vision was not realized in full, and aspects of it were subverted.
Shared open courtyard areas intended to be accessible in the middle of every block
were in some cases blocked off by buildings. The rich clus-
tered into certain areas and built these sections up higher
with fancy custom architecture (including works by Antoni
Gaudí). Still, much of the Eixample worked as intended, creating a better, more open part of the city—for a while, at least.

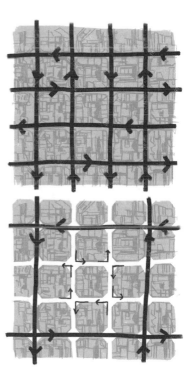

The rise of the automobile presented new problems for
the Eixample. The wide, straight streets were not originally
designed for cars but are nonetheless more suited to them
than pedestrians. Even the chamfered corners are helpful for drivers, allowing them to see around the edges of
buildings at intersections more easily. With the increased
presence of autos, however, the air and noise pollution
Cerdà had sought to avoid made its way into the Eixample.

Out of growing concern for public health and safety,
Barcelona has started to experiment with a strategy of creating superblocks by adapting the old grid in a new way.
Each superblock consists of a three-by-three grid of nine
regular blocks. Within these megablocks, vehicular traffic is limited and streets are largely handed back over to
cyclists and pedestrians in part to encourage less sedentary
lifestyles and improve public health. Barcelona plans to redistribute millions of
square meters of car-centric space using this approach. Aside from deliveries,
transit, and other local access exceptions, vehicles are primarily routed around

these superblocks. As urban retrofit plans go, this one is relatively simple and low-cost—it mainly involves repurposing existing open space and changing around some signs and signals. In many ways, the superblock strategy is an extension of the Eixample's original design intent, which was aimed at creating healthier open spaces to be shared equally by all citizens.

# STANDARD DEVIATIONS

## *Growth Patterns*

"TO AN OVERHEAD OBSERVER, THE STREET PATTERN OF Detroit presents a strange mosaic of conflicting systems, which seem to start and end with no apparent reason, and to have no relation to each other," observed the narrator of a 1960s educational film titled *Detroit's Pattern of Growth*. "However, the twists and turns have their historic explanations." The movie goes on to discuss the specific urban patterns of Detroit but in the process reveals a much deeper truth about how cities can be understood through the eccentricities of their roadways.

Any gridded modern city has deviations and exceptions. These sometimes weave around topographical obstacles, but there are other factors that can contribute to quirks in a city's layout. In Detroit, a confluence of factors has contributed to its "strange mosaic": there's an orthogonal network running roughly along cardinal axes, an application of the classic Jeffersonian system; a conflicting network that parallels the Detroit River, a waterway that connects nearby Lake Erie and Lake St. Clair; and angled streets that seem to defy both of these conventions. At a glance, it all looks like a big mess, which can be attributed to centuries of incremental development. Examining it piece by piece, though, one can start to puzzle out key turning points along the way.

In 1701, French explorer Antoine Laumet de la Mothe Cadillac set out to establish Fort Pontchartrain du Détroit, a defensible outpost for New France in what is now Michigan. This modest town was situated at a narrow point in the Great Lakes waterway system that was already a nexus of Native American travel and trading trails. Some of these informal trails would continue to be used and eventually evolved into major spoke streets radiating out of the city's core.

Over the decades, French rule gave way to British control. Later, after Detroit passed into American hands, the Great Fire of 1805 burned the town to the ground. Some saw this as an opportunity to not just build anew, but to build better. Named for its champion, Judge Augustus B. Woodward, the Woodward Plan called for dividing the land into a series of triangles bisected by lines. Each triangle would have three main roads passing through it, one from each end point to the center of the opposite side. Public parks were to be placed where these paths intersected in the middle of each larger triangular superblock and at the points of the triangles. The city could grow outward indefinitely by adding more triangles that would fit neatly together into an expansive mosaic. But this triangle-based geometry

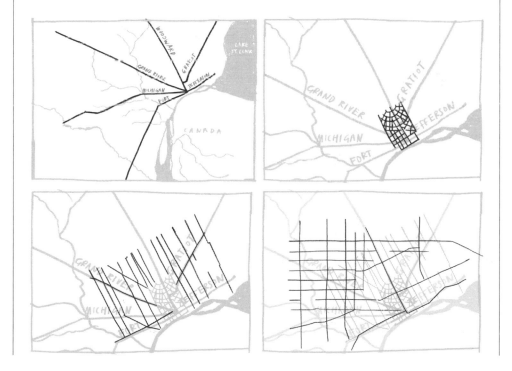

didn't play well with existing rectilinear property lines. It was also criticized by some as being overly urban. Only a few bits and pieces of this generally unpopular plan were implemented before the city turned back toward more traditional rectilinear layouts of roads and lots.

As the city grew, local farms spread out from the river on plots aligned with the water. These long, thin lots allowed farmers to access the river for irrigation and transportation purposes. The edges of these holdings created obvious paths for running roads *perpendicular* to the waterway. On the whole, farmers were fine with border roads but resisted having streets cross through their property. As a result, there are many jogs and bends in Detroit's roads that *parallel* the water. This system of long streets extending out from the water also intersected oddly with Detroit's spoke streets and angular core, further complicating the city.

Adding more confusion to an already complex system, a network of north-south and east-west routes also had to be integrated into Detroit as the city grew outward. This framework of square-mile superblocks includes numbered mile roads like the famous 8 Mile Road.

Where all of these various approaches intersect, strange junctures and elaborate turns stitch the city grids back together. The net effect can be a real pain for drivers, but within this complex tapestry, one can trace the city's history, its position as a trading hub, the aftermath of a devastating fire, the allocation of its farming real estate, and the imposition of a modern cardinal grid. Cities are rarely the product of a single planner, grand plan, or time period. Urban realities are rarely that simple.

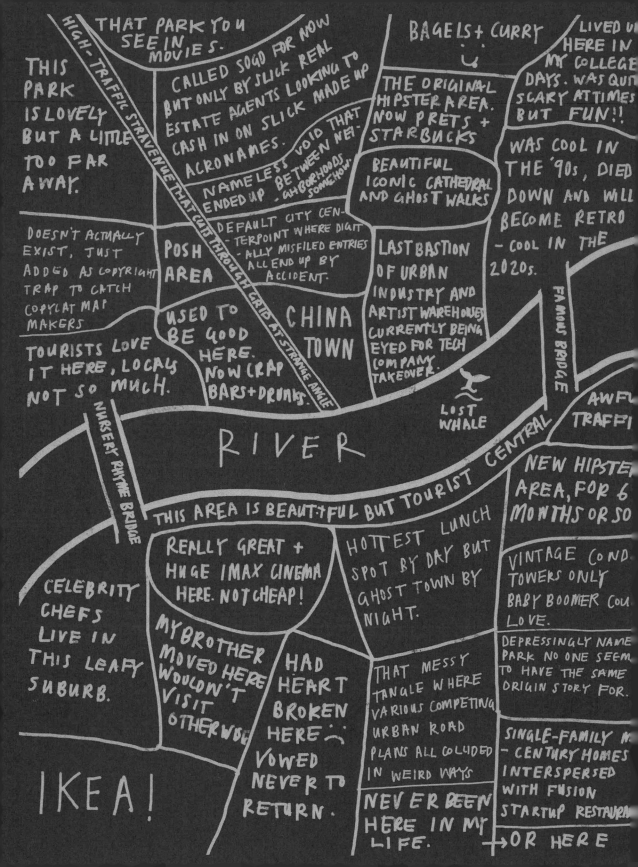

THAT PARK YOU SEE IN MOVIES.

HIGH-TRAFFIC STRAVENUE THAT CUTS THROUGH GRID AT STRANGE ANGLE

THIS PARK IS LOVELY BUT A LITTLE TOO FAR AWAY.

CALLED SOGO FOR NOW BUT ONLY BY SLICK REAL ESTATE AGENTS LOOKING TO CASH IN ON SLICK MADE UP ACRONAMES.

NAMELESS VOID THAT ENDED UP BETWEEN NEIGHBORHOODS SOMEHOW.

BAGELS + CURRY

LIVED UP HERE IN MY COLLEGE DAYS. WAS QUITE SCARY AT TIMES BUT FUN!!

THE ORIGINAL HIPSTER AREA. NOW PRETS + STARBUCKS

WAS COOL IN THE '90s, DIED DOWN AND WILL BECOME RETRO-COOL IN THE 2020s.

BEAUTIFUL ICONIC CATHEDRAL AND GHOST WALKS

DOESN'T ACTUALLY EXIST, JUST ADDED AS COPYRIGHT TRAP TO CATCH COPYCAT MAP MAKERS

DEFAULT CITY CENTERPOINT WHERE DIGITALLY MISFILED ENTRIES ALL END UP BY ACCIDENT.

POSH AREA

LAST BASTION OF URBAN INDUSTRY AND ARTIST WAREHOUSES CURRENTLY BEING EYED FOR TECH COMPANY TAKEOVER.

FAMOUS BRIDGE

USED TO BE GOOD HERE. NOW CRAP BARS + DRUNKS.

CHINA TOWN

TOURISTS LOVE IT HERE, LOCALS NOT SO MUCH.

LOST WHALE

NURSERY RHYME BRIDGE

R I V E R

TOURIST CENTRAL

AWFUL TRAFFIC

THIS AREA IS BEAUTIFUL BUT

NEW HIPSTER AREA, FOR 6 MONTHS OR SO

CELEBRITY CHEFS LIVE IN THIS LEAFY SUBURB.

REALLY GREAT + HUGE IMAX CINEMA HERE. NOT CHEAP!

HOTTEST LUNCH SPOT BY DAY BUT GHOST TOWN BY NIGHT.

VINTAGE COND. TOWERS ONLY BABY BOOMER COU LOVE.

MY BROTHER MOVED HERE WOULDN'T VISIT OTHERWI

HAD HEART BROKEN HERE. VOWED NEVER TO RETURN.

THAT MESSY TANGLE WHERE VARIOUS COMPETING URBAN ROAD PLANS ALL COLLIDED IN WEIRD WAYS

DEPRESSINGLY NAME PARK NO ONE SEEM TO HAVE THE SAME ORIGIN STORY FOR.

SINGLE-FAMILY M-CENTURY HOMES INTERSPERSED WITH FUSION STARTUP RESTAURA

IKEA!

NEVER BEEN HERE IN MY LIFE.

→ OR HERE

# DESIGNATIONS

## *The*

## POWER

## *of*

## NAMES.

**LEFT:** *Subjective map of the city (inspired by Chaz Hutton)*

# CITATIONS NEEDED

## *Informal Geonyms*

SEARCH THE INTERNET FOR BUSTA RHYMES ISLAND AND you'll turn up a small patch of land sitting in a small residential pond in the small state of Massachusetts. The surrounding town of Shrewsbury is a sleepy one and probably the last place most people would expect to find an island named after a rapper. The islet itself is a quiet little piece of land a few dozen feet across with a rope swing and some blueberries, which were planted by the man who named it, area resident Kevin O'Brien.

O'Brien, a fan of canoeing and intricate high-speed rapping, had been paddling out to the island for years. When a friend asked O'Brien what the island was called, Busta Rhymes came to mind, and the name stuck—at least on Google Maps. When O'Brien submitted an application to the US Board on Geographic Names (BGN), however, the name was officially rejected, though not for the reasons one might initially suspect.

The BGN dates back to 1890 and is responsible for deciding what the federal government is going to call a piece of land. Under the Secretary of the Interior, they are tasked with determining official names and settling naming-related disputes. The board itself doesn't actually come up with names, but it is empowered to approve them. The BGN also tracks millions of names in its database along with locations, physical descriptions, and bibliographic references. To accomplish its mission, the BGN brings together people from different departments and agencies, including the Library of Congress, the US Postal Service, and even the Central Intelligence Agency.

The BGN tends to favor places named after geographical features—an aspect of how an island, river, or mountain looks—rather than people. But the board will consider commemorative names if certain conditions are met. In order for a body of land to be named after a celebrity, there are extra requirements, including the fact that the person needs to have been deceased for at least five years.

One of the ideas behind this rule is that emotions are too raw in the period immediately following a death, hence the required cooling-off period before potential commemoration. Just six days after President John F. Kennedy was assassinated, his successor Lyndon B. Johnson announced that Cape Canaveral would be renamed Cape Kennedy. The former name had been around for generations, and locals didn't exactly embrace this change. Their frustration grew over the years until the Florida legislature gave in and voted to change the name back. This shift back and forth led the BGN to introduce a mandatory delay at the federal level.

Different states and cities also have their own names and naming rules. When the BGN considers a federal name for a place, one of the things taken into account is what locals call it officially or colloquially. So Busta Rhymes Island can't be official until the rapper passes away, but if the name stays in use until it becomes eligible, that will count in its favor should O'Brien submit it again. For now, the place may not be federally recognized, but it does have its own Wikipedia page, which seems like a notable start. Woo hah!!

# HYBRID ACRONAMES

## *Neighborhood Monikers*

LIKE MANY OTHER PLACES, THE BAY AREA HAS ITS FAIR share of shortened neighborhood names. The area south of Market Street in San Francisco is called SoMa. The part of town north of the Panhandle is known as NoPa. Around the intersection of North Oakland, Berkeley, and Emeryville, real estate brokers have pitched properties as being located in NOBE. There have also been attempts to brand a stretch of downtown Oakland as KoNo (a reference to Koreatown Northgate), though few people call it that. This convention of shortening and combining names has taken off in recent decades in cities around the

United States, but there isn't really a name for this phenomenon—these unofficial "acronames" (or "acromanteaus" as wordsmith and *The Allusionist* podcaster Helen Zaltzman calls them) aren't quite acronyms or portmanteaus. They are something else, and they aren't just a fad.

These names can serve a financial purpose for the people interested in selling properties at higher prices. Where Prospect Heights and Crown Heights intersect in New York City, real estate agents found that they could list properties in the more affordable Crown Heights neighborhood at Prospect Heights prices by lumping the areas together and calling the result ProCro. Brokers have rebranded parts of Harlem as SoHa and entire swaths of the Bronx as SoBro. There have been attempts to stop the proliferation of these kinds of names in New York and elsewhere, but it's hard to ban or criminalize informal names.

In cities like Boston, DC, Seattle, and Denver, you can find areas like LoDo, SoDo, and SoWa, all of which trace back to one acroname in New York City: SoHo, short for south of Houston Street in Manhattan, a name that goes back to 1962 and an urban planner named Chester Rapkin. On behalf of the New York City Planning Commission, Rapkin was tasked with looking into conditions in an area that had once been called Hell's Hundred Acres. At the time, it was known as the South Houston Industrial Area—less ominous but still not very appealing.

The area that would become known as SoHo was zoned for industrial manufacturing. The neighborhood had a lot of vacancies, and its brick buildings and cast-iron facades were seen by many as eyesores out of sync with the rest of Manhattan. In the 1960s, under the influence of the infamously ruthless "master builder" Robert Moses, tearing down and rebuilding was the norm, but SoHo avoided this fate. Rapkin suggested another path: preserve and renovate local industrial structures for ongoing manufacturing uses. In conversations at the time, he and his colleagues began to refer to the area as SoHo. Rapkin had no idea this name would stick or spawn a widely used convention.

Artists started renting manufacturing spaces in SoHo for use as studios and in many cases lived in them in order to save money on rent. In the 1970s, the neighborhood became renowned as an arts district. The buildings weren't designated as residences, but people found a loophole: artists were effectively classified as "machines" who "manufactured" art. Machines, of course, could stay in factories overnight. Performers, painters, and musicians were soon hosting art openings and other hip happenings in these loft spaces, attracting media attention.

SoHo came to be seen as a blueprint that urban planners could build on to create appealing new mixed-use areas in neighborhoods like Tribeca (a shortening of Triangle Below Canal Street). Like SoHo, Tribeca became cool and desirable. These areas became associated with industrial chic; high-end boutiques and condos began popping up. Spaces were minimalist and functional at first but evolved to become more luxurious as the rich installed marble bathtubs and expensive furniture into spaces filled with exposed bricks and metal beams. Many lofts in these old industrial buildings are worth millions of dollars today. It's a familiar story in cities around the world now: artists move in, then get priced out, and the cycle repeats.

A new and trendy acroname (or any novel moniker) is now often seen as a leading indicator of imminent change. For better or worse, the act of renaming has become a harbinger of gentrification. In the end, neighborhoods change. Their names can change, too, but whether a new name sticks or fails to catch on is generally up to the people who actually live there, not the real estate agents trying to make a buck.

# CALCULATED OMISSIONS

## *Unlucky Numbers*

IN 2015, THE CANADIAN CITY OF VANCOUVER ISSUED A bulletin requiring developers to number floors of new buildings using a "normal mathematical sequence of numbers." "Four, thirteen, [and] any other number people want to skip for whatever reason, we're putting back in," declared Pat Ryan, the city's chief building official. Numerical skipping was getting out of hand. In one case, a condo tower marketed as having sixty floors only had fifty-three—floor 13 was omitted, as was every floor ending with the numeral 4, which led to a lot of gaps in the numbering scheme. The new rule was for public safety: in an emergency, responders need to be able to navigate a building without worrying about creative numbering systems. For the developers, skipping numbers wasn't about selling buildings as being taller than they actually were, but it was still a function of the bottom line—some groups of buyers have very strong feelings about numbers.

In China (and places like Vancouver with large Chinese populations), the numeral 4 is frequently avoided because the Mandarin word for "four" sounds like the Mandarin word for "death." In Cantonese-speaking regions in China, 14 and 24 are considered even unluckier than 4 because the Cantonese word for "fourteen" sounds like "will certainly die" and the Cantonese "twenty-four" sounds like "easy to die." In some buildings, the entire set of fortieth floors is bypassed. A study of Vancouver real estate prices found that houses with the numeral 4 in their address sell at a 2.2% discount on average while ones with the numeral 8 (which sounds like "prosperity" in Chinese) sell at a 2.5% premium, which may sound small but can add up to tens of thousands of dollars.

In many parts of the world, 13 is considered an especially unlucky number. The fear of 13 is particularly old and pervasive, though there are competing theories as to why. It was rumored that Hammurabi omitted the thirteenth law from his code, though this theory has since been debunked. Loki, the Norse trickster god, was the thirteenth (and an uninvited) guest at a dinner held in memory of Baldur, a fellow god he had slain. Judas the betrayer was supposedly the thirteenth person to sit down at the table with Jesus at the Last Supper. Whatever their origins, associations

with unlucky and lucky numbers seem to take root in cities and find their way into the numbering systems of built environments—except when municipalities push back. The Otis Elevator Company at one point estimated that 85% of the elevator panels they create omit the thirteenth floor. Sometimes, the number 13 is left out in favor of 12A or M (the thirteenth letter in the alphabet). In other buildings, the thirteenth floor is relegated to mechanical or storage functions or given a special designation (such as the pool level or the restaurant floor). On the plus side, those interested in a thirteenth- or fourteenth-floor view in Vancouver may find themselves with a fortunate opportunity to get a unit for a few percentage points less than their superstitious neighbors.

# DELIBERATED ERRORS

## *Fictitious Entries*

"A MAP IS NOT THE TERRITORY IT REPRESENTS," WROTE philosopher Alfred Korzybski in the 1930s. As if to prove his point, the General Drafting Corporation drew up a map of New York State that included a fictitious town that existed only on paper. Agloe, as it was called, was added as a kind of geographical trap to identify future copycats, a blip on the map situated between the towns of Roscoe and Beaverkill near the Pennsylvania border.

While many creative works are easy to protect with copyright, factual projects can be trickier. Facts can't be copyrighted, so works that collect them like dictionaries and maps are easier to copy without getting caught. One workaround used by industry professionals is to include a false "fact" or entry. Makers of the *New Columbia Encyclopedia* added an entry for Lillian Virginia Mountweazel, a fountain designer turned photographer who never existed. A similar solution can be found in copies of the *New Oxford American Dictionary,* where the word *esquivalience* is found—"The willful avoidance of one's official responsibilities (late 19th cent.: perhaps from French *esquiver*, 'dodge, slink away')." This definition, too, is a fake.

In the case of Agloe, the story took an unexpected turn. A few years after the General Drafting Corporation published its map with the embedded trap, Rand McNally released a map that also featured this made-up place, which naturally led the first company to accuse them of copyright infringement. It seemed open-and-shut, but Rand McNally doubled down and asserted the town was real. The case went to court.

Rand McNally's defense was simple: the existence of the Agloe General Store. Apparently, the owners of this actual store had seen a version of the original map, so when they went to set up shop in the area, they named it after the fictional town. This once-fake place had become a modest reality, a "town" that at its peak was home to a store and a pair of houses. The town is long gone now, but it left behind a sign along the road that reads, WELCOME TO AGLOE! HOME OF THE AGLOE GENERAL STORE. COME BACK SOON!

# MISPLACED LOCATIONS

## *Null Island*

NULL ISLAND IS LOCATED IN THE SOUTH ATLANTIC OCEAN where the prime meridian meets the equator—or it would be if it actually existed. Situated at 0 degrees north and 0 degrees east, Null Island has become an unlikely hub in the realm of geographic information systems (GIS). When data is corrupted or entered improperly, a coordinate location of zero longitude and zero latitude can result. This can lead programs to identify all kinds of odds and ends as being located at this remote nonplace. Since Null Island doesn't actually exist, there is no one there to be impacted by or complain about this problem, but not all geographical defaults are quite so innocuous.

A remote farm in the middle of Kansas found itself the victim of a similar GIS glitch back in the early 2000s, suddenly making this rural plot the center of much unwanted attention. Over the years, the family who owns the land and the people who have rented it from them have been accused of theft, fraud, and other scams, and have been visited by tax collectors, federal marshals, and local ambulances. All of this attention traces back to a mapping company that decided to geolocate any unspecified points within the United States to a specific location near the geographical center of the country, which resulted in hundreds of millions of entries pointing at this one particular farm way out in the countryside. The default point was eventually moved to the center of a body of water to avoid further hassle for the property owners.

Since there is no one on Null Island to be disturbed by knocks at the door from unwanted visitors, enthusiasts have come to embrace its nonexistence rather than try to erase it from databases. In fact, it has become so popular that fans have created maps of this default spot as well as a national flag and fake history to provide some backstory. In reality, there is no island to visit, but there is a marker: Station 13010, dubbed Soul, is situated at point 0,0, where it collects air and water temperature data as well as wind speed and direction information for PIRATA, the Prediction and Research Moored Array in the Atlantic. "Null Island is a curious blend of real and imaginary geography, of mathematical certainty and pure fantasy," writes Tim St. Onge of the Library of Congress, "or it's just the site of a weather observation buoy. However you see it, we have the GIS world to thank for putting Null Island on the map."

# PAVED WAYS

## *Tucson Stravenues*

THE FIRST WORDS IN ROUTE OR PLACE NAMES OFTEN TELL short stories that provide poetic glimpses into local history. Some tell uplifting tales, like Victory Peak, but there are depressing ones, too, including Cape Disappointment, Pointless Mountain, Loveless Lake, and Hopeless Way. One has to wonder: What did someone go through before landing on Broken Dreams Drive or Suffering Street? When did they give up on Despair Island? What were their dreams on Nightmare Island? What (or who) came to an end at Termination Point? Who would feel compelled to travel down Why Me Lord Lane, Emptiness Drive, or

Shades of Death Road? Damien Rudd, author of *Sad Topographies,* has quite the collection of these humorous and macabre monikers.

While less explicitly loaded with meaning, simple road numbers can tell stories, too. Fun fact: Second is the most common street name in the United States. Third is the second-most common, First is the third, and Fifth is the sixth. Inexplicably, Fourth is the fourth. A lot of streets that would be called First end up with names like Main, which is presumably why we have this counterintuitive order.

The latter part of a road name can provide information as well. Names for routes all have regional variations and exceptions, but there are fairly persistent conventions even longtime drivers may not realize.

ROAD (Rd): any route connecting two points

STREET (St): has buildings on both sides, perpendicular to avenues

AVENUE (Ave): perpendicular to streets, may have trees on one side

BOULEVARD (Blvd): wide city street with median and side vegetation

WAY (Way): small side route

LANE (La): narrow and often rural

DRIVE (Dr): long, winding, and shaped by natural environments

TERRACE (Ter): wraps up and around a slope

PLACE (Pl): no through traffic or a dead end

COURT (Ct): ends in a circle or loop (like a plaza or square)

HIGHWAY (Hwy): major public route connecting larger cities

FREEWAY (Fwy): has two or more lanes in each direction

EXPRESSWAY (Expy): divided highway for faster traffic

INTERSTATE (I): often goes between states but not always

TURNPIKE (Tpke): usually an expressway with a tollbooth

BELTWAY (Bltwy): wraps around a city like a belt

PARKWAY (Pkwy): usually has parkland on the side

CAUSEWAY (Cswy): runs on an embankment across water or a wetland

This list is not definitive, and with naming conventions, nothing is ever complete. Take Tucson, Arizona, for instance, where the grid looks fairly commonplace

ROAD (Rd): any route
connecting two points

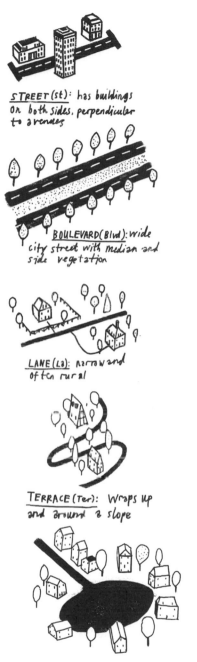

STREET (St): has buildings
on both sides, perpendicular
to avenues

AVENUE (Ave): perpindicular
to streets, may have trees
or buildings

BOULEVARD (Blvd): wide
city street with median and
side vegetation

WAY (Way): small side route

LANE (La): narrow and
often rural

DRIVE (Dr): Long, winding
and shaped by natural
environments

TERRACE (Ter): Wraps up
and around a slope

PLACE (Pl): no through traffic
or dead end

COURT (Ct): ends in a circle or
loop (like a plaza or square)

at a glance—most roads running east-west are called streets while roads running north-south are labeled as avenues. There is, however, a hybrid type unique to this city: the stravenue, a portmanteau of street and avenue used for diagonal roads (abbreviated Stra). In the grand scheme of official designations, this relatively recent term coined in 1948 hints at a potential avenue for people interested in leaving a memorable mark on the built environment if they don't wish to go down the route of naming roadways after various states of death and despair.

# ACCESSIBLE VOIDS

## *Nameless Places*

MOST PEOPLE MAY NOT KNOW WHAT TO CALL THAT PATCH of curvy land trapped between a freeway and its on-ramps. In his 2010 "field guide to invisible public space" titled *The Typology of New Public Sites,* Baltimore artist Graham Coreil-Allen dubbed these byproducts of urban expansion *freeway eddies.* In more official contexts, places like this often have less-inspiring, more esoteric names—like gores, which separate merge lanes from freeways. So it's easy to see why someone looking to draw attention to these would come up with catchier monikers.

In addition to other less "gory" names, Coreil-Allen's book offers an array of captivating designations, like corner surprises, boxes of uncertainty, displaced forests, and suggested swallets, each with its own distinct definition but with something in common. On a city map, these all tend to be overlooked and unmarked—the unnamed spaces between the things that typically get labeled; they are the non-things, the nothings. Coreil-Allen saw something in them, though, and singled them out for inspection and reflection, photographing and describing his findings and even giving tours of them.

Some of these places are clearly designed, like gores or berms, but they are often overlooked. Most of these spaces, though, are leftovers in planned areas that were created incidentally through the process of car-centric urban development. These "new public sites" aren't always (or even often) attractive in an aesthetic sense, but they have potential for public use. Coreil-Allen highlights this potential, which is normally associated with conventional and intentional squares and parks. His argument is that naming these sites makes them more visible.

The project is partly about raising the profile of public spaces, but it's also about getting people engaged with them. "The mere act of identifying the sites and representing them through physical installations, dispersed media and promoted events," Coreil-Allen argues, "raises awareness of the spaces while also making them more physically and digitally accessible."

*The Typology of New Public Sites* is not a policy brief for urban planners or a comprehensive guide for urban explorers. Still, reading the definitions and looking at the images is a useful mental exercise in rethinking what we see (or don't) as we move through urban environments. The swirling spaces trapped between highways might never be public parks or places for civic rallies, but perhaps they have some uses yet to be imagined by someone who sees them as something more than interstitial voids.

# LANDSCAPES

W E HUMANS EXPECT A BIT OF VEGE-tation even in our most austere cityscapes. Sometimes we allow nature to be nature, but often our desire for control prunes and shapes plant life into an unrecognizable facsimile of nature. At its best, greenery in cities is harmonious and inspiring. At its worst, it's wasteful, unsustainable, and overly dependent on constant human intervention. Either way, it's fascinating to view our humanity through the lens of our relationship with plants, particularly in the places where plants don't naturally grow.

LEFT: *Converted High Line greenway on elevated rail line in New York City*

# GRAVEYARD SHIFTS

## *Pastoral Parks*

FROM A DISTANCE, THE TOWN OF COLMA, CALIFORNIA, looks a bit like a sprawling city in miniature—but instead of skyscrapers for the living dotting its landscape, the skyline is made up of mausoleums, monuments, and tombstones dedicated to the deceased. In Colma, the dead outnumber the living by a thousand to one. Located just ten miles south of San Francisco, the town has elements of conventional public parks like rolling green hills and manicured hedges, but it is also a true necropolis—a place dedicated primarily to the dead. This town houses the remains of well more than a million and a half people, which dwarfs the living population of less than two thousand. Residents acknowledge this oddity with their town motto, "It's great to be alive in Colma." Urban expansion has slowly crept up all around it, but Colma still feels shockingly rural. This uncanny place is the product of a historical shift away from urban burial practices toward a new kind of open memorial park.

Around the world, the dead have long coexisted with the living in population centers, interred in town squares or urban churchyards. Historically, such burial grounds often served as public mixed-use spaces to hang out in or graze livestock on, but the overlapping functions in these places have been known to create issues. Bodies were often buried in stacks to save space, then later unearthed by floods. By the early 1800s, outbreaks of disease and escalating real estate prices began to push the dead out of cities, which led new graves to be dug on plots increasingly distant from urban populations. This shift changed not only the location of gravesites but also the way they were designed and experienced.

Near Cambridge, Massachusetts, Mount Auburn Cemetery was among the first rural American "cemeteries," a name derived from the Greek word for "sleeping chamber." The carefully planned landscape drew on English garden traditions and pushed cemetery design in a radical new direction. "If the city of the living was designed for speed and efficiency and business," suggests Keith Eggener, author of *Cemeteries,* "the city of the dead was instead understood as a kind of quiet peaceful Arcadia—a kind of evocation of paradise or heaven on Earth." This type of cemetery was particularly popular in an era before there were a lot of public parks, art museums, or botanical gardens in or around American cities. The picturesque Mount Auburn would not only go on to inspire other cemeteries but also large public parks like Frederick Law Olmsted's Central Park in New York City, which in turn inspired a whole new generation of urban parks.

The area that is now home to Colma used to be largely dedicated to farming. As San Francisco's cemeteries started to fill up in the late 1800s, churches and other organizations began buying plots for burials south of this growing regional metropolis. In the early 1900s, San Francisco even put a moratorium on new urban burials and cut off funding for cemetery maintenance. A few years later, the city passed an ordinance forcing existing graves out as well, which led to the mass disinterment of 150,000 bodies. Many of these were unearthed, shipped out, and then reburied in the area that would come to be called Colma. Families that could afford a ten-dollar fee could move headstones along with their deceased loved ones while other corpses were simply put into mass graves.

For the markers left behind in San Francisco, though, this wasn't the end of the story. Many individual headstones from old graveyards ended up being reused as building material around the city. Intact headstones and fragments of them can be found all over San Francisco. Some wound up at Ocean Beach, arrayed to reduce coastal erosion, while others ended up in Buena Vista Park, lining trails and gutters. The dead may have been moved out of the metropolis for the living, but ghosts of their history still linger in parks and other public spaces.

# TRAILING SPACES

## *Converted Greenways*

THE HIGH LINE IS A REMARKABLE PARK BUILT ON A stretch of repurposed elevated rail in Manhattan that winds between buildings and even through them. Started in the 2000s, this raised greenway was groundbreaking in many ways, but the basic notion of a pathway park connecting neighborhoods has been around for a long time. Even before cities filled in around old transit corridors, many had long, thin urban parks that defied the surrounding grids of streets and sidewalks.

In the 1870s, the firm of famed landscape architect Frederick Law Olmsted began to wrap his Emerald Necklace around a section of Boston. His vision was to connect a series of parks across the city along streams, paths, and parkways, form-ing a chain of green spaces linking freshwater ponds, natural groves, picturesque meadows, and arboretums. Much of this was possible at the time thanks to swaths of undeveloped marshland. Breaking new ground became increasingly difficult as cities filled in, but these marshy areas offered fresh opportunities for growth.

Meanwhile, in places like New York City, freight trains were also competing for undeveloped urban space but often with devastating side effects. One route on Manhattan's West Side was dubbed Death Avenue because of the hundreds of pedestrians killed in the late 1800s and early 1900s. Eventually, the city, the state, and the railroad company agreed to elevate the rail line in 1929. Within a few years, new tracks began running high above the streets below.

With the rise of trucking, rail usage started to decline in the 1960s, and sections of this elevated rail were torn down. Then, in 1983, two key factors set the stage for the High Line's future: a foundation was formed to preserve and develop the raised tracks, and Congress amended the National Trails System Act, which simplified the process of turning old rails into trails. But the High Line would still narrowly escape demolition for decades; at one point, it was put on the chopping block by

Mayor Rudy Giuliani, who went so far as to sign a demolition order for the sections that remained. A new organization, Friends of the High Line, thwarted this edict by raising awareness around the potential of the elevated tracks and soliciting design ideas for reuse. The group received hundreds of submissions from around the world, including proposals for roller coasters and lap pools. In the end, something more practical but still visionary won out.

While it is both a trail and a park, the High Line was also promoted as being more than just a conventional pathway or an ecologically sensitive landscape. It changes and shifts along its length, opening up to offer seating, gathering, performance, and other public spaces with spots carved out for vendors as well as the hundreds of species of plants interspersed along its mile-and-a-half span. The long, thin park pushes people together, which helps it feel lively and active, if a bit crowded at times. Some of its successful, density-driving strategies are a byproduct of the space, but they can be traced back to other New York precedents in a city famous for its cozy pocket parks. The multistage High Line has been a hit and has spurred adjacent development—improving or gentrifying the area depending on one's perspective.

Other cities have drawn up similar plans, some explicitly attempting to emulate the High Line with varying degrees of success. In London, a proposed Garden Bridge to span the Thames ultimately fell through despite a lot of high-level political support and the involvement of high-profile designers. It drew some inspiration and perhaps some of the wrong lessons from New York's precedent. Unlike the High Line, the Garden Bridge would have been an entirely new structure that connected two points rather than a reused one winding through the heart of a city. Tens of millions of pounds were spent before it was scrapped. In Chicago, the 606 greenway has become a fully realized rails-to-trails conversion that (despite valid criticisms concerning gentrification) is popular and successfully connects a series of neighborhoods. A Los Angeles River greenway is also in the works.

From Minneapolis to Paris, a number of extensive rails-to-trails conversion projects have already taken shape, and more are underway. Germany alone has thousands of miles of rail trails. Today, many cities are transforming urban riverbanks, viaducts, underpasses, and even old freeways into parks, bike paths, pedestrian routes, and combinations thereof. Cities derive different benefits from different kinds of open recreational and leisure spaces, but linear parks and green-ways often offer a particularly appealing combination of opportunities—they can wind along existing paths, connect parts of a city, and serve not just as places to relax and play but also as transportation corridors and connectors that diversify mobility options for urban dwellers.

# C<small>OURTING</small> P<small>ALMS</small>

## *Street Trees*

O<small>N THE CAMPUS OF THE</small> U<small>NIVERSITY OF</small> N<small>EBRASKA IN</small> Lincoln, spraying evergreen trees with fox urine and glycerin is a decades-old practice used to deter would-be Christmas tree thieves. In the cool outdoors, the smell is not very noticeable, but if a student or other local resident chops down a tree to take inside for the holidays, the mixture heats up and the odor becomes unbearable. Putting tags on the smaller trees that are more likely to be taken helps warn potential thieves of the rancid smell that awaits. "I think it's helping things," Jeffrey Culbertson of the UNL landscape services told the *Daily Nebraskan*. "I'll get two or three phone calls asking if we really sprayed it or we just put the tag on it because they can't smell anything. So I always find that funny—do they want to know we didn't spray it so they can take the tree, or why are they calling to ask?" Christmas tree theft is a seasonal problem, but throughout the year, many other tree and plant varieties are also snatched from public spaces.

Elms, oaks, maples, and other trees and shrubs line many city streets, providing shade and converting carbon dioxide into oxygen, but fortunately for people who enjoy such things, most of these varieties are less attractive targets for thieves—at least compared to the palm tree, which, in fact, is not a tree at all. Colloquially called palm trees, Arecaceae are actually a family of perennial plants that come in thousands of species, but the ones that look particularly treelike have special significance in urban environments. Despite being relatively poor converters of carbon dioxide, they have long been fashionable in states like Texas and California. A combination of factors, including their dense, easy-to-excavate root balls and their general desirability, has made urban palm tree theft a serious issue.

Thieves can sell a mature palm for tens of thousands of dollars. Like pine trees in the cold American Midwest, the value of palms in the warmer South and West is tied not to their utility but to their place in our collective imagination, which has shifted over the centuries. Hundreds of years ago, devout Spanish Christians planted palms in California for their fronds, which were used on Palm Sunday. By the time California became a state in 1850, Orientalism, a Western fascination with all things exotic, contributed to an interest in these pseudo-trees. Palms also came to be associated with the tropics, which in turn conjured images of luxury, leisure, and escape. By the early 1900s, numerous fancy hotels in major cities around the world featured palm courts—even the mighty RMS *Titanic* had one on board.

As palm fever swept the world, these plants came to be especially popular in Los Angeles. Wealthy homeowners would plant palms to frame their front entrances, while rich suburbanites took things a step further by planting them along public street verges. During the Great Depression, Los Angeles tasked unemployed people through the Works Progress Administration with putting up municipal palms along major boulevards, which led to a preponderance of these plants throughout the city.

These days, palms in Southern California and elsewhere are growing older and, in some cases, suffering from a devastating kind of wilt as well. Rather than replacing them, cities like Los Angeles are rethinking the role of palms, which provide a lot less in terms of ecological benefits than other plant species, including actual trees. New palms will no doubt be planted in spots where their symbolic role is seen as particularly important, but the landscape of Los Angeles and other palm-laden cities may have a lot fewer palms to steal in the coming decades, at least if ecologically oriented urbanists have anything to say about it.

# Lawn Enforcement

## *Owned Backyards*

In recent decades, some homeowners have taken to hiring companies that will paint brown patches of grass or even entire lawns green. Some choose to do this for aesthetic reasons when faced with droughts or water restrictions; others are forced to take this strangely drastic action because of local governments or neighborhood associations that simply won't tolerate anything short of a green yard that befits their unified vision of suburban subdivisions.

It's easy to make light of lawn-related rules, but the ramifications can be quite stark for people who cannot meet the exacting standards imposed on them. Over a decade ago, a homeowner in Hudson, Florida, was jailed for having a brown lawn. He was later freed in part because press coverage raised awareness of his plight, which led area residents to take up his cause and resod his lawn. This retiree had tried to satisfy his homeowner's association by replanting three times, but each new yard failed to take, and a warrant was eventually issued for his arrest. His is not an isolated case. More recently in the Florida city of Dunedin, the local Code Enforcement Board moved to foreclose on a retired homeowner for failing to pay tens of thousands of dollars in lawn-related code violation fines. At five hundred dollars a day, the steep penalties added up quickly while the owner was out of state caring for his dying mother and later traveling to deal with her estate after she passed.

Few extreme cases like these result in jail time or foreclosures, but they highlight how seriously American municipalities take lawns, a preoccupation that seems at odds with a culture that stereotypically values self-determination. Houses with their lawns and picket fences are supposed to be symbols of a modern American dream, yet this "private" property is highly policed by others. In fact, from the start, lawns had little to do with liberty and even less to do with American suburbia. Their origins trace back to wealthy elites across the Atlantic Ocean.

According to Paul Robbins, author of *Lawn People,* modern lawns are derived not from ancient gardening traditions but from idealized landscape paintings created by Italian Renaissance artists. English elites became enthralled with these, which led life to imitate art as landed aristocrats began to emulate these picturesque scenes right in their own backyards. Grass was nice and soft to walk on, but lawns were also about showing power and privilege. Only a rich person could afford to let their fields be unproductive and hire scythe-wielding peasants to keep their lovely but useless grass nice and short. As European colonists sailed to the New World, they brought this tradition with them.

Andrew Jackson Downing, one of America's earliest and most prominent landscape architects, advocated for lawns as a place for order amid the chaos of cityscapes. In 1850, he wrote that "when smiling lawns and tasteful cottages begin to embellish a country, we know that order and culture are established." As the first suburbs emerged, the middle class began adopting lawns, bolstered in part by this idea of the lawn as an organizing moral force. It was also efficient—grass was a cheap and easy way to brighten up large patches of land.

Today, grass is the most irrigated crop in the United States. "Even conservatively," estimates research scientist Cristina Milesi, "there are three times more acres of lawns in the U.S. than irrigated corn." In a typical American city like Columbus, Ohio, lawns have been found to cover a quarter or more of the metropolitan landscape, and that doesn't include other grass-covered areas like soccer fields and golf courses. Americans spend billions of dollars a year maintaining lawns. Arrayed in neat rows or tucked in planters, other plants and flowers become decorative flourishes against the largely blank green canvas of a lawn.

The role of lawns may be changing, though, particularly in places impacted by climate change and other local environmental factors. In California, the effects of drought have been particularly visible in recent years when it comes to grass. Back in 2015, Governor Jerry Brown declared that the Golden State would need to cut water use by a quarter. "We're in a new era," he explained, and cautioned citizens that "the idea of your nice little green grass getting water every day—that's gonna be a thing of the past." In some southwestern states, governments are even paying citizens to tear out lawns and replace them with alternative landscapes. Xeriscaping (from the Greek *xeros* for "dry" and sometimes called zeroscaping) is on the rise, leading to yards that have few plants and require little to no water or other maintenance. If the old paradigm was neighbors shaming one another over less-than-green lawns, the new one may be neighbors giving one another grief over having too much grass.

Aside from their water usage, lawns displace other types of plants that support key natural ecosystems and insect species vital to humans, including pollinators. "If we can't provide for the nature that literally sustains us at home, how can we ever hope to steward that nature beyond our front door into parks and farm fields and marshes and deserts and forests and prairies?" asks Nebraska author and garden designer Benjamin Vogt. When we default to a lawnscape, he argues, "we might as well be paving over everything with asphalt, because [a] lawn has no flowers, and it certainly has no shrubs or small trees which create hedgerows, perhaps some of the best bee nesting habitat around." For the sake of humans as well as other species, it's probably time for people to get off the damn lawn.

# LOFTY TREESCRAPERS

## *Ungrounded Plants*

EMBELLISHED WITH NAMES LIKE "GARDEN TOWER" AND "urban forest" by the global architecture firms behind them, lush skyscrapers with plant-adorned facades create visual and conceptual appeal by blending elements of nature and cities. Plant-filled architectural renderings are on the rise in the age of social media, thanks in part to a growing concern with urban greenery. From landscape-wrapping groundscrapers to tree-wrapped high-rises, lush plants add color while also offering the appearance of sustainability, which can appeal to potential investors and other buyers as well as sales-oriented developers. A trend that began with green roofs has spilled over the edges, hanging off the sides of structures like a modern vision of Babylon. Still, many of these "treescrapers" are more art than architecture, and most never get off the drawing board, let alone the ground.

A pair of towers in Milan, Italy, collectively called the Bosco Verticale ("Vertical Forest"), is a rare example of a finished project in the realm of largely unbuilt conceptual treescrapers. The construction of these twinned residential towers designed by Boeri Studio began in 2009. Each of them is hundreds of feet high and supports an impressive array of plants, including thousands of trees and shrubs. This greenery was added in part to help filter air, reduce noise pollution, and provide shade but also to support habitats for various species of birds and insects. The project was awarded LEED Gold certification. It also won the International Highrise Award in 2014 and was named the 2015 Best Tall Building Worldwide by the Council on Tall Buildings and Urban Habitat. "The Bosco Verticale is a new idea of skyscraper, where trees and humans coexist," exclaimed architect Stefano Boeri. "It is the first example in the world of a tower that enriches biodiversity of plant and wildlife in the city"—the world's first true vertical forest.

Critics, however, were quick to point out that the environmental cost of hoisting the plants and the embodied energy involved in structurally supporting them significantly offsets sustainability gains, including carbon sequestration. Other reported problems include higher-than-expected costs to tenants, structural issues with some specific trees, and general construction delays, though some of these setbacks are par for the course in big urban building projects. Once completed, the greenery also took time to fill in and arguably never came to look quite as lush in reality as it did in the renderings. There is also a lot of flat green lawn and hardscape surrounding the towers, a potential missed opportunity for packing in taller plants on the ground that could provide shade and be easier to care for. Some of the issues encountered in erecting the Vertical Forest towers were project specific and were resolved in various ways, but certain challenges are endemic to treescrapers in general.

When tons of trees are put up on buildings, extra concrete and steel reinforcement are required to handle their added weight, irrigation systems are needed to water the plants, and additional wind load complexity has to be taken into account. Once installed on upper floors, trees are subject to high winds, though they often seem to remain improbably straight and tall in renderings. Wind can also interrupt photosynthetic processes, while heat and cold can wreak havoc on many species of trees—especially the tall and lush varieties seen in many drawings. Different sides of a given building are also subject to different environmental conditions. Variable winds and maximum sun exposure make putting the same type of greenery on all sides impractical, though that doesn't stop a lot of architects from showing illustrations where various sides are treated equally. On top of all of these considerations, plants are living things that need to be fertilized, watered, trimmed, cleaned up after, and periodically replanted.

Renderings often represent an idealized vision of a building, so if an image does not quite match reality, it is not a huge surprise. Architects have been known to omit details like railings on balconies to make buildings look sleeker. But illustrations have power. They can create unrealistic expectations and lead to unsustainable solutions, not to mention adding to the workload of the structural engineers, landscape architects, ecologists, and botanists who are essential in refining and executing such demanding designs.

In general, thinner layers of soil that support mosses, succulents, herbs, and grasses are often much more practical to deploy and maintain than the more intensive support systems needed for bigger shrubs and trees. More minimal, lighter-touch solutions may not be as photogenic, but they demand less in terms of water, nutrients, and ongoing management while still providing ecological benefits.

At the heart of all of this is a larger question about what role greenery should play in cities. There are architectural projects that deftly integrate different kinds of living plants into buildings of all shapes and sizes, but treescrapers tend to lift trees out of shared public spaces and put them up where they can be seen by many but enjoyed by few. They can become more like window dressing—green ornaments rather than ecological assets or social activators. Civic greenery can bring a lot of benefits to urban environments, but it is perhaps most useful to citizens when grounded in reality.

# SYNANTHROPES

PEOPLE BUILT CITIES FOR THEM-selves—huge works of concrete, metal, and glass were designed to house squishy bipeds. There was less concern for the feathered, furry, and spineless. Still, in the words of Ian Malcolm from *Jurassic Park*: "Life finds a way," even if the animals that have managed to thrive in cities aren't always applauded for their adaptability. Familiarity has bred contempt. Many citizens kick at pigeons, poison snails, and war with raccoons. Still, these wild species of animals, known as synanthropes—from the Greek *syn* ("together with") and *anthropos* ("man")—persist among us, often unnoticed despite the ways they inform the nature of modern metropolises.

LEFT: *Urban raccoon, also known as a trash panda (not to scale)*

# NATURALIZED DENIZENS

## *Common Squirrels*

LIKE PIGEONS AND RACCOONS, EASTERN GRAY SQUIRRELS may seem like a universal feature of many cities, but for a long time, they were nowhere to be found in urban environments. The present abundance of metropolitan squirrels is not accidental but driven by humans who put them into parks, then fed and sheltered them, which allowed them to become successful synanthropes.

Philadelphia was an early squirrel adopter, reintroducing this native species to a public park in the mid-1800s. Like many Eastern Seaboard cities at that time, the area was highly urbanized, and squirrels brought an element of wildness back into the industrialized landscape. A few other East Coast cities also added squirrels to their parks, but the urban squirrel population remained small overall. Philadelphia had only three squirrels in 1847, which were carefully fenced in to keep out predators. But even with human care, these captured critters did not fare well. A wild squirrel requires deciduous nut-bearing plants in order to survive. The feed provided by the city often proved to be either insufficient or nutritionally worthless, so early urban squirrels mostly either perished in captivity or were sold as pets. It would take a shift in how cities treated green spaces for them to thrive.

Prior to various transformation efforts of the late 1800s, large public open spaces had largely served as multipurpose fields used for everything from cattle grazing to militia training. Slowly, though, they came to be understood as potential places for leisure, with parks crafted to mimic the natural world. Designers like Calvert Vaux and Frederick Law Olmsted pushed designs for New York's Central

Park and Prospect Park in this new direction and worked with existing hydrological and geological features. They turned ponds and marshes into artificial lakes and preserved natural rock outcroppings in an attempt to balance a sense of wild nature with an orderly and enjoyable experience of urban escape.

These new natural-looking parks were filled with hedges, lakes, and streams as well as oak trees, which provided plenty of acorns for squirrels. It was into this redesigned landscape that the squirrels were reintroduced in New York in 1877. Within a few years, an initial population of a few dozen squirrels grew into an uncountable horde, with estimates putting their population in the thousands by 1920. In Central Park and beyond, squirrels became as commonplace as the leaves on the oak trees they built their nests in. As this new approach to urban parkland spread to other cities, the idea of populating parks with squirrels traveled, too. Eastern gray squirrels were reintroduced in cities like Philadelphia and New Haven in the east as well as San Francisco, Seattle, and Vancouver in the west. North American squirrels were also shipped overseas to countries including England, Italy, Australia, and South Africa.

These squirrels benefited not just from these lush new environments that resembled natural habitats but also from a growing sense that humans were morally obliged to care for wild species, especially those deemed peaceful and friendly. Squirrels in particular provided a level of interaction uncommon among undomesticated creatures as they flipped their tails and solicited food in a civilized-looking way. For a long time, humans were largely unconcerned about the booming and spreading squirrel population, which thrived on the largesse of city dwellers and suburbanites. Unfortunately for their bipedal benefactors, however, squirrels don't always play nice with human infrastructure.

By some estimates, as many as a fifth of all power outages are squirrel related. Squirrels build nests in trees but also other treelike structures, such as utility poles and power transformers. Equipped with teeth that never stop growing, squirrels regularly chew things like bark, branches, nuts, and power cables to keep their incisors in check. Inevitably, some unlucky squirrels gnaw through powerline insulation or chomp on exposed wires with deadly results for the animals and frustrating outages for humans. One particularly infamous squirrel is credited with helping to crash an exchange of the US stock market.

America's exported squirrels have also wreaked havoc overseas. In Great Britain, the eastern gray squirrels introduced in 1876 quickly began to displace the native red squirrel and drove it close to extinction. There are only a few small pockets of red squirrels left in northern England and Scotland despite a massive eradication campaign to keep the American invaders out of the Scottish Highlands. In Europe, eastern grays are officially an invasive species.

As squirrels spread during the twentieth century, ecologists, wildlife managers, and park officials began to reexamine conventional approaches to wild animals, including which species should be targeted for hunting or encouraged to thrive. In newer ecological models, there was no discussion of which species seemed cuter, cuddlier, or more civilized. Instead, a balance was promoted between predator and prey species that was ideally maintained with the least human intervention possible. Approaches based on this thinking flourished in national parks and then made their way into cities.

Species like hawks, which prey on squirrels, are now a regular part of the urban landscape in places like New York City, and feeding squirrels has become increasingly frowned on by ecologists. Providing bread and other unnatural foods can lead to a variety of health problems for the squirrels. It can also make them overly dependent on humans and possibly prone to unstable population booms. In many places, feeding squirrels and other urban critters is banned outright—with good reason. Thanks in part to modern parks, squirrels are now fully capable of thriving on their own, and it's time for humans to step back and allow them to be the wild species they always were.

# GHOST STREAMS

## *Fish Stories*

BURIED IN A 1971 EDITION OF THE *NEW YORK TIMES* LIES a letter to the editor in which the author recounts catching and subsequently eating a three-pound carp in the basement of a Manhattan building. "We had a lantern to pierce the cellar darkness," he writes, "and fifteen feet below I clearly saw the stream bubbling and pushing about, five feet wide and upon its either side, dark greenmossed rocks." He goes on to paint a vivid scene of this six-foot-deep subterranean rivulet splashing cool water upward as he cast his line, then waited with baited hook to feel a tug from below. This story sounds apocryphal, but it's not out of the realm of possibility.

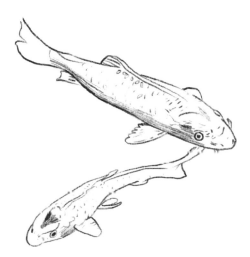

Hundreds of waterways crisscross the earth under Manhattan, legacies of a historical landscape surrounded by and infused with water. Paved in the early 1800s, Canal Street was originally a waterway. Even the great Empire State Building sits close to the site of what was once Sunfish Pond, one of hundreds of water bodies that used to span the city. Though this historical home to squirming eels has long since vanished, an old feeder stream still forces the iconic skyscraper above to use pumps to proactively mitigate basement flooding.

"Across the country, buried beneath the pavement you walk on, an invisible network of waterways flows through the darkness," writes Brynn O'Donnell, a freshwater ecosystem scientist who studies urban biogeochemistry. "These are ghost streams, and they're haunting us." Burying urban streams is a strategy as old as cities. Waterways are often co-opted to become part of drainage and sewage systems. In some modern metropolitan cores, as many as 98% of urban streams have been pushed underground and built over, which can be a real problem. Waterways are critical for healthy cities. "Streams typically teem with life: algae, fish, and invertebrates," explains O'Donnell, and these species are helpful in managing pollutants and mitigating negative impacts to downstream bodies of water. Waterways, though, need light and air for their occupants to thrive and be of use to species living above the surface.

Some cities have taken to "ripping up pavement, shattering pipes, and hammering away the concrete to exhume ghost streams," notes O'Donnell. "Daylighting, as the procedure is called, opens the streams up to the sun and restores the adjacent land connection." Unearthing streams is challenging and expensive, but it is an important step in balancing local ecosystems—not just for humans but also for the creatures who live around, among, and beneath us.

# HOME TO ROOST

## *Unloved Doves*

SOMETIMES REFERRED TO AS FLYING RATS, PIGEONS HAVE earned quite a reputation for their bothersome presence in the urban landscape, though they were not always considered pariahs. This now-ubiquitous metropolitan bird used to be rarer and even had regal associations. Historically, pigeons were birds of the aristocracy. Researchers believe they were domesticated in the Middle East millennia ago, then were spread around Europe by the Romans. Habitats for these birds were even built into the architecture of Roman houses—one common element of traditional Tuscan villas was an integrated lookout tower and pigeon house.

In the 1600s, pigeons were brought to Canada from Europe; from there, they spread across the United States. Governors and dignitaries would exchange them as gifts and house them in domestic pigeon roosts. As they became more common and made their way into the wild, pigeons began to lose their exotic appeal and fell out of favor with the upper class.

The pigeon's shifting status is reflected in the language we use to talk about these birds. For a long time, the terms *pigeon* and *dove* were used interchangeably for various bird species belonging to the Columbidae family. Over time, sentiment around the two diverged as the dove was increasingly imbued with positive attributes and the pigeon became associated with negative ones. The legacy of this divergence is easy to spot today. It's hard to imagine Pigeon beauty bars, silky smooth Pigeon Chocolate, or the Holy Spirit descending from heaven in the form of a glorious pigeon.

Pigeons are largely unwelcome in cities today, to the point where a huge industry has evolved around deterring them. There are numerous design strategies and technologies aimed at keeping these feathered nonfriends from occupying urban spaces and outdoor surfaces, including spikes, wires, netting, and even miniature electrified fences. Such innovations largely fail to do what they are designed to do, though. They mostly just move pigeons around, pushing the birds to adjacent structures. Of course, these strategies would never have been seen as necessary if it weren't for humans, who bred pigeons and spread them around the world in the first place, then laid out all of the food waste that allows them to thrive. Ultimately, pigeons are not a species so much as a human construct, and we are responsible for our cities being infested by dirty pigeons rather than blessed by beautiful doves.

# RACCOON RESISTANCE

## *Trash Pandas*

THE HIGHER SHE GOT, THE MORE PEOPLE TUNED IN TO watch a lone raccoon slowly make her way up a downtown office tower in St. Paul, Minnesota, in 2018. The so-called MPR raccoon got its nickname thanks to Minnesota Public Radio employees who began tracking and publicizing her ascent from their offices across the street. She quickly attracted social media attention and eventually news crews. Television stations set up live feeds from the ground below, then turned spotlights on the raccoon as day turned into night, arguably prolonging the saga by scaring the dazed creature even farther up the building. As she climbed, the raccoon took advantage of the rocky aggregate on the facade's precast concrete panels, moved horizontally at times to rest on windowsills, and eventually discovered that one particular rounded corner offered an opportunity to ascend easily to the very top. In the end, the building was challenging but not insurmountable for a species that has demonstrated an uncanny ability to overcome human-made obstacles.

In the early 1900s, comparative psychology researchers at various US universities had already begun to figure out just how smart and adaptive raccoons could be. Scientists at different institutions crafted puzzle boxes for animals and independently concluded that raccoons were more capable problem solvers than many common species, more akin to monkeys in their cognitive abilities than domesticated animals like cats and dogs. Raccoon test subjects not only solved puzzles through trial and error, but they could also figure them out by watching humans solve them first. Unlike many species driven by survival instincts like hunger or fear, raccoons would sometimes solve challenges simply out of curiosity and ignore food rewards at the end.

As for the wild raccoons that followed humans from the countryside into cities, curiosity and hunger have often put them at odds with urbanites. These persistent creatures frequently poke and pry at barriers, tilt and topple trash cans, and even break into buildings in search of food and shelter. While the MPR raccoon incident cast a literal spotlight on this common synanthrope, Minnesota's Twin Cities don't attract nearly as much raccoon-related attention as another North American metropolis, which has something of a love-hate relationship with the species.

When Toronto unveiled its "raccoon-resistant" compost bins in 2016, reactions were mixed—some residents feared that local "trash pandas" would be starved out while others applauded this innovative design. The novel locked bin was rolled out as a new weapon in the city's ongoing war on raccoons, the latest volley in a protracted interspecies struggle over municipal waste removal infrastructure.

"Toronto's new organic waste bin had to meet strict design requirements," explained Amy Dempsey in a report for the *Toronto Star*. "It had to withstand rain, snow, flash freezing and water pooling," among other things, and "had to have a handle with enough resistance to keep raccoons out, but still suitable for people with disabilities. It had to be light so as not to cause injury, but heavy enough so as not to be easily toppled over." And, of course, it had to keep out raccoons. The ensuing design featured bigger wheels and a rodent-resistant rim with a rotating handle and a German-made locking mechanism. Dozens of raccoons were pitted against the test model and they all failed to get in. Emboldened by these results, the city began deploying hundreds of thousands of these bins, and for the most part, they seem to have worked, though there is  video documentation of racoons knocking some of the bins over, loosening their locks, and eating the tasty leftovers inside—these are very industrious omnivores. Some researchers are concerned that in attempting to foil their foraging, humans may well be encouraging animals to become even more innovative.

So far, raccoons seem to be surviving and even thriving despite human-designed interventions. Like squirrels and pigeons, raccoons are highly adaptable and inhabit so many global cities in part because humans introduced them both deliberately and inadvertently. These intrepid mammals may have started out in deciduous forests, but they have since made their way into mountains and coastal marshes and metropolitan environments. They can be found across Europe, in Japan, and around the Caribbean. In all likelihood, they will continue to be persistent urban creatures, having proved many times over to be especially adept at adapting to and overcoming our architecture and infrastructure.

# UNMANNED LANDS

## *Wildlife Corridors*

THE IRON CURTAIN IS MOSTLY KNOWN AS AN OMINOUS border that spanned thousands of miles and separated East from West for decades during the Cold War, but it has different associations for many nonhuman species. In the no-man's-land that was created as a buffer zone between the eastern and western edges of the countries on either side of this conflict, something surprising emerged. Absent human intervention and disruption, an accidental wildlife refuge formed across a range of countries and climates. Following the fall of the Berlin Wall, conservationists on both sides of this former divide saw an opportunity to establish a European greenbelt with the old Iron Curtain as its backbone. This space could help connect habitats across borders and link national parks and nature preserves along its length. In a world of gridded cities, rural agricultural subdivisions, and countrysides crisscrossed by paved highway systems, such long uninterrupted stretches of relatively natural landscape can be a real boon to myriad animal species.

Wildlife corridors, which provide habitats and pathways for animals, are a class of human infrastructure designed for nonhuman species. Such solutions vary immensely in scale, scope, and design depending on their specific purpose. There are crab bridges, squirrel wires, fish ladders, and freeway overpasses for mountain lions. Some corridors help expand territories available to wide-roaming mammals while others facilitate seasonal migrations for various bird and fish species, the latter of which require contiguous waterways to move from one place to the next.

In the United States, there are estimated to be close to two million water flow barriers that create serious obstacles for migratory fish and the humans who rely on them. Aside from fish ladders and other workarounds, extreme-seeming solutions like fish cannons, which physically launch fish into the air, have been employed to help certain species overcome various artificial obstacles. In the long run, though, quick fixes and quirky technology can only do so much. Fish cannons may bridge gaps temporarily, but they are not enough to reconnect patchwork habitats and migration paths disrupted by human infrastructure.

Animals are unlikely to see a return of the world as it was before cities, highways, and dams anytime soon, but for their part humans cannot just plow ahead with development and expect wildlife to cope. In some cases, the best approach may be simply for humans to get out of the way, but people need to understand that cities and nature are all part of the same ecosystem and that proactive strategies will be needed to help various species survive in a human-centric world.

IT IS A
5 MINUTE
WALK TO
SUBWAY

KIDS
PLAY
AREA
7 MINS

RECYCLING
CENTER
10 MIN
WALK

PUBLIC

*Chapter 6*

# URBANISM

**T**HERE IS A CONSTANT DIALOGUE between cities and their citizens. Master plans and big designs aside, cities employ a wide array of targeted, top-down strategies in public spaces, using objects, lights, and sounds to shape the behavior of residents. These are embraced by some and criticized by others. Bottom-up citizen interventionists reshape the city by taking matters into their own hands to solve the problems they feel officials have neglected. These can be controversial at times and have unintended side effects. The conversation goes back and forth, with each side stealing and adapting design strategies from the other.

PREVIOUS: *Discouraging spikes, guerrilla signage, and open hydrant*

# HOSTILITIES

T HERE IS ALWAYS AN ASPECT OF coercion to design. In the commercial world, design is used to get you to buy things you don't need or use your iPhone in a prescribed way. Cities use design to shape our behavior, too. They employ both subtle and overt forms of influence in public spaces to make life more difficult for "undesirable" populations and to curb "antisocial" behavior. Whether you are the target or a beneficiary of hostile design, it's crucial to recognize when we're replacing human interaction with hard, physical, nonnegotiable solutions.

LEFT: *Skateboarders defying ban in Philadelphia's LOVE park*

# LOVED PARK

## *Dubious Skateblockers*

"THANK YOU! MY WHOLE DAMN LIFE HAS BEEN WORTH IT just for this moment," exclaimed ninety-two-year-old architect Edmund Bacon (the father of actor Kevin Bacon) as he skateboarded (with some assistance) through the Philadelphia park he had designed decades prior. Officially named John F. Kennedy Plaza, everyone calls this place LOVE Park because of the typographical sculpture that spells out the word *LOVE* at its center. This Modernist public space was designed to be relatively open, simple, and rational, which incidentally made it a perfect place to skateboard.

Skaters experience cities differently than other people. As they move through urban environments, they see all the wheel marks from other board-riding citizens and all the skate-stopping nobs bolted onto rails, buildings, and street furniture designed to foil them. Philadelphia architect Tony Bracali is not a skateboarder, but he appreciates the way skaters have adapted their sport to the built environment. It was Modernists like Le Corbusier who favored rectilinear steel, glass, and concrete forms that in turn made cities perfect places to skateboard. "Modernists were the ones that reinterpreted a bench in a park as a slab of granite," Bracali notes, adding that this design paradigm involved a turn away from "flowing landscapes [with] grassy areas" toward "paved open plaza spaces," which produced great surfaces, ledges, and edges for skateboarders.

Philadelphia's LOVE Park was just such a space, with its linear marble benches, straight-edged planters, elongated steps, and square stone tiles that could be tilted up to form ramps. Built in the 1960s to little fanfare in an era of suburbanization, LOVE Park didn't get a lot of love in downtown Philadelphia initially, but in the 1980s, skateboarders began to realize its full potential and made it their own personal playground. By the 1990s, it was a hot background for skating photo shoots and films, which enticed pro skaters to move to the city to conquer its contours.

The park was even featured in a Tony Hawk skateboarding video game. All of this attention helped draw skateboarding competitions to the city.

All of this activity, though, was illegal. Police would run skaters out of the park, give them tickets, and even take their boards away. Fines escalated over the years, and in 2002, the park was renovated in part to make it less skate friendly. Granite benches were replaced with more ornate and unskateable alternatives; grassy landscapes were introduced to break up long hard surfaces. DC Shoes, a California-based shoe company geared toward skaters, even offered the city a million dollars to return the park to its previous condition and offset any damage caused by skaters, but the appeal was rejected.

LOVE Park wasn't the only target of anti-skater activity in that era. Small skater-stopping attachments started showing up in other cities in the early 2000s. These fixtures are usually simple metal brackets that disrupt the smooth surfaces and edges a skateboard can slide and glide along, but sometimes they're more ornate, at times even disguised as little pieces of urban art. Along the Embarcadero in San Francisco, skate stoppers have taken the form of delightful metal sculptures of tidal sea creatures. These add-ons can be seen adorning benches, railings, and other edges that would otherwise appeal to skateboarders.

For his part, Edmund Bacon never intended for LOVE Park to become a skateboarding hub, but he was a big supporter of this unexpected usage. "The wonderful thing to me," he explained, "is that these young people discovered that they themselves could creatively adapt to the environment." A park that had been relatively empty had found an unusual means of activation, and Bacon loved it—a love that led him to ride a board in defiance of the law during the 2002 LOVE Park protests. But even with the park's original designer literally and figuratively on board, the city wouldn't budge.

More than a decade later, just before LOVE Park went through another renovation, the city's mayor offered up a small gift of acknowledgment to urban skaters in 2016. He suspended the skating ban and opened up the park for five days in largely subzero conditions for one last skate session. Despite the weather, dozens of skaters came out. Some pried up soon-to-be-removed granite tiles as keepsakes—heavy stone reminders of a place so central to their sport. Others broke branches off trees to build fires and stay warm, then skated the park one last time without having to worry about anyone handing out citations or trying to take away their boards.

Each time the park changed, skaters found new ways to work with or around the new design, but the real legacy of LOVE Park was its influence on *intentional* skateparks, which borrowed elements from its design. Still, there is something artificial about a designated skatepark, at least to some skaters—finding new edges, rails, and other opportunities to skate in the built environment is part of the sport.

# URINE TROUBLE

## *Discouraging Spikes*

WHEN THE GROCERY CHAIN TESCO INSTALLED METAL spikes outside one of its shops in central London, public reaction was swift and intense. The company explained that the spikes were installed to discourage sleeping, loitering, and other "antisocial" behaviors outside their entrance, but many people interpreted their intervention as a hostile attack on the most vulnerable members of society. Activists even poured concrete over the spikes as an act of awareness-raising protest. Anti-homeless spikes have long been used to keep "undesirable" populations from rough sleeping on low walls, in front of commercial buildings, or in other sittable spaces. Spikes and other protrusions that discourage resting or sleeping are among the most prominent and easy to spot examples of what's commonly known as "defensive design" or "hostile architecture."

Not all spiky protrusions are meant to deter sleepers or sitters. Horizontal spikes and angled urine deflectors can often be found in dark corners and alleys that aim to make things unpleasant for anyone attempting to take a pee in a public space. One city in Germany has even deployed liquid-reflecting paints to achieve a similar effect. Renowned for its bustling nightlife, the St. Pauli district in Hamburg has long had issues with unpleasant street smells and stained walls. So a group of local businesses got in touch with the inventors of a special hydrophobic paint that would bounce liquids back at urinators. They sprayed coats of this paint on the sides of buildings along with signs reading, HIER NICHT PINKELN! WIR PINKLEN ZURÜCK. ("Don't Pee Here! We Pee Back.")

These kinds of anti-urination strategies are not new. A passage from 1809 highlights the plight of a prospective urinator: "In London a man may sometimes walk a mile before he can meet with a suitable corner; for so unaccommodating are the owners of doorways, passages and angles, that they seem to have exhausted invention in the ridiculous barricadoes and shelves, grooves, and one fixed above another, to conduct the stream into the shoes of the luckless wight who shall dare to profane the intrenchments." Old rusty spikes and shelves can still be found in the winding alleyways of London and other cities. An angled urine deflector on the Bank of England building occupies a promising niche where critics of modern capitalism might be tempted to relieve themselves. So you would do well to keep it in your pants, you luckless wight.

Given the long history and modern prevalence of defensive designs, the outrage and days of protests against Tesco's spikes took the company by surprise. Subsequent criticism of anti-homeless spikes around London reached a crescendo when then-mayor Boris Johnson called them "ugly, self-defeating and stupid," which arguably also describes certain British prime ministers. In

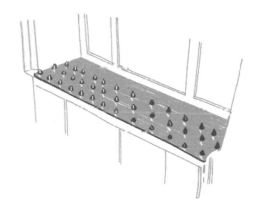

the end, these particular spikes were removed from Tesco only a few days after they were installed. Still, such urban deterrents are widespread in London and around the world and are often overlooked—at least until activists or media outlets call attention to them.

# OBSTINATE OBJECTS

## *Discomforting Seats*

IT WOULD BE EASY TO THINK OF HOSTILE ARCHITECTURE as a failure of design, but *Unpleasant Design* editors Selena Savić and Gordan Savičić suggest that if the design does what it is supposed to, it is arguably a success. Many public benches are specifically crafted to let people take a short break without being able to fully relax. Unpleasant public seats at parks, bus stops, and airports are made to keep people from getting too comfortable. Discomfort is something we tend to think of as an unwanted byproduct of bad design, but in this case, the discomfort is the point.

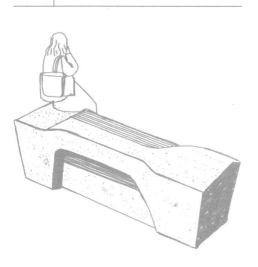

"A classic [example] is the bench with armrests in between" seats, says Savić, which "lets you rest your arm . . . but at the same time restrict[s] any other kind of use." Armrests are the most common method of preventing people from sleeping in places where the establishment only wants them to sit. "Leaning" benches are also popular at bus stops. These lack a backrest and are often elevated and tilted to prevent actual sitting. There's even a rumor that the seats in certain fast food chains were designed to serve as "fifteen-minute chairs" that are intentionally too uncomfortable to sit in for a long period of time and thus encourage customer turnover.

The object that Savić considers a particular masterpiece of unpleasant design is the Camden bench. Unlike spikes, which scream their hostile intent, the Camden bench is innocuous in its appearance, although it's rather lumpy and not particularly inviting. Designed by Factory Furniture for the London borough of Camden, the bench is a strange, angular, sculpted, solid chunk of concrete with rounded edges and slopes in unexpected places.

The complex shape of this seating unit makes it virtually impossible to sleep on. It is also anti-dealer because it features no slots or crevices to stash drugs in; it is anti-skateboarder because the edges on the bench fluctuate in height to make grinding difficult; it is anti-litter because it lacks cracks that trash could slip into; it is anti-theft because recesses near the ground allow people to tuck bags behind their legs away from would-be criminals; and it is anti-graffiti because it has a special coating to repel paint. On top of all of this, the object is so large and heavy that it can also serve as a traffic barrier. One online critic called it the perfect "anti-object."

But perhaps the most common form of hostile seating is even subtler: the utter lack of it in some places. When you notice there is no place to rest for blocks and blocks, that is a design choice, too. In many cases, hostile design decisions and so-called sit-lie ordinances are paired together to create an environment that is unwelcoming to anyone seeking respite.

# CITIES OF LIGHT

## *Dissuasive Illumination*

BRIGHT STREET LIGHTS ARE GENERALLY SEEN AS A POSitive part of our shared public spaces; they illuminate our way and help keep streets safe after dark. As urbanist Jane Jacobs pointed out in her 1961 manifesto *The Death and Life of Great American Cities,* more "eyes on the street" can raise visibility and shared responsibility with help from active storefronts, lively sidewalks, and, of course, street lighting so people can both see and be seen.

The idea of lighting public spaces is nothing new—ancient Romans lit the streets of their cities with oil lanterns while the Chinese channeled volcanic gas through bamboo pipes to illuminate ancient Beijing. In the 1400s and 1500s, citizens of cities like London and Paris were instructed to put candles and lamps outside their homes or in their windows to provide communal street light. In many European cities, people out at night were also required to carry torches or lanterns, not to see but to be seen as having no shadowy intent. In hindsight, this can look like progress, but there is a darker side to street lighting depending on one's perspective.

In 1667, a new lieutenant general of police was installed in Paris by royal decree, and he mandated the rollout of more extensive and permanent public street lighting in the service of law and order. Not all Parisians were pleased, in part because of the associated installation and upkeep costs. Some citizens also enjoyed the relative freedom to engage in illicit activities in the dark corners of the so-called City of Light and resented being exposed.

Public street lights were also the target of vandalism by political dissenters. In the 1700s and 1800s, revolutionaries would smash them in order to move around more freely in the shadows. During the French Revolution, the tables were turned and some lampposts were used as gallows for hanging officials and aristocrats, leading to the French phrase *"À la lanterne!"* ("To the lamppost"), a call to execution akin to "String 'em up" in English.

These days, lighting is still employed as a defensive design strategy, often to target certain demographics like loitering teens. One classic tactic is to turn up light levels to make places uncomfortably bright. There are also other more refined and arguably devious strategies. In Mansfield, England, the Layton Burroughs Residents' Association installed pink lights that highlight skin blemishes, which made them hostile to self-conscious acne-afflicted youths. Blue lighting has been installed in some public restrooms in the United Kingdom to deter intravenous drug users by making it harder for them to see their veins. In Japan, blue lights have been tested in subway stations on the theory that their calming effect might reduce suicide rates. It's hard to measure the effectiveness of social control through special colored lighting, but that hasn't stopped cities from trying out a broad spectrum of potential applications.

# Targeting
# Demographics

## *Disruptive Sounds*

A lot of sounds in noisy urban areas are byproducts of everyday activities, but some of them are designed to deter specific activities like loitering. Many businesses play classical music outside their entryways not to attract sophisticated Mozart fans but to dissuade youths who are presumably traumatized by old-people music.

Not all of these sonic interventions are meant to be heard by everyone, though. High-pitch acoustic deterrents have been used to keep teens away by playing frequencies that only younger ears can hear. People lose their ability to hear high frequencies as they age, so, in theory, these annoying noises can only be heard by persons up to their late teens or mid-twenties. One such electronic device, called the Mosquito, is marketed as being capable of discouraging loitering, vandalism, violence, drug dealing, and substance abuse. It has been alternately lauded for its effects and criticized for indiscriminately infringing on the rights of young people.

The Mosquito was invented in 2005 by Howard Stapleton, and he tested it on his own children, who apparently confirmed that it was very annoying indeed. He got the idea for this device as a child when he complained about hearing irritating factory sounds that his father was unable to hear. Stapleton grew up to become a security advisor and was inspired to develop the Mosquito by his daughter after she was harassed by some boys at a local convenience store in Barry, South Wales. The owner of the store had been planning to blast out classical music to deter such groups of troublemakers when Stapleton offered a free prototype of his Mosquito. Unlike loud classical music, the Mosquito wouldn't bother all the shoppers coming and going, just the young people lingering out front.

As with many well-intentioned designs deployed in the public sphere, critics have cited a number of potentially harmful secondary effects of acoustic deterrent strategies. One major concern is that prolonged exposure could damage the hearing of young children, particularly because parents can't perceive the problem themselves. Some have also noted the potential impacts for sensitive populations—people with tinnitus or autism, for example. In various buildings and municipalities both in and beyond the United Kingdom, devices like the Mosquito have been banned entirely. As with a lot of contentious designs for public spaces, this solution was developed to target one group without thorough consideration of how it might impact a whole host of others.

# EXTERIOR MOTIVES

## *Deceptive Deterrents*

WHEN THE CITY OF SEATTLE INSTALLED A NEW ROW OF bicycle racks beneath an urban overpass, it was easy for most people to assume that this infrastructure was innocuous enough. Yet to some observers, this particular location seemed curiously out of the way and unlikely to be useful for cyclists. So a local resident decided to investigate with a public records request, the results of which were later published in Seattle's alternative newspaper *The Stranger*. They discovered that this overtly unassuming cycling infrastructure was actually the product of a "homelessness emergency response" effort funded with money for homeless-related initiatives. It was clear that the city wanted to use these racks to eliminate a potential encampment spot, but authorities had kept the purpose of this effort concealed beneath a veneer of completely different functionality.

The obvious hostility of things like sharp spikes, bright lights, and targeted sounds can help make some hostile designs easier to identify and thus criticize. Armrests on benches are a bit trickier to critique because they are at least arguably useful in some cases whether or not that is a driving factor of their design. Some additions, though, are particularly insidious, their ulterior design intent masked in an overt effort to dupe onlookers. Sprinklers planted in paved or rocky areas are a classic example of this extreme. They are made to look like city-greening infra-structure, but they are positioned to put off unwanted populations. These disguised designs can take many forms—from utilitarian bike racks to elaborate public "art."

All urban designs have an element of coercion. Still, citizens deserve transpar-ency about the intended functions of things rather than camouflage or obfuscation. In some instances, city agencies have openly made the case that deterrents are needed for safety reasons. In Portland, an array of boulders placed along a busy freeway was explained by the Oregon Department of Transportation as being a risk-reducing intercession in a high-traffic area where sleepers could be struck and injured or even killed by vehicles. Interventions like this can be controversial, but in this case, the relevant agency was open about their intentions, which allowed for public discourse and scrutiny.

For better or worse, defensive designs limit the range of activities people can engage in. They can also create real problems for the elderly or disabled. Some of the goals of unpleasant designs can seem noble, but they follow a potentially dangerous logic with respect to public spaces. When supposed solutions address symptoms of a problem rather than the root causes, that problem is not solved but only pushed down the street to the next block or neighborhood. Spikes beget spikes, and tar-geted individuals are just moved around without addressing underlying issues. In many cases, these efforts can shift vulnerable populations to less visible and more dangerous areas. Regardless of whether one sees a given design as exclusionary but also serving a greater good or believes it to be hostile and offensive, it is important to be aware of the decisions that are being made for all of us.

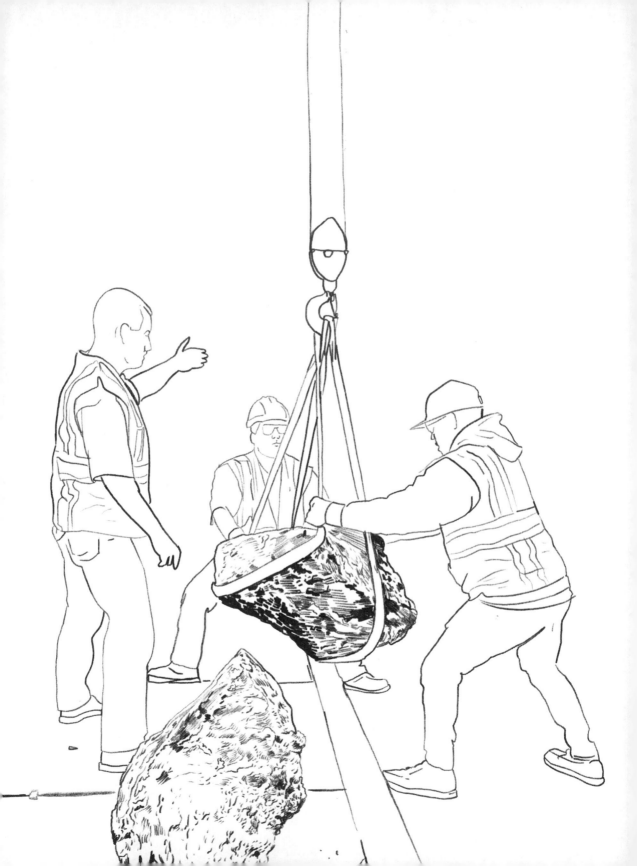

# INTERVENTIONS

SOME LARGE-SCALE PROJECTS LIKE subway networks and city-spanning sewage systems can only be effectively tackled by a government. But any efforts to correct, modify, or adapt urban infrastructure to better serve the needs of an ever-changing citizenry can be bogged down by bureaucracy. Sometimes, small-scale bottom-up interventions implemented by everyday urban dwellers can fill in the gaps. These can be anything from an improved sign to an unsanctioned bike lane. Some changes are motivated by altruism while others are initiated out of blatant self-interest. Spotting these DIY interventions can be a challenge, especially the ones designed to look official and take advantage of our trust in authority.

LEFT: *Municipal workers moving embattled boulders placed by citizens*

# Guerrilla Fixation

## *Unsanctioned Shield*

Every city dweller has seen something in their built environment that needs fixing, but few take the initiative to fix it themselves. In the 1980s, when artist Richard Ankrom drove past his Los Angeles freeway exit and got lost, he didn't think much of it at the time, but this missed turn stuck with him. Years later, he was passing by the same spot and noticed the continued absence of an exit sign that would help him and other drivers get to where they needed to go. Where others might have asked someone in a position of authority to fix the problem, Ankrom saw an opportunity to put his artistic skills to work. He decided to make his own sign and hang it above the 110 as an act of "guerrilla public service"—and he would keep his intervention a secret.

For his plan to work, the sign had to look like it belonged there, which meant measuring the exact dimensions of other official signs. Ankrom also held up color swatches to match the paint and read the *California Manual on Uniform Traffic Control Devices* to determine the right typeface. He even sprayed a thin layer of gray paint over his copycat sign to make it blend in better with the smog-glazed signage around it. Ankrom wrote his name on the back with a black marker like a painter signing a canvas (except he put it out of sight so it wouldn't risk drawing attention to his piece).

After a lot of work and planning, Ankrom and a group of friends assembled near the target location on the morning of August 5, 2001. To pull off the operation, the artist cut his hair and bought a set of work clothes, an orange vest, and a hard hat. He even applied a magnetic sticker to his truck to make it look like the vehicle of a Caltrans contractor to avoid raising suspicion that might lead to his arrest. Using a ladder, Ankrom made his way up to the catwalk thirty feet above the freeway and spent the next half hour installing the sign. He worried the whole time that he might get caught or, worse, drop a tool on one of the speeding drivers below. In the end, the installation went off without a hitch and no one was the wiser.

The whole affair remained a secret until a friend leaked it to the press nearly a year later, at which point Caltrans sent people out to inspect Ankrom's handi-work. To everyone's surprise, the sign passed inspection and remained in place for eight more years. "He did a good job," admitted a Caltrans spokesperson, "but we don't want him to do it again." When the sign finally had to be updated years later, Caltrans not only replaced Ankrom's creation but also added a few more I-5 North exit signs along the 110.

The reaction of authorities to these kinds of "fixes" can vary significantly from project to project. Police departments and city councils sometimes defend or at least overlook guerilla actions, as in the case of a guy known for repairing play-grounds in Reno and another who repainted a neglected crosswalk in Baltimore. But other illicit crosswalk painters have been less fortunate—interventionists in Muncie, Indiana, and Vallejo, California, have found themselves placed under arrest for their actions. Authorities argue that not every intervention is appro-priate, helpful, and safe.

Many cases fall somewhere in between the extremes of going unnoticed or landing someone in jail. Often an intervention is removed without anyone getting arrested. When a New York group called the Efficient Passenger Project put up signage to help inform riders of the best exits and fastest routes to change trains, the Metropolitan Transit Authority promptly took them down. Like Ankrom, the EPP mimicked the colors, typographies, and layouts of official MTA signage. The MTA, however, was concerned that the signage would be a little *too* helpful and lead to overcrowding in certain train cars, which could compound congestion and make transfers tougher for everyone. In the end, the success and persistence of these kinds of interventions often comes down to not only design choices but also to the responses of official actors and community members—good intentions and thoughtful designs will only take a project so far.

# DRAWING ATTENTION

## *Viral Signage*

SOME GUERRILLA SIGN MAKERS GO OUT OF THEIR WAY TO
make their creations look official by precisely matching the typefaces and placement strategies of municipal authorities. Others don't want to be hemmed in by a
city's bad design choices and boldly present something they believe to be better,
intentionally drawing attention to perceived design problems by publicly imple-
menting potential solutions.

Like most people who have driven around Los Angeles, designer Nikki Sylianteng found many of the city's street-parking signs to be virtually indecipherable. A
whole stack of vertically arrayed parking signs can often be found on a single post.
Some contain overlapping information or seemingly conflicting imperatives while
others simply display too much data to usefully address the question every driver
wants answered: can I park here right now? Confusing parking signs aren't unique
to LA, but some of the most confounding examples can be found there.

Sylianteng explains that "the problem is that signs are cluttered with unnec-
essary information—the why—when the important stuff—the what—is nowhere
near clear." Her approach was to eliminate consequences for violations and other
caveats, and focus instead on "when you can and can't park, and for how long."
She tried to conform as much as possible to official standards by matching sizes,
colors, and materials, then manipulating her graphics within that framework.
The idea here was less to make her signs blend in and more to make it easier for
the city to adopt her solution if the design proved successful. She also put up
examples and solicited feedback from "drivers, city officials, traffic engineers, and
the colorblind community" to find out what was and wasn't clear and to verify
her most important assumption: that this was a problem shared by many. With
the final design deployed in test locations, she observed a 60% improvement in
compliance with parking regulations. The project has inspired officials in cities

as far away as Brisbane, Australia, to address similarly confusing signage with clearer graphics.

This isn't the only urban signage project to start small and go big. When Matt Tomasulo put up a series of walking direction signs in Raleigh, North Carolina, his intention was to raise awareness of just how quickly people can get between places on foot. He was frustrated with friends who would drive a few minutes because they perceived their destination to be beyond a reasonable walking distance. Tomasulo figured that by showing people how many minutes it would actually take, he might get more people walking. He researched existing city policies and regulations before taking action and concluded that his design intervention aligned in principle with the city's walkability policies and goals outlined in its comprehensive plan.

Tomasulo considered getting permits, but the process would have been long and expensive, so he settled on printing a trial solution himself. Careful not to permanently disrupt or damage any infrastructure, he zip-tied his signs to existing poles along city streets. These signs simply and clearly indicated the direction and average walking time between major locations, with directives such as IT'S A 7-MINUTE WALK TO RALEIGH CENTRAL CEMETERY in sans serif font on top of an arrow pointing the way. The project was quickly picked up on social media and by the urbanist blogosphere. All of the exposure initially caused the signs to be taken down, but the city quickly relented under public pressure. Like Sylianteng's project, Tomasulo's design quickly spread to other cities. He also put up templates and guides on a website for other municipalities looking to try out new wayfinding signs.

Both of these signage projects are examples of "tactical urbanism"—low-cost, low-risk interventions with potentially high-impact urban effects. They each also evolved in legal gray areas—putting up signs without permission is usually illegal, but such installations can garner positive public attention and political support. Neither of these designers set out to create global solutions, though both have influenced other cities directly and indirectly. As many tactical urbanists have discovered, when it comes to improving the urban landscape, it can be better to seek forgiveness than permission.

# ASKING PERMISSION

## *Open Hydrants*

IT'S A CLASSIC CITY SCENE: KIDS PLAYING OUTSIDE IN the spray of open fire hydrants spilling water onto the sizzling streets of the Big Apple. While it may be part of our shared cultural imagination, prying open a fire hydrant is usually considered an illegal act, and fines can be imposed for tampering with this vital city infrastructure. Still, it's common to find firefighters in many cities today helping people open hydrants safely in a controlled fashion during the dog days of summer. The New York City government has sanctioned these openings in different ways and at different times for more than a century, which highlights the gray area between illicit and city-sanctioned interventions.

When a heat wave swept the East Coast in 1896, cities were hit especially hard as urban heat island effects drove up already soaring temperatures. Densely paved and packed places were devastated; Lower Manhattan had more than one thousand deaths. In a time before air conditioners or the widespread use of electric fans, citizens suffered in the sweltering heat. Some even slept on rooftops or fire escapes, which led to injuries and deaths from rolling off of buildings.

In the midst of the crisis, Police Commissioner (and future president) Theodore Roosevelt helped facilitate the distribution of free ice, particularly in poorer areas of the city. Bans on sleeping in city parks were suspended to let overheated citizens spend nights out in the open. Fire hydrants were also opened to help clean up and cool off the streets. Grateful tenement-dwelling families came out in droves to get relief from cramped living conditions and poor air circulation.

Over the next century, citizens illegally opening hydrants became something of a New York tradition on hot summer days, though at times it was a controversial one. The high pressures of an unmodified flow can hurt people by knocking them down or pushing them into the street. The release of that force can also lower the water pressure for area residents, not to mention firefighters who need that pressure to fight fires. The uncontrolled spray of a single hydrant can push out thousands of gallons per minute and waste a lot of good, clean water.

In 2007, the NYC Department of Environmental Protection (DEP) rolled out a program to educate people about the dangers of opening hydrants on their own. During peak summer months, they hired youths to join HEAT (Hydrant Education Action Team) and explain to communities the risks as well as alternative options. "Hydrants can be opened legally if equipped with a city-approved spray cap, which releases only 20 to 25 gallons per minute," explains the DEP. "Spray caps can be obtained by an adult 18 or over, free of charge, at local firehouses." In the end, what started out as a city-sanctioned effort became an illegal guerrilla activity, then evolved into an approved DIY action that bridged the two extremes. A century of dialogue between a city and its citizens combined with official and informal efforts culminated in a commonsense solution that everyone could get behind.

# SEEKING FORGIVENESS

## *Embattled Boulders*

IT ALL STARTED WHEN TWO DOZEN BOULDERS SUDDENLY appeared on a San Francisco sidewalk in late 2019. At first, no one was sure what to make of these massive stones that were a few feet tall and wide, and too big to be carried by a single rogue individual. Most people assumed that these additions had to be the work of the city, which has a history of using rocks to deter rough sleepers. But it soon came to light that this wasn't a top-down imposition but rather a bottom-up intervention—the work of a group of neighbors seeking to disrupt illegal activities along the sidewalk. These residents had pooled together $2,000 to buy and place twenty-four huge stones on a public footpath just off of Market Street in the Mission District.

Reactions were swift. Some locals came out in favor of the boulders, citing frequent criminal activity along this stretch of sidewalk. Various activists, however, quickly came out against the rocks, arguing that the money could have been put to better use on more humane and substantive efforts to deal with underlying issues. Detractors began petitioning the city to remove the boulders.

When officials failed to take action, one local artist posted a classified ad on Craigslist offering the two dozen boulders for free to anyone who wanted them. In a tongue-in-cheek tone, Danielle Baskin represented herself as their owner, writing, "We're getting rid of our beautiful collection of landscape rocks [and] realized we don't have enough space for them in our own home. We left them outside by the curb." The stones, her post boasted, "have a lot of character—hues of tan and grey with some fresh moss."

As the debate around the boulders heated up, some activists took matters into their own hands and began to roll the rocks into the adjacent roadway. Caught up in the middle, a spokesperson for the San Francisco Department of Public Works expressed concern about these big obstructions now clogging up the street. So city workers stepped in—not to remove the stones as many assumed they would, but to put them back on the sidewalk. Their placement was apparently deemed to be compliant with city ordinances as there was enough space to walk beside them.

The boulder battle didn't end there, however. In the days that followed, activists continued to push the rocks back into the street while DPW workers continued to roll in with heavy machinery to hoist them back up onto the sidewalk. While the city brought in cones and yellow tape to deter the vigilantes, chalk messages began to appear in defense of the homeless people displaced by these stones. "It is a great theft if we don't give to those in greater need than ourselves" and "I got neighbors. They more like strangers. We could be friends." Some residents took issue with these and other anti-boulder messages, arguing that the stones were meant to deter dangerous drug dealers rather than rough sleepers.

Finally, enough was enough, and city officials stepped forward to bring this Sisyphean battle to an end. "At the request of the residents, we will be taking the boulders out," San Francisco Public Works Director Mohammed Nuru told the *San Francisco Chronicle*. Asked why, he explained that "some of the residents felt that they were being targeted" by opponents of the boulders. In short: residents who helped pay for putting the boulders in place went from feeling threatened by drug dealers to being afraid of harassment from urban activists who had been fired up by the spotlight cast on the back-and-forth, rock-rolling battle. The stones were removed and put into storage at taxpayer expense. In the aftermath, the future of this contested section of sidewalk remains uncertain. Nuru added that the DPW "will support whatever the residents want to do," which could mean even bigger rocks that would be more difficult to remove.

For now, the physical situation has come full circle—the rocks are gone, leaving only some scratches on the sidewalk where they once rested. This conflict, though, reverberated across the city, galvanizing citizens interested in addressing issues like crime and homelessness. The rocks may not have had the effect their placers intended, but they started a larger conversation around urban issues and created an outsized impact in an unexpected way.

# LEGITIMIZING ACTION

## *Middle Way*

OAKLAND RESIDENT DAN STEVENSON WAS NEVER THE type to call the cops on drug dealers or prostitutes in his neighborhood. He took a lot of this criminal behavior in stride, but he drew the line at the piles of garbage that kept appearing across from his house. When the city installed a permanent traffic diverter at the intersection next door, no amount of signage kept litterers from dumping unwanted furniture, clothing, bags of trash, and all kinds of waste on this new patch of concrete and dirt. Litter attracts litter and dumping begat more dumping while calls to the city had little effect.

So Dan Stevenson and his wife, Lu, discussed options and decided to try something unusual: they would clear out the junk and install a statue of the Buddha.

When asked by *Criminal*'s Phoebe Judge why they chose this particular religious figure, Dan explained, "He's neutral." Someone like Christ, he noted, could be considered "controversial," but the Buddha, they figured, was not likely to be a source of contention. So Lu went to a hardware store to pick out a statue, and then Dan drilled into it, epoxied some rebar inside the figure to anchor it to the ground, and installed it in the neglected space next to his home.

For a time, the Buddha simply sat there, unmoving and unchanging, but months later, Dan noticed it had been painted white. Offerings of fruit and coins soon followed. The Buddha continued to evolve over time; the statue was set on a pedestal, painted gold, and eventually enshrined in architecture. Members of the Oakland Vietnamese Buddhist community began appearing in the early morning to light incense and pray at the statue. Tourists, too, came to visit the Buddha, sometimes arriving on buses that could barely fit down this small residential street. When city authorities considered removing the statue, the community pushed back. Crime has also gone down in the neighborhood, though how much of this shift can be attributed to the statue is debatable.

A lot of the care and evolution of this space traces to Vina Vo, a Vietnamese immigrant who takes care of the statue and shrine with help from the community. Vo lost family and friends and the village shrine she grew up with in the Vietnam War. She fled the country in 1982 and made her way to Oakland, where she heard about this statue in 2010. Someone suggested that Vo could take care of it and transform the space around the figure into a hub for gathering and prayer like the places of worship she had left behind decades prior. Over the years, more structures have appeared around the Buddha, containing signs, lights, flags, bowls of fruit, and additional sculptures. At night, the growing shrine complex is lit up with swirling LEDs visible from blocks away; up close, the smell of incense fills the air.

Today, a broom leans against the shrine and the surrounding ground is regularly swept. One could argue that the original Buddha constituted a work of hostile architecture intended to dissuade certain undesirable activities. Ultimately, though, it has become a place of positivity and community, appreciated by neighbors both Buddhist and otherwise. "It's become this icon for the whole neighborhood," says Dan Stevenson. He has observed that there are a lot of "people that are not Buddhist that really come and just talk in front of him . . . It's just cool." As it turns out, Buddhas beget Buddhas—new statues and shrines have begun appearing at other nearby intersections, echoing the Buddhist philosophy that everyone needs to work on their own salvation and not depend on others (like city officials) to do it for them.

# CATALYSTS

S OME URBAN INTERVENTIONS ARE
meant to solve local everyday problems while
others are intended to provoke responses and inspire
debate. When done right, such catalysts can accomplish more by starting a dialogue around issues of
shared spaces and accessibility than any one-off,
site-specific solution ever could. A captivating statement made in the built environment by the right
activist or artist can be so compelling to the general
public that the powers that be are forced to pay attention and, in some cases, be persuaded to change.

LEFT: *Curb cut at a residential street corner for accessibility*

# Ramping Up

## *Cutting Curbs*

PEOPLE WHO DON'T USE WHEELCHAIRS OR PUSH KIDS IN strollers tend to take curb cuts for granted, but these small pedestrian ramps running up to and down from sidewalks at urban intersections were few and far between fifty years ago. When activist Ed Roberts was young, most sidewalks dropped off vertically at intersections and made it difficult for him and other wheelchair users to get between blocks without assistance.

Growing up in the 1940s and '50s, Roberts was the oldest of four children living with his family in a small city near San Francisco. He was diagnosed with polio at age fourteen, which left him almost entirely paralyzed below the neck. He spent much of his time inside an iron lung—a huge machine that helped him breathe. Outside, he needed assistance to get around. His mother sometimes had to enlist strangers to lift him up or down stairs and curbs in public.

When Roberts applied to the University of California, Berkeley, in 1962, the school initially turned him down, in part because they weren't sure where he could live safely on campus with his iron lung. In the end, he was accepted and moved into the campus hospital. His story made national news, and more students with disabilities began to appear on campus, often helped by paid attendants who would heft wheelchairs up staircases and into lecture halls.

All of this was happening during the 1960s, "a time of lots of protests, and lots of reform, and lots of change," recalls Steve Brown, cofounder of the Institute on Disability Culture. On the Berkeley campus, the hospital housing disabled students also became the headquarters for an exuberant and irreverent group of organizers known as the Rolling Quads. Like similar groups around the country, they began advocating for civil rights for people with disabilities—rights to education, employment, respect, and greater inclusion in public life.

At the time, the physical world was not broadly accessible—some ramps existed in places where disabled veterans had pushed local governments and institutions to include them, but these were exceptional. As the 1960s and '70s unfolded, a new wave of young disabled activists was done waiting for official action. To this day, rousing stories circulate about Roberts and the rest of the Rolling Quads riding out in Berkeley under the cover of night with attendants and using sledgehammers to bust up curbs and build their own ramps to force the city into action. Eric Dibner, who was an attendant for disabled students at Berkeley in the 1970s, says, "The story that there were midnight commandos is a little bit exaggerated, I think. We got a bag or two of concrete and mixed it up and took it to the corners that would most ease the route." While it did happen at night, the physical intervention may have been minimal, but it made a powerful and lasting point.

On a day-to-day basis, most of the progress made by the Rolling Quads was more bureaucratic in nature and included petitioning the Berkeley City Council in 1971. Ed Roberts, by then a political science graduate student, was part of these protests. He and his allies insisted that the city build curb cuts on every street corner in Berkeley, a call to action that sparked the world's first widespread curb cuts program on September 28, 1971, when the city council declared that "streets and sidewalks be designed and constructed to facilitate circulation by handicapped persons within major commercial areas." The motion carried unanimously.

By the mid-1970s, the disability rights movement had grown and spread, pushing not just for curb cuts but also for wheelchair lifts on buses, ramps alongside staircases, elevators with reachable buttons in public buildings, accessible bathrooms, and service counters low enough to let a person in a wheelchair be attended to face-to-face. In 1977, protesters simultaneously descended on federal office buildings in ten cities to push the government to act on neglected rules protecting the disabled in all facilities taking federal money. The protest in San Francisco turned into a monthlong sit-in complete with continual news coverage of people in wheelchairs refusing to leave until action was taken. A few years later, demonstrators in wheelchairs publicly cracked concrete curbs in Denver with sledgehammers in the same activist spirit as the Rolling Quads.

Activists learned that these kinds of public displays were powerful tools for capturing public attention. When the sweeping Americans with Disabilities Act of 1990 was hung up in the House of Representatives, disabled demonstrators left their wheelchairs and crawled up the marble steps of the Capitol building to make sure the bill was passed by physically demonstrating the challenges they faced in a built environment that excluded them.

The ADA wasn't the first federal legislation designed to remove barriers for disabled people, but its reach was unprecedented. It mandated access and accommodation for the disabled in all places open to the public, including businesses and transportation infrastructure. It had qualifiers, to be sure—the ADA required only what was "reasonable" for employers and builders. This added a little ambiguity and a lot of wiggle room, and to this day, there aren't curb cuts at every intersection, even in Berkeley. Still, it was a momentous step in the right direction. At the bill's signing ceremony in 1990, President George H. W. Bush spoke powerfully about it in relation to the recent fall of the Berlin Wall, which had divided communist East Germany from the West. "And now I sign legislation, which takes a sledgehammer to another wall, one which has for too many generations separated Americans with disabilities from the freedom they could glimpse but not grasp. And once again we rejoice as this barrier falls, proclaiming together, we will not accept . . . excuse [or] tolerate, discrimination in America."

Ed Roberts, who UC-Berkeley officials once thought was too disabled for their university, finished his master's degree, taught on campus, and cofounded the

Center for Independent Living, a disability services organization that became a model for hundreds of others around the world. He also married, fathered a son, divorced, won a MacArthur genius grant, and ran California's Department of Rehabilitation for nearly a decade. Roberts was an internationally recognized advocate of independence for the disabled when he went into cardiac arrest and died at age fifty-six. Today, his wheelchair is stored at the Smithsonian's National Museum of American History and is prominently displayed on their website. But the most widespread and arguably most meaningful memorials to his legacy can be found at thousands of street corners around the United States that remind us that tactical interventions can change hearts, minds, and ultimately cities.

# CYCLING THROUGH

## *Clearing Cars*

IN THE 1960S, A YOUNG STUDENT NAMED JAIME ORTIZ Mariño left his home country of Colombia to get a degree in architecture and design in the United States. When he returned to Bogotá, he found himself drawing on that experience abroad and viewing his city in a new light. Mariño recalls being "shocked to see that we Colombians were following the American path of urban development"—a path that had led to US cities being dominated by automobiles. He felt strongly that something needed to be done to prevent that history from repeating in Bogotá.

In the spirit of the era, Mariño came to see bicycle rights as civil rights. For him, cycling embodied individuality as well as "women's rights, urban mobility, simplicity, the new urbanism, and, of course, environmental consciousness." Having also been exposed to protest culture in the United States, Mariño organized local cyclists to put up signs and get permission to temporarily close two major streets, leaving them open for cyclists and pedestrians. Thus, the first Ciclovía was born, and from there, its influence spread. Four decades later, on Sundays and public holidays, a vast interconnected network of Bogotá's streets is shut down to automotive traffic, creating an extensive "paved park" for runners, skaters, and cyclists. These weekly Ciclovía events draw as many as two million people out into the streets—about a third of the city's population—to enjoy the seventy-plus miles of repurposed road space.

Urban and regional development professor Sergio Montero believes that Ciclovías can show urban dwellers and designers a new world of possibilities. The problem, as he sees it, is that citizens are used to cities being car-centric. "People have internalized that that is how cities look and so assume that's normal . . . that the streets are dedicated to cars." Ciclovías help break that cycle, illustrating by example how spaces can have many other uses when domineering motorized vehicles are prohibited. The persistence of Bogotá's Ciclovía through various administrations can be attributed in large part to its sheer popularity. Public engagement and support have gone a long way to keeping it going, and it has spurred global offshoots and other efforts by guerrilla cyclists.

While some activists have successfully promoted similar citywide projects, other groups are working incrementally to make everyday improvements to cycling infrastructure. In the Bay Area, a group called SF Transformation, or SFMTrA (not to be confused with SFMTA, the official San Francisco Municipal Transportation Agency), responded to a series of tragic cycling deaths by erecting a set of traffic cones to form a protected bike lane. Such guerrilla interventions are usually temporary and ultimately get taken down by municipal authorities. In one case, though, when the group installed a set of soft-hit posts alongside Golden Gate Park to create a safer bike lane, the city reacted by making the change official. The group's aim was not only to make cyclists safer in this specific spot but also to show how inexpensive and easy it can be to make real and persistent improvements. Guerilla activists in other cities have tried similar interventions with mixed success. In Wichita, Kansas, one group glued a series of 120 toilet plungers to a street as a temporary bike barrier to raise awareness. In Seattle, city authorities at first removed a set of activist-installed lane-marking posts but then apologized for doing so and ultimately ended up installing permanent replacements.

Pollution, health, noise, and space are factors in pro-cycling initiatives, but these efforts also speak to larger questions about urban design history and the very nature of cities. "We must first remember that all cities were car-free little more than a century ago," writes *Carfree Cities* author J. H. Crawford. "Cars were never necessary in cities and in many respects they worked against the fundamental purpose of cities: to bring many people together in a space where social, cultural and economic synergies could develop. Because cars require so much space for movement and parking, they work against this objective [by causing] cities to expand in order to provide the land cars need."

Even as cyclists and pedestrians continue the long fight for their share of urban space, new forms of transportation are also complicating things. Personal electric scooters potentially offer another low-energy, space-saving mode of urban transportation, but as e-scooter sharing services have grown in popularity, these devices have become controversial. Part of the problem is that some users leave them on sidewalks where they can obstruct pedestrians. In Cincinnati, a group called YARD & Company experimentally spray-painted a series of "Bird cages" (referring to Bird, one of the companies building and deploying scooters) onto paved areas. The idea was to encourage people to park e-scooters in safer designated spaces, keeping them clear of cyclists and pedestrians.

Criticisms of e-scooters aside, reducing the number of cars in cities in favor of more bicycles and other multimodal transit options is generally viewed as a net positive for citizens and the environment. Still, it is worth keeping a critical eye on what replaces car-oriented space. Activist-led interventions tend to favor the lifestyles of those activists. Cyclists naturally tend to promote cycling infrastructure. The best interventions, however, involve the whole community and use local input to drive designs that will serve a variety of residents with different experiences, priorities, and points of view.

# DRIVING AWAY

## *Appropriating Parklets*

WHEN DESIGNERS FROM THE REBAR GROUP IN SAN FRAN-cisco unrolled strips of sod onto a stretch of curbside pavement, they had no idea it would spark a global movement. The group was inspired in part by the work of Gordon Matta-Clark, an artist who purchased a series of small unbuildable parcels and inaccessible voids in New York City back in the 1970s. He had been fascinated by underutilized and leftover places like verges and the thin strips between houses that were easy to overlook. Decades later, the Rebar Group similarly sought to understand cities in a different way by doing something new with what urban sociologist William H. Whyte referred to as the "huge reservoir of space yet untapped by imagination."

Surveying their cityscape for underused real estate, Rebar saw parking spots as an opportunity to experiment—these were, after all, rentable spaces that often went unrented, which seemed like a waste. They inserted a few coins, added grass, seating, and a potted tree, then stood back to watch as people engaged with their parklet. As one participant later recalled, when a suspicious parking official started asking questions, the parklet's makers successfully argued their way out of a ticket by explaining that they had paid for the spot and were thus occupying it legally even if they were using it in an unorthodox way.

What started as a temporary urban installation quickly grew in impact as images of the parklet spread. Rebar began fielding requests for similar interventions and responded by publishing guide material for those wishing to replicate or expand on their work in other cities. When parklet makers have encountered pushback, many of them have found it is easier to sell city officials on temporary or pilot projects rather than expensive and permanent changes. If all else fails and a parklet isn't deemed a success for whatever reason, these kinds of low-cost installations are relatively easy to roll up and replace. The City of San Francisco, meanwhile, has gotten on board, accommodating an annual Park(ing) Day and backing a broader initiative to encourage the reclaiming of paved spaces through the Pavement to Parks Program.

Many parklet designs have grown more elaborate and include everything from mini-golf greens to climbable sculptures. Outside of more official parklet-creation channels, some parkleteers have also continued to find loopholes and workarounds, like turning Dumpsters into greenery-filled mobile parks (or "parkmobiles"), then securing a legal Dumpster-parking permit for longer-term curbside placement. The parklet that started as an experiment evolved into a prototype and then developed into a broader typology.

Several factors have helped spread the idea of the urban parklet. In the United States, some estimates put the number of parking spaces as high as two billion. With so many more spots than there are cars, some argue that underutilized, city-subsidized spots in high-density areas can usefully extend the social space of sidewalks and create more room for activities. From the perspective of urban economics, these mini-parks can also be a boon to adjacent shops—indeed, some cities cede spaces to local businesses willing to put in the work and money to create adjacent parklets.

While this might all sound like a great synergistic strategy that benefits everyone, there are reasons to be wary of these kinds of overtly Instagrammable projects. Better economic prospects for certain local businesses can lead to higher rents in neighborhoods like San Francisco's Mission District, where parklets are popular. So while parklets may be amenities for some, they can be seen as gentrifiers by others. Also, as Gordon C. C. Douglas points out in *The Help-Yourself City,* even where parklets are technically public, they "may not appear at all welcoming or accessible to those who are unwilling or unable to buy something." A parklet near a coffee shop that aesthetically matches the business can look and feel more like a private extension than a public amenity, something built by and for latte-sipping elites rather than being equally open and inviting to everyone.

The success and official acceptance of parklets and similar projects raises questions about who is served by a given type of design approach, not to mention the fact that some demographics are less likely to be arrested for trying out guerrilla interventions in the first place. "The official embrace of the cultural values behind many DIY urban design activities," argues Douglas, can come "at the expense of existing communities" who may have less of a voice in the matter. In the case of the Mission, incoming gentrifiers may be more enamored with new parklets (and associated hip businesses) than longtime residents.

Douglas's basic point is that both official and do-it-yourself urbanists need to consider the neighborhood they're adapting to their personal taste. One should be careful about assuming that any popular "improvements" will be unambiguously good, be they creative placemaking parklets or bike lanes or farmers' markets. For better or worse, all city-reshaping projects come with cultural implications and associations. When it comes to evaluating these kinds of urban interventions, Douglas suggests maintaining a "critical eye on the social qualities of the spaces we are building, on who benefits and who is excluded." Among other things, this means truly involving impacted communities in design processes.

# Grafting On

## *Grassroots Gardening*

A subversive urban agriculture group in San Fran-
cisco has turned the simple activity of gardening into an act of creative civil disobe-
dience by converting ornamental trees into fruit-producing greenery. The process
goes something like this: a small incision is made in existing street trees that allows
industrious grafters to add living branches from other fruit-bearing trees. These
Frankensteined branches become part of the existing tree and eventually bear
edible fruits. This approach is a form of "guerrilla gardening" a term rooted in
green urban activism that can be traced back to the Big Apple.

In the early 1970s, Lower Manhattan activists began turning vacant lots into
community gardens starting with small tactical interventions, then expanding to
larger projects. An artist who lived in the city's Lower East Side named Liz Christy
cofounded a group called the Green Guerrillas. This crew began to throw "seed
bombs" packed with fertilizer, seeds, and water over fences into abandoned lots.
Stepping things up, they also took over an entire vacant property on the corner
of Bowery and Houston and cleared out the site to plant flowers, trees, fruits, and
vegetables. The group then appealed to the city's Housing Preservation and Development Department to make the Bowery Houston Community Farm and Garden
official. The place has since been renamed in honor of Liz Christy and continues
to be maintained by a group of dedicated community volunteers.

The idea of turning unused space into community plots has taken off and
branched out around the world. Guerrilla gardening has come to refer to a whole
range of informal greening projects, including ongoing seed-bombing initiatives
aimed at populating deserted lots, road medians, and other barren places with
living plants. The contents of these green grenades can vary greatly. Some include
native species selected for ecological reasons or sets of seeds carefully chosen to
flower in sequence. Others activists and artists have taken to growing greenery on

vertical surfaces, a process akin to painting wall murals. By mixing ingredients like buttermilk, gardening gel, and crumbled moss, creators produce a kind of organic "paint," then apply it to surfaces like old concrete walls. The results are living artworks that slowly grow into bold and highly visible statements.

Many of these efforts are arguably more about attention-grabbing artistry than about making a lasting impact on the ecology of cities, but not all guerilla gardening projects are so flashy. Many successful interventions persist because they are thoughtfully planned and executed with sensitivity to local environments. Californian guerilla gardener Scott Bunnell has spent years planting drought-tolerant species like aloe vera, agave, and other varieties of exotic succulents along road medians and highways. In large part, he has received praise for the efforts of his group, the SoCal Guerilla Gardening Club. They have even petitioned officials for access to municipal water to keep these regionally appropriate plants alive and well.

Back in San Francisco, one might expect a similarly positive response from authorities to the fruit-tree grafting, but the city's Guerrilla Grafters intentionally keep a low profile to avoid official scrutiny. They do not create maps so people can find trees they have worked on. The results of their interventions are only visible once they literally bear fruit. This stealthy approach is motivated by a well-grounded fear that the city would actively undo their work. On the surface, turning a decorative tree into a fruit-bearing one seems like a positive contribution, but from the city's perspective, such additions undermine municipal goals.

While the city of San Francisco has thousands of apple, plum, pear, and other fruit trees—and more than 100,000 public trees in total—these are intentionally rendered sterile to avoid attracting animals and making messes. Productive fruit trees mean more work for city maintenance crews, which have to clean up fallen and rotting fruit. For their part, the grafters argue that they are helping to address urban food scarcity as well as raise awareness about the accessibility of fresh fruit. Tensions like these can be found at the intersection of a lot of top-down plans and bottom-up approaches—conflicts between different visions for what a city can and should be and how it should serve its citizens.

Other cities like Toronto offer potential templates for mediating such tensions in the form of nonprofits like Not Far from the Tree. For years, this organization has paired volunteer pickers with a network of fruit-bearing trees on properties around the city. Volunteer-picked fruits are then divided among residents who register fruit trees, people who pick the fruits, and an array of food banks, community kitchens, and other such institutions—a hat trick of sorts that taps into a massive, distributed urban orchard.

# BUMPING OUT

## *Collaborative Placemaking*

MUCH LIKE THE DESIRE PATHS PEOPLE MAKE THROUGH grassy areas, the tracks humans and vehicles leave in the snow can show urban observers and designers how people actually move through cities. In some parks, officials have used pedestrian tracks in winter to decide where to pave paths when summer comes around. As cars make their way through the ice and snow on winter roads, they also carve out routes that clear narrow corridors and leave snowy neckdowns (or "sneckdowns") on either side. Author and activist Jon Geeting has been photographing these snowy curb extensions in Philadelphia for years to highlight how little space cars really require on roads and advocate for underutilized areas to be productively converted. His documentation has done more than just create interest around these places—it has actually helped urban activists reshape specific intersections both in and beyond Philadelphia.

Geeting first became interested in city planning issues while biking the streets of New York City around 2007 when the city was "really aggressively transforming the streets with things like car-free Times Square and the pedestrian plaza program." It was, he recalled in an interview with Kurt Kohlstedt for *99% Invisible,* "a pretty exciting time to be following this arena of politics." He also started reading *Streetsblog,* whose founder, Aaron Naparstek, originally coined the term *sneckdown*. Geeting later moved to and began documenting sneckdowns in Philadelphia. The images he made there were used in a campaign to convince the city to modify a confusing and dangerous intersection. The resulting transformation at Twelfth and Morris streets shortened pedestrian crossing times, calmed vehicular traffic, and added more green space. Geeting credits other local urban advocates with turning his images into action, including Sam Sherman, "one of Philly's original urbanist agitators," who brought some of Geeting's photos to the commerce and streets departments to make his case to city officials.

Since then, Geeting has worked on other sneckdown-driven pedestrian plazas with his neighborhood association in Fishtown, but the idea of documenting sneckdowns and using similar methods to drive urban change has spread. Citizens in other cities have begun taking photos of snowy formations at intersections and using them to push for official redesigns.

In the absence of snow, some citizens have developed alternative techniques to gather data on how much space cars need. A few years back, one Toronto resident deployed leaves and chalk to artificially extend curbs into the street in his neighborhood. His "leafy neckdowns" looked like fallen leaves overflowing roadside gutters, but they effectively narrowed the visible roadway. Chalked lines were sketched out to further guide drivers within the reconfigured space. Some people still drove through the leaf piles, but many drivers stayed within the artificially narrower space created between them and opposing curbs. The project's instigator concluded that building permanent neckdowns in the same spots could free up to two thousand square feet of space.

While photographing snow is legal, most cities frown on people obstructing sections of streets, even temporarily. But activists who do projects like this are treading on familiar ground, whether they are laying down some leaves or rolling big and controversial boulders around. These kinds of guerrilla urbanist approaches are well documented in *Tactical Urbanism: Short-term Action for Long-term Change* by authors Mike Lydon and Anthony Garcia. Citing Lydon, Geeting notes that in many cases "citizen-led interventions tend to have some staying power, and often aren't removed even if done illicitly."

Back in Philadelphia, Geeting is pleased that his city "now has a process for citizen-initiated pedestrian plazas, which gives people a way to advance ideas even if their local elected official disapproves." Not every metropolis offers that option, however; in places without such a clear path, he observes that making "changes to streets illicitly can be a good way for citizens to call attention to problems that a city administration may not be aware of, or may be ignoring." If you imagine a solution, "chances are that other people probably have as well, and temporarily testing it out is a great way to meet those people, and start organizing for more permanent changes." There's no one right way to shape a city, but taking action, observing results, sharing knowledge, and engaging in collaborative advocacy with other citizens is a good place to start.

# Outro

THAT'S IT! THAT'S EVERYTHING YOU'LL EVER NEED TO know about a city. Just kidding! No guide is ever complete, this one included. We could have probably written a whole book just about manhole covers. Each week on the *99% Invisible* podcast, we tell a story that reveals something surprising about the design of our world. Inevitably, someone with specialized or local knowledge writes in to lightly chastise us for neglecting to mention a cool fact that wasn't in the episode. Sometimes they offer an insight or a perspective that's completely new to us, but often our research uncovered that aspect and we chose not to include it. In the service of telling a cogent and compelling story, we have to wrap it up at some point, and things are always left on the cutting room floor, including some fascinating but tangential side stories that we encounter along the way. The same goes for this book.

As this guide to the city evolved, different odds and ends we intended to explore no longer seemed to fit. There was a whole multistory arc about extreme urban camouflage that included a fake suburb with entire houses and sidewalks draped over an airplane factory, artificial towns used for police and other emergency personnel training, and even empty cities designed to impress neighbors across tense borders. We could have covered both spite and nail houses, buildings that become physical manifestations of conflict and defiance. There were more human-centered stories as well, like a man who tragically lost his son on the streets of Mumbai and has since dedicated his time to fixing the city's potholes or the woman in Philadelphia who puts up plaque stickers to commemorate humdrum and humorous happenings, little fun facts that typical historical marker makers skip over. We also ended up leaving out many tales of everyday traffic cones, survey markers, and the placebo crosswalk buttons that placate foot-tapping pedestrians waiting to walk. Eventually, enough is enough, less really is more, and it's wise to affix the city-approved spray cap on the open fire hydrant so a thousand gallons of water don't knock you off your feet (see page 328).

Luckily for you, there is an ongoing conversation about these subjects and many more on the *99% Invisible* podcast and website—some of the stories we cut from the book will be developed as episodes or turned into articles instead. For more than ten years, a group of us at the show and our collaborators have followed our collective curiosity down unexpected desire paths, all in an effort to stoke our audience's interest in the everyday. We hope that with this guide we have infected you with our enthusiasm and you will continue to join us as we explore the overlooked aspects of the built world. Please forgive us if it takes us a little longer to get to our destination because we are stopping to read every plaque along the way.

# ACKNOWLEDGMENTS

T<small>HERE IS A DECADE OF RESEARCH, INSIGHTS, AND KNOWL</small>-edge that make up the more than four hundred episodes of the *99% Invisible* podcast, which served as a foundation for this guide. We weren't satisfied with the idea of releasing a collection of uninspired transcripts of past episodes, however. So even stories with roots in the show were picked apart, reexamined in light of the larger picture we wanted to paint, and written from scratch. Then we wrote another two hundred pages of essays that have no precedent on the podcast, and organized it all to create something bigger, new, and different.

For the stories inspired by previous reporting, as well as the stories that are new to this volume, we are grateful to the brilliant team at *99% Invisible.* Thank you for the stellar work you have contributed over the years and for continuing to put out an amazing show while we were busy creating this book. In addition to the authors, *99% Invisible* is Katie Mingle, Delaney Hall, Emmett FitzGerald, Sharif Youssef, Sean Real, Joe Rosenberg, Vivian Le, Chris Berube, Irene Sutharojana, and Sofia Klatzker. There is no better crew in all of podcasting. Some of you eat green mole, and some of you don't, but we love you all the same. Additionally, we give heartfelt thanks to past team members Avery Trufelman, Sam Greenspan, and Taryn Mazza.

The staff makes incredible stories, but we also rely on a network of outside producers, some of whose work served as the basis for essays in this volume. Special thanks to Julia DeWitt, Matthew Kielty, Dan Weissmann, Sam Evans-Brown, Logan Shannon, Jesse Dukes, Stan Alcorn, Will Coley, Christophe Haubursin, Zach Dyer, Joel Werner, Chelsea Davis, Ann Hepperman, Amy Drozdowska, Dave McGuire, as well as fellow Radiotopians Benjamen Walker (*Theory of Everything*), Nate Dimeo (*The Memory Palace*), Phoebe Judge and Lauren Spohrer (*Criminal*). Thanks also to all the interviewees and other people who've talked to us over the years and shared their interests and expertise with our audience.

Thanks to Daniel Scovill and Adam Winig of Arcsine for generously offering the show a home and being the reason we are based in beautiful downtown Oakland, California.

Even though our podcast is about design, the fact that our medium is audio means we rarely have the opportunity to work with visual artists. We feel so lucky to have found Patrick Vale and that he allowed us to chain him to a desk for months, cranking out beautiful illustrations for this book with periodic sanctioned ventures out into the world in order to sketch sidewalk utility graffiti and other unconventional cityscapes. Liz Boyd was our indefatigable fact checker, who not only made sure the dates and places were correct, but also brought clarity and confidence to each story. Helen Zaltzman read early drafts and encouraged us to put in more jokes. Michelle Loeffler helped us build the extensive bibliography.

Thanks as well to the team at HMH, especially our editor Kate Napolitano, who was our coach and our cheerleader. Jay Mandel at WME took Roman to seventeen meetings over the course of two days to sell this book. Every writer should have an agent that good.

## ROMAN

*99% Invisible* was born at KALW in San Francisco. There are so many people to thank from that humble but mighty radio station, but in particular the show wouldn't exist without former General Manager Matt Martin. He was instrumental in the creation of the "tiny radio show about design" and also selflessly allowed it to grow and develop on its own as a podcast. Few people are that generous. I wouldn't be in radio at all if it weren't for Nicole Sawaya and Alan Farley at KALW. The Bay Area was so lucky to have had these two servants to the mission of public radio. They are dearly missed.

The podcast is a founding member of a collective of podcasts called Radiotopia. It is a project of PRX, a company that is responsible, in one way or another, for everything good and innovative in public radio. Jake Shapiro was the boss when PRX and I founded Radiotopia and Kerri Hoffman is in charge now. Jake's forward thinking and ambition made the creation of Radiotopia possible. Kerri's dedication, fairness, intelligence, savvy, and warmth keep it going today. The day-to-day operation and creative growth of the collective is shepherded by Julie Shapiro, who loves audio storytelling more than anything and that fact can always be heard in everything she touches. Thank you to the whole Radiotopia team and all our sister and brother podcasts.

I will always be grateful to Mae Mars for supporting the creation of *99% Invisible* and me as a broadcaster. It was a crazy leap that was never mocked or questioned, even when there was no evidence that it would work out. Her intelligence and kindness can be heard in her voice featured in many early episodes. My boys Mazlo and Carver were the first breakout stars of the show, appearing in the first ads as three-year-olds who always had something to say. I'm convinced that all the early advertising money the show earned was largely thanks to them. They have grown into thoughtful, kind, curious, and lovely young men. I feel so honored that I get to be their dad.

Thanks to my mom and my Betty, and my sister, Leigh Marz (with a *z*), and her family, Michael and Ava. I don't know any other middle-aged man whose sister is his best friend, but I think it speaks to the character of Leigh and our mother that this is the case. After all the places we've been, we all ended up here together in the Bay Area, thousands of miles from where we started. I feel lucky to have been born into our little family.

I wouldn't have been able to finish this book without the love and support of my partner, Joy Yuson. Thanks for inviting me out in the world and sharing with me all the beautiful things you enjoy. I'm in awe of your capacity to talk to every person, eat any food, explore every beach, and read every plaque. I'm your biggest fan.

## KURT

I HAD BEEN A FAN OF THE SHOW FOR YEARS WHEN ROMAN asked me to join *99% Invisible.* That invitation brought me into collaboration with my future coauthor as well as a stellar crew of other curious and creative storytelling colleagues. Leading up to that, a host of talented people made this leap possible, including those who tenaciously helped build and grow a different, older project—an online urban art, architecture, and design publication that was my primary (pre)occupation for years prior to *99pi.*

When *WebUrbanist* launched in 2007, friends and family were cautiously supportive but also understandably skeptical about independent web publishing as a professional pursuit. But thanks in part to contributing authors, especially Delana Lefevers, Steve Levenstein, and SA Rogers, this digital magazine evolved and thrived, becoming the first in a series of popular design-centric web publications. Technical experts, including Mike Waggoner and Jeff Hood, kept the sites up and running through thick and thin and fielded frantic late-night pleas for assistance. Andrea Tomingas and Gabe Danon helped redesign and rebuild *WebUrbanist* from layout to logo a few years back. Meanwhile, what sustained all of this most fundamentally was a loyal and enthusiastic readership to whom I remain deeply grateful.

I was fortunate to have generous and patient teachers along the way, including Jeffrey Ochsner and Nicole Huber, who greatly expanded my understanding of urban design and served as my Master of Architecture thesis advisors at the University of Washington, Seattle. Foundational, too, was my time at Carleton College with professors and peers who taught me to observe and understand the world around me through the lenses of philosophy, history, and art.

For my love of reading, writing, traveling, and learning, I am eternally appreciative of my parents, Professors David Kohlstedt and Sally Gregory Kohlstedt, who thankfully brought their work home with them every night. In more ways than I can list, they have supported me throughout the years, sometimes quite directly by answering technical questions about shear forces as they apply to road signs (thanks, Dad!) and responding to inquiries about sackcloth textile design history (thanks, Mom!). And for all of those times I said your jobs were boring when I was a dumb kid: my humblest apologies. Gratitude as well to my brother, Kris, who graciously let me crash at (and work out of) his place in Chicago at key times in my life, and his wife, Courtney, the sister I always wanted. Finally, thanks to Michelle Loeffler, who worked on this book at essentially every step of the process, filling ever-expanding roles (researcher, editor, translator, irony checker) as the project evolved. I'll catch you all on the flip side!

## FIN

LAST, BUT CERTAINLY NOT LEAST, THANK YOU TO ALL THE beautiful nerds who supported *99% Invisible* through the years. When podcasting was considered little more than a hobby and no radio station other than KALW put our stories on the air, you gave us the financial and emotional support that allowed us to thrive. We will never forget that.

# BIBLIOGRAPHY

## CHAPTER 1: INCONSPICUOUS

### UBIQUITOUS
### Official Graffiti: *Utility Codes*

Burrington, Ingrid. *Networks of New York: An Illustrated Field Guide to Urban Internet Infrastructure.* Brooklyn, NY: Melville House, 2016.

Cawley, Laurence. "What do those squiggles on the pavement actually mean?" *BBC News,* February 18, 2014.

Common Ground Alliance. *Best Practices: The Definitive Guide for Underground Safety & Damage Prevention.* Alexandria, VA: CGA, 2018.

Healy, Patrick. "Why You Should Call 811 Before Digging." *NBC Los Angeles,* September 15, 2010.

"Holocaust: Pipeline Blast Creates Horror Scene in L.A." *The Evening Independent* (Los Angeles), June 17, 1976.

Kohlstedt, Kurt. "Decoding Streets: Secret Symbols of the Urban Underground." *WebUrbanist* (blog), February 27, 2014.

UK Health and Safety Executive. *Avoiding Danger from Underground Services.* HS(G). 3rd ed. Bootle, UK: HSE Books, 2014.

### Initialed Impressions: *Sidewalk Markings*

Alden, Andrew. *Oakland Underfoot: Fossils in the City's Hardscape* (blog). Accessed September 28, 2019.

Cushing, Lincoln. "Sidewalk Contractor Stamps." Berkeley Historical Plaque Project, 2012.

Cushing, Lincoln. "Sidewalk Stamps Make Local History More Concrete." *Berkeley Daily Planet,* June 14, 2005.

Klingbeil, Annalise. "Concrete connection to Calgary's past preserved in sidewalk stamps." *Calgary Herald,* January 6, 2017.

Saksa, Jim. "Streetsplainer: What the heck do those 'The space between these lines not dedicated' street markers mean?" *WHYY* (PBS), May 10, 2016.

### Planned Failure: *Breakaway Posts*

American Association of State Highway and Transportation Officials. *Roadside Design Guide.* Washington, DC: AASHTO, 2011.

*Breakaway Timber Utility Poles.* VHS, MPEG video. Federal Highway Administration. Washington, DC, 1989.

McGee, Hugh W. *Maintenance of Signs and Sign Supports: A Guide for Local Highway and Street Maintenance Personnel.* Washington, DC: Office of Safety, Federal Highway Administration, January 2010.

### A Little Safer: *Emergency Boxes*

Harrell, Lauren. "41 Brand Names People Use as Generic Terms." *Mental Floss* (blog), May 9, 2014.

Jones, Cynthia. "Rapid Access: Gainesville Fire Department." Knoxbox (website). The Knox Company, June 26, 2014.

"Key Secure: Master Key Retention with Audit Trail." Knoxbox (website). The Knox Company. Accessed September 28, 2019.

### CAMOUFLAGE
### Thornton's Scent Bottle: *Stink Pipes*

Barker, Geoff. "Cleopatra's Needle or 'Thornton's Scent Bottle.'" Museum of Applied Arts & Sciences website, June 13, 2012.

Fine, Duncan. "The Sweet Smell of Success—Hyde Park Obelisk Celebrates 150 Years." City of Sydney website, December 11, 2007.

"History of Hyde Park." City of Sydney website, updated November 1, 2016.

"Tall Tale About City's Aspiring Ambitions." *Daily Telegraph* (Sydney), December 19, 2007.

Winkless, Laurie. "Do You Know What a Stinkpipe Is?" *Londonist* (blog), updated December 14, 2016.

### Exhaustive Outlets: *Fake Facades*

Manaugh, Geoff. "Brooklyn Vent." *BLDGBLOG,* December 22, 2011.

Rogers, SA. "Buildings That Don't Exist: Fake Facades Hide Infrastructure." *WebUrbanist* (blog), April 29, 2013.

Ross, David. "23-24 Leinster Gardens, London's False-Front Houses." Britain Express (website), accessed September 28, 2019.

Siksma, Walther. "Ehekarussell." *Atlas Obscura* (blog), accessed October 14, 2019.

Slocombe, Mike. "23/24 Leinster Gardens, Paddington, London W2—Dummy houses in the heart of London." *Urban 75* (blog), January 2007.

### Catalytic Diverters: *Ventilation Buildings*

"#93 Holland Tunnel Ventilation System." American Society of Mechanical Engineers website, accessed September 28, 2019.

"Erling Owre, 84, Tunnel Architect; Consultant to 'Engineers' Firm Dead—Supervised Holland, Queens Tubes." *New York Times,* February 1, 1961.

Gomez, John. "Brilliant design in Modernist towers that ventilate the Holland Tunnel: Legends & Landmarks." NJ.com website, April 10, 2012, updated March 30, 2019.

"Holland Tunnel." American Society of Civil Engineers, Metropolitan Section (website), accessed October 23, 2019.

"Pure Air Is Assured for the Vehicular Tunnel; There Will Be No Danger of Asphyxiation from Motor-Car Monoxide in the Big New Boring Under the North River, as Shown by Remarkable Experiments in Ventilation." *New York Times,* February 17, 1924.

"Tests Show Safety of Vehicle Tunnel; Ventilating System for Proposed Tube Under Hudson Tried Out in Pittsburgh. Smoke Bombs Exploded But Air Remains Pure, as It Also Does When Autos Are Run Through Test Tube." *New York Times,* October 30, 1921.

### Neighborhood Transformers: *Electrical Substations*

Bateman, Chris. "The transformer next door." *spacing* (blog), February 18, 2015.

Collyer, Robin. "Artist Project/Transformer Houses." *Cabinet Magazine,* Spring 2006.

"History of Toronto Hydro." Toronto Hydro website, accessed September 28, 2019.

Levenstein, Steve. "Power Houses: Toronto Hydro's Camouflaged Substations." *WebUrbanist* (blog), February 5, 2012.

Mok, Tanya. "Toronto Hydro's not so hidden residential substations." *blogTO,* May 12, 2018.

"Power Restored After Huge Hydro Vault Fire Leads to Blackout." *CityNews* (Toronto), December 16, 2008.

### Cellular Biology: *Wireless Towers*

"Concealment Solutions." Valmont Structures website, accessed February 4, 2020.

Lefevers, Delana. "Faux-ny Phone Towers: Cleverly Concealed Cellular Sites." *WebUrbanist* (blog), March 26, 2010.

Madrigal, Alexis C. "How the 'Cellular' Phone Got Its Name." *The Atlantic,* September 15, 2011.

Oliver, Julian. "Stealth Infrastructure." *Rhizome* (blog), May 20, 2014.

U.S. Federal Communications Commission. Telecommunications Act of 1996. Public Law 104-104. Washington, DC: GPO, 1996.

Young, Lauren. "Take a Look at America's Least Convincing Cell Phone Tower Trees." *Atlas Obscura* (blog), May 17, 2016.

### Resourceful Artifice: *Production Wells*

Comras, Kelly. "The Brothers Behind Disney's Magical Landscapes." The Cultural Landscape Foundation's website, February 2, 2018.

Gilmartin, Wendy. "Beverly Hills' Fugliest Oil Well, AKA the 'Tower of Hope.'" *LA Weekly,* May 22, 2012.

Harold, Luke. "Venoco to vacate oil well at Beverly Hills High." *Beverly Press* (Los Angeles, CA), June 7, 2017.

King, Jason. "Urban Crude." *Landscape and Urbanism* (blog), November 22, 2009.

Levenstein, Steve. "School Fuel: Monumental Beverly Hills High's Tower of Hope." *WebUrbanist* (blog), April 18, 2010.

"Pico Blvd. Drill Sites" *STAND—L.A.* (blog), accessed January 31, 2020.

Schoch, Deborah. "Toasting Industry as Art." *Los Angeles Times,* September 13, 2006.

Tuttle, Robert, and Laura Blewitt. "California Oil Dreams Fade as Iconic Beverly Hills Derrick Comes Down." *Bloomberg,* April 26, 2018.

Wiscombe, Janet. "Drilling in Disguise: On Long Beach's Artificial Islands, Oil Comes Out and—Just as Important—Water Goes In." *Los Angeles Times,* November 15, 1996.

## ACCRETIONS

### Seeing Stars: *Anchor Plates*

American Institute of Architects, San Francisco Chapter Preservation Committee. "Architectural Design Guide for Exterior Treatments of Unreinforced Masonry Buildings during Seismic Retrofit." November, 1991.

Michalski, Joseph. "Star Bolts . . . They Aren't Just Decoration!" *ActiveRain* (blog), February 8, 2011.

"The Secret Life of Buildings: Star Bolts." *Solo Real Estate* (blog), accessed September 28, 2019.

Toner, Ian. "Your House and Your Facade: A Separation Agreement." *Toner Architects* (blog), June 13, 2013.

### Scarchitecture: *Urban Infill*

Kohlstedt, Kurt. "Ghost Lanes: Angled 'Scarchitecture' Reveals Historic Urban Roads & Railways." *99% Invisible* (blog), April 17, 2017.

Manaugh, Geoff. "Ghost Streets of Los Angeles." *BLDGBLOG,* December 4, 2015.

Migurski, Michal. "Scar Tissue." *tecznotes* (blog), May 17, 2006.

User: the man of twists and turns. "The Ghost Streets of LA." *MetaFilter* (blog), December 5, 2017.

### Lines of Sight: *Relay Nodes*

"CenturyLink Building." Newton Bonding website, accessed September 29, 2019.

"Fiber Optics." *Today's Engineer,* November 2011.

Harding, Spencer James. *The Long Lines.* Self-published, MagCloud, 2017.

Kohlstedt, Kurt. "Vintage Skynet: AT&T's Abandoned 'Long Lines' Microwave Tower Network." *99% Invisible* (blog), October 20, 2017.

LaFrance, Albert. "The Microwave Radio and Coaxial Cable Networks of the Bell System." *Long Lines* (blog), last modified April 11, 2013.

Lileks, James. "The CenturyLink building in downtown Mpls is losing its distinctive antenna." *Star Tribune* (Minneapolis), October 2, 2019.

"Long Lines Sites in U.S." Google Maps website, accessed September 29, 2019.

Teicher, Jordan. "The Abandoned Microwave Towers That Once Linked the US." *Wired,* March 10, 2015.

User: chrisd. "Discarded AT&T Microwave Bunkers for Sale." SlashDot website, September 11, 2002.

### Thomassons: *Maintained Remains*

Akasegawa, Genpei. *Hyperart: Thomasson.* Translated by Matthew Fargo. Los Angeles: Kaya Press, January 2010.

*Hyperart: Thomasson* (blog), accessed October 29, 2019.

Trufelman, Avery. "129: Thomassons." *99% Invisible* (podcast, MP3 audio), August 26, 2014.

### Accumulative Controversy: *Love Locks*

Bills, John William. "The Heartbreaking Origin of 'Love Locks.'" *Culture Trip* (blog), last modified February 12, 2018.

Daley, Beth. "From ancient China to an Italian chick flick: the story behind Venice's love lock burden." *The Conversation,* September 29, 2014.

"The Great Wall & Love Locks." Penn State: ENG 118 (course website), June 11, 2015.

Griffin, Dan. "Love locks weigh heavily on Dublin City Council discussions." *Irish Times* (Dublin), June 18, 2019.

Grundhauser, Eric. "Not-So-Loved Locks: 6 Love Lock Sites That Caused Both Controversy and Cuddling." *Atlas Obscura* (blog), June 2, 2015.

Jovanovic, Dragana. "The Bridge of Love Where the Romance of Padlocks Began." *ABC News,* February 13, 2013.

Mallonee, Laura C. "In Place of Love Locks, a Paris Bridge Gets Street Art." *Hyperallergic* (blog), June 11, 2015.

O'Callaghan, Laura. "Tourism crackdown: Rome bans toplessness, messy eating and Instagram staple 'love locks.'" *Express* (London), June 10, 2019.

Pearlman, Jonathan. "Melbourne to remove 20,000 'love locks' from bridge due to safety concerns." *The Telegraph,* May 18, 2015.

Rubin, Alissa J., and Aurelien Breeden. "Paris Bridge's Love Locks Are Taken Down." *New York Times,* June 1, 2015.

### Spolia of War: *Constructive Reuse*

"Corner Cannons." *Dartmouth History* (blog), May 15, 2014.

DeWitt, Julia. "174: From the Sea, Freedom." *99% Invisible* (podcast, MP3 audio), July 28, 2015.

Evans, Martin H. "Old cannon re-used as bollards." Westevan website, updated July 25, 2017.

"The fight to save a hidden part of Britain's war history." *CBC Radio-Canada,* November 10, 2017.

Hall, Heinrich. "Spolia—Recycling the Past." *Peter Sommer Travels* (blog), August 26, 2013.

"The history of bollards." Furnitubes website, August 22, 2013.

Johnson, Ben. "French Cannons as Street Bollards." Historic UK website, accessed October 2, 2019.

"A Load of Old Bollards." *CabbieBlog,* July 24, 2015.

"Plaza de la Catedral." TripAdvisor website, Havana, accessed October 3, 2019.

"The Stretcher Railing Society: For the promotion, protection and preservation of London's ARP stretcher railings." Stretcher Railing Society website, accessed September 29, 2019

## CHAPTER 2: CONSPICUOUS

### IDENTITY

### Vexillology Rules: *Municipal Flags*

"City of Pocatello to Form Flag Design Committee." City of Pocatello website, February 2, 2016.

Harris, Shelbie. "Pocatello no longer has the worst city flag on the continent." *Idaho State Journal,* September 19, 2017.

Kaye, Edward B. "The American City Flag Survey of 2004." *Raven: A Journal of Vexillology* 12 (2005): 27–62.

Kaye, Ted. *Good Flag, Bad Flag: How to Design a Great Flag.* Trenton, NJ: North American Vexillological Association, 2006.

Kohlstedt, Kurt. "Vexillology Revisited: Fixing the Worst Civic Flag Designs in America." *99% Invisible* (podcast, MP3 audio), February 22, 2016.

Mars, Roman. "140: Vexillionaire." *99% Invisible* (podcast, MP3 audio), November 11, 2014.

Mars, Roman. "Why city flags may be the worst-designed thing you may never notice." TED talk, Vancouver Convention Centre, March 2015.

Schuffman, Stuart. "It's time for a new San Francisco flag." *San Francisco Examiner,* July 16, 2015.

### Public Bodies: *Civic Monuments*

"Audrey Munson Is Out of Danger." *New York Times,* May 29, 1922.

Donnelly, Elisabeth. "Descending Night." *The Believer,* July 1, 2015.

Geyer, Andrea. *Queen of the Artists' Studios: The Story of Audrey Munson.* New York: Art in General, 2007.

Jacobs, Andrew. "Neighborhood Report: New York Up Close; Rescuing a Heroine from the Clutches of Obscurity." *New York Times,* April 14, 1996.

Shilling, Donovan A. *Rochester's Marvels & Myths.* Victor, NY: Pancoast Publishing, 2011.

Trufelman, Avery. "200: Miss Manhattan." *99% Invisible* (podcast, MP3 audio), February 15, 2016.

### Fonts of Knowledge: *Historical Plaques*

Allen, Kester. "Read the Plaque." Read the Plaque website.

"Gold Fire Hydrant—1906 Earthquake." Roadside America website, accessed February 4, 2020.

Kohlstedt, Kurt. "Always Read the Plaque: Mapping Over 10,000 Global Markers & Memorials." *99% Invisible* (blog), May 13, 2016.

Loewen, James W. *Lies Across America: What Our Historic Sites Get Wrong.* 20th anniversary edition. New York: The New Press, 2019.

"London's Blue Plaques." English Heritage website, accessed February 4, 2020.

"Michael J. Smith." Read the Plaque website, accessed February 4, 2020.

Neno, Eric, and Nell Veshistine. "60B: Heyward Shepherd Memorial." *99% Invisible* (podcast and MP3 audio), September 10, 2012.

### Distinguished Features: *That Fancy Shape*

Anderson, Christy. *Renaissance Architecture*. Oxford, UK: Oxford University Press, February 2013.

Jones, Owen. *The Grammar of Ornament*. London: Day & Sons, 1856.

Tate, Carolyn E. *Yaxchilan: The Design of a Maya Ceremonial City*. Austin: University of Texas Press, August 2013.

Trufelman, Avery. "The Fancy Shape." *99% Invisible* (podcast and MP3 audio), March 17, 2014.

## SAFETY

### Mixed Signals: *Traffic Lights*

Grabowski, Charley. "Tipperary Hill." *Apple's Tree* (blog), November 14, 2007.

"International Road Signs Guide." Auto Europe website, accessed October 7, 2019.

Kirst, Sean. "In Syracuse, an Irish lesson for the prime minister: Rocks against red lift green on Tipp Hill." *Syracuse.com* (blog), updated March 23, 2019.

Kirst, Sean. "On Tipp Hill, longtime neighbor keeps watch over Stone Throwers' Park." *Syracuse.com* (blog), updated March 23, 2019.

McCarthy, John Francis. "Legends of Tipp Hill: In Syracuse's Irish neighborhood, facts rarely get in the way of a good story." *Syracuse.com* (blog), updated March 22, 2019.

Pilling, Michael, and Ian Davies. "Linguistic relativism and colour cognition." *British Journal of Psychology* 95, no. 4 (2004): 429–55.

Richarz, Allan. "According to Japanese Traffic Lights, Bleen Means Go." *Atlas Obscura* (blog), September 12, 2017.

Scott, Tom. *All the Colours, Including Grue: How Languages See Colours Differently*. YouTube video, posted June 7, 2013.

"Stone Throwers' Park." City of Syracuse website, accessed February 4, 2020.

Tulloch, Katrina. "Green-over-red stoplight: Stone throwers remembered for stubborn Irish spirit." *Syracuse.com* (blog), updated January 30, 2019.

### Visibility Aids: *Retroreflective Studs*

Colvile, Robert. "Percy Shaw: Man with his eye on the road." *The Telegraph* (UK), November 30, 2007.

"Guidelines for the Use of Raised Pavement Markers: Section 2. RPM Guidelines." Federal Highway Administration website, accessed February 4, 2020.

Irish, Vivian. "Percy Shaw OBE (1890–1976)—a successful inventor and entrepreneur." Yorkshire Philosophical Society website, accessed October 8, 2019.

Migletz, James, Joseph K. Fish, and Jerry L. Graham. *Roadway Delineation Practices Handbook*. Washington, DC: Federal Highway Administration, 1994.

"Percy Shaw O.B.E. 15th April 1890 to 1st September 1976." Reflecting Roadstuds website, accessed October 8, 2019.

Plester, Jeremy. "Weatherwatch: Percy Shaw and the invention of the cat's eye reflector." *The Guardian*, December 3, 2018.

Richards, Gary. "Caltrans says bye-bye to Botts' dots." *Mercury News* (San Jose, CA), August 23, 2017.

Stein, Mark A. "On the Button: The Quest to Perfect Botts' Dots Continues." *Los Angeles Times*, August 11, 1991.

Swinford, Steven. "End of the road for cats eyes?" *The Telegraph*, September 4, 2015.

Vanhoenacker, Mark. "Reflections on Things That Go Bump in the Night." *Slate* (blog), January 23, 2014.

Winslow, Jonathan. "Botts' Dots, after a half-century, will disappear from freeways, highways." *The Orange County Register* (Anaheim, CA), May 21, 2017.

### Checkered Past: *Recognition Patterns*

"Chief Constable Sir Percy Sillitoe." *Rotary International, Howe of Fife* (blog), September 26, 2017.

Harrison, Paul. *High Conspicuity Livery for Police Vehicles*. Hertfordshire, UK: Home Office, Police Scientific Development Branch, 2004.

Killeen, John. "The difference between Battenburg high-visibility markings and Sillitoe chequers on Police, Fire & Ambulance vehicles." *Ambulance Visibility* (blog), April 27, 2012.

Scott, Mike. "Designing Police Vehicles: It's Not Just 'Black and White.'" *Government Fleet* (blog), March 18, 2010.

"The Sillitoe Tartan." Glasgow Police Museum website, accessed October 10, 2019.

"Tartan Details—Sillitoe." The Scottish Register of Tartans website, accessed October 11, 2019.

U.S. Fire Administration. *Emergency Vehicle Visibility and Conspicuity Study*. Emmitsburg, MD: U.S. Department of Homeland Security, 2009.

### Memorable but Meaningless: *Warning Symbols*

Baldwin, C. L., and R. S. Runkle. "Biohazards Symbol: Development of a Biological Hazards Warning Signal." *Science* 158, no. 3798 (1967): 264–265.

Cook, John. "Symbol Making." *New York Times Magazine*, November 18, 2001.

Frame, Paul. "Radiation Warning Symbol (Trefoil)." Oak Ridge Associated Universities website, accessed February 4, 2020.

Haubursin, Christophe, Kurt Kohlstedt, and Roman Mars. "Beyond Biohazard: Why Danger Symbols Can't Last Forever." *99% Invisible* and Vox Media, January 26, 2018.

Hora, Steven C., Detlof von Winterfeldt, and Kathleen M. Trauth. *Expert Judgment on Inadvertent Human Intrusion into the Waste Isolation Pilot Plant*. Albuquerque, NM: U.S. Department of Energy, 1991.

Human Interference Task Force. "Reducing the likelihood of future human activities that could affect geologic high-level waste repositories." Report for the Office of Nuclear Waste Isolation, May 1984.

Kielty, Matthew. "114: Ten Thousand Years." *99% Invisible* (podcast and MP3 audio), May 12, 2014.

Lerner, Steve. *Sacrifice Zones: The Front Lines of Toxic Chemical Exposure in the United States*. Cambridge, MA: MIT Press, 2012.

### Signs of Times: *Shelter Markers*

"Abo Elementary School and Fallout Shelter." US National Park Service website, updated December 27, 2017.

"The Abo School." *Atomic Skies* (blog), July 12, 2013.

Kennedy, John F. "Radio and television report to the American people on the Berlin crisis." John F. Kennedy Presidential Library and Museum, July 25, 1961.

Klara, Robert. "Nuclear Fallout Shelters Were Never Going to Work." *History* (blog), September 1, 2018.

McFadden, Robert D. "Obituary: Robert Blakely, Who Created a Sign of the Cold War, Dies at 95." *New York Times,* October 27, 2017.

Mingle, Katie. "121: Cold War Kids." *99% Invisible* (podcast and MP3 audio), July 1, 2014.

## S I G N A G E

### Broad Strokes: *Hand-Painted Graphics*

Fraser, Laura. "The New Sign Painters." *Craftsmanship Quarterly,* Spring 2017.

Levine, Faythe, and Sam Macon. *Sign Painters.* Hudson, NY: Princeton Architectural Press, 2012.

Rich, Sara C. "The Return of the Hand-Painted Sign." *Smithsonian,* November 2, 2012.

Walker, Benjamin. "74: Hand Painted Signs." *99% Invisible* (podcast and MP3 audio), March 8, 2013.

### Tube Benders: *Neon Lights*

Auer, Michael J. "The Preservation of Historic Signs." Preservation Brief 25, for the U.S. National Park Service, October 1991.

Downs, Tom. *Walking San Francisco: 30 Savvy Tours Exploring Steep Streets, Grand Hotels, Dive Bars, and Waterfront Parks.* Berkeley, CA: Wilderness Press, 2008.

Harper, Pat, Janice Neumann, and Barbara Dargis. "Struggle over business signs." *Chicago Tribune,* June 26, 2009.

Ribbat, Christoph. *Flickering Light: A History of Neon.* Translated by Mathews Anthony. London: Reaktion Books, 2013.

Roosblad, Serginho. "San Francisco Was Once Aglow with Neon." *KQED News,* February 8, 2018.

Seelie, Todd. "Oakland's Historic Tribune Tower and the Renegade Artist Who Keeps It Glowing." *Atlas Obscura* (blog), May 6, 2016.

Trufelman, Avery. "193: Tube Benders." *99% Invisible* (podcast and MP3 audio), December 13, 2015.

Tse, Crystal. "Hong Kong Is Slowly Dimming Its Neon Glow." *New York Times,* October 13, 2015.

### Sky Dancers: *Inflatable Figures*

Bettleheim, Judith, and John Nunley. *Caribbean Festival Arts.* Seattle: University of Washington Press, 1988.

Dean, Sam. "Biography of an Inflatable Tube Guy." *Medium* (blog), October 20, 2014.

Greenspan, Sam. "143: Inflatable Men." *99% Invisible.* (podcast and MP3 audio), December 2, 2014.

"INFORMATIONAL LETTER 0019-2009—ATTENTION GETTING DEVICES." City of Houston—Public Works. Effective January 1, 2010.

Laughlin, Nicholas, Attillah Springer, and Georgia Popplewell. "Masman: Peter Minshall." *Caribbean Beat,* May/June 2009.

### Outstanding Directors: *Production Placards*

Ferguson, Kevin. "The story behind LA's mysterious yellow and black filming location signs." *Off-Ramp* (podcast and MP3 audio), January 30, 2015.

Kohlstedt, Kurt. "L.A. Misdirection: Secret Codes on Yellow Filming Location Signs." *99% Invisible* (blog), March 7, 2016.

Millar, Diangelea. "Film set signs specialize in misdirection." *Los Angeles Times,* July 10, 2013.

Roberts, Randall. "Pop duo YACHT talks about yellow film location signs and visual language in 'L.A. Plays Itself.'" *Los Angeles Times,* September 24, 2015.

### Minded Businesses: *Absent Advertising*

Burgoyne, Patrick. "São Paulo: The City That Said No to Advertising." *Bloomberg,* June 18, 2007.

Curtis, Amy. "Five Years After Banning Outdoor Ads, Brazil's Largest City Is More Vibrant Than Ever." *New Dream* (blog), December 8, 2011.

Garfield, Bob. "Clearing the Air." *On the Media* (podcast and MP3 audio), May 29, 2008.

Ghorashi, Hannah. "Tehran's Mayor Replaces Ads on All 1,500 City Billboards with Famous Artworks." *ARTnews,* May 7, 2015.

Leow, Jason. "Beijing Mystery: What's Happening to the Billboards?" *Wall Street Journal,* June 25, 2007.

Mahdawi, Arwa. "Can cities kick ads? Inside the global movement to ban urban billboards." *The Guardian,* August 12, 2015.

Plummer, Robert. "Brazil's ad men face billboard ban." *BBC News,* September 19, 2006.

Queiroz Galvão, Vinícius. "Retirada de outdoors revela favela na avenida 23 de Maio." *Folha de S. Paulo,* April 19, 2007.

Rogers, SA. "Super Clean City: São Paulo Entirely Scrubbed of Outdoor Ads." *WebUrbanist* (blog), March 3, 2010.

"Visual pollution: Advertising firms fret over billboard bans." *The Economist,* October 11, 2007.

Wentz, Laurel. "Sao Paulo's Ingenious Move for Return of Banned Billboards." *AdAge,* October 30, 2017.

Winterstein, Paulo. "Scrub Sao Paulo's Graffiti? Not So Fast, London's Tate Says." *Bloomberg,* August 24, 2008.

## CHAPTER 3: INFRASTRUCTURE

## C I V I C

### Bureaucracy Inaction: *Incidental Bridge*

Henn, Jurgen. "The end of 'Overheight when Flashing.'" *11 FOOT 8* (blog), May 8, 2016.

Henn, Jurgen. "Raising 11foot8." *11 FOOT 8* (blog), accessed January 4, 2020.

Henn, Jurgen. "Very hungry canopener bridge defeats fancy, new warning system." *11 FOOT 8* (blog), July 7, 2016.

Klee, Miles. "Farewell to the Legendary Truck-Destroying Bridge that Captivated a Nation." *Mel Magazine* (blog), accessed February 4, 2020.

Krueger, Sarah. "Durham's 'can opener bridge' being raised." WRAL-TV website, accessed October 28, 2019.

"Section 2C.22 Low Clearance Signs." In *Manual of Uniform Traffic Control Devices*. Federal Highway Administration website, updated February 5, 2017.

### Good Delivery: *Postal Service*

"Benjamin Franklin, First Postmaster General." U.S. Postal Service website, accessed October 23, 2019.

Gallagher, Winifred. *How the Post Office Created America: A History*. New York: Penguin Press, 2016.

"Mail Service and the Civil War." The USPS website.

Mingle, Katie. "244: The Revolutionary Post." *99% Invisible* (podcast and MP3 audio), January 24, 2017.

Ostroff, Hannah S. "In the Grand Canyon, the U.S. Postal Service still delivers mail by mule." *Smithsonian Insider* (blog), August 25, 2016.

Ritholtz, Barry. "Congress, Not Amazon, Messed Up the Post Office." *Bloomberg*, April 4, 2018.

Thomas, JD. "The Postal Act: A Free Press, Personal Privacy and National Growth." The Accessible Archives website, February 20, 2011.

## WATER

### Rounding Down: *Manhole Covers*

Brooks, David. "City inevitably must replace unique triangular manhole covers." *The Telegraph* (Nashua, NH), July 18, 2012.

Camerota, Remo. *Drainspotting: Japanese Manhole Covers*. New York: Mark Batty Publisher, 2010.

Gordenker, Alice. "Manhole covers." *Japan Times*, December 16, 2008.

"Japanese manhole covers: how design became a tool to collect more city taxes." *Brand Backstage* (blog), July 8, 2018.

Bagalye, Rachel. "Art at Your Feet: Japan's Beautiful Manhole Covers." *DIGJAPAN* (blog), April 25, 2016.

Scales, Lauren. "London's History in Manholes." *Londonist* (blog), January 2015.

"A short history of manhole covers." Metro Rod website, December 7, 2017.

Sturdevant, Andy. "Minneapolis' sense of itself revealed in artist-designed manhole covers." *MinnPost*, July 10, 2013.

Williams, David B. "Seattle Map 3 = Manhole Covers." *GeologyWriter* (blog), October 7, 2014.

Wullur, Melissa. "The Story Behind Japanese Manhole Covers." *Wonderland Japan WAttention* (blog), accessed October 8, 2019.

Yasuka. "Contemporary Art: Japanese Manhole Covers." *KPC International* (blog), March 31, 2014.

### Upwardly Potable: *Drinking Fountains*

Ackroyd, Peter. *London Under: The Secret History Beneath the Streets*. New York: Knopf Doubleday Publishing Group, November 2011.

"Benson Bubblers." City of Portland Water Bureau website, May 2013.

Davies, Philip. *Troughs & Drinking Fountains: Fountains of Life*. London: Chatto & Windus, 1989.

Docevski, Bob. "The Great Stink: That time when London was overwhelmed with sewage stench." *The Vintage News* (blog), September 5, 2016.

Gutman, Marta. *A City for Children: Women, Architecture, and the Charitable Landscapes of Oakland, 1850–1950*. Chicago: The University of Chicago Press, 2014.

Mann, Emily. "Story of cities #14: London's Great Stink heralds a wonder of the industrial world." *The Guardian*, April 4, 2016.

Mingle, Katie. "188: Fountain Drinks." *99% Invisible* (podcast and MP3 audio), November 10, 2015.

### Reversing Course: *Waste Management*

Driesen, David M., Robert W. Adler, and Kirsten H. Engel. *Environmental Law: A Conceptual and Pragmatic Approach*. New York: Wolters Kluwer, 2016.

Loe, Claire. "Reversing the Chicago River, Again." *Helix* (blog), February 25, 2015.

Moser, Whet. "Dyeing the Chicago River Green: Its Origins in the Actual Greening of the River." *Chicago Magazine*, March 16, 2012.

O'Carroll, Eoin. "Is the dye in the Chicago River really green?" *Christian Science Monitor*, March 16, 2009.

Sudo, Chuck. "What Are the Property Management Ties to Dyeing the Chicago River Green on St. Patrick's Day?" *Bisnow* (blog), March 9, 2017.

Weissmann, Dan. "86: Reversal of Fortune." *99% Invisible* (podcast and MP3 audio), August 8, 2013.

Williams, Michael, and Richard Cahan. *The Lost Panoramas: When Chicago Changed Its River and the Land Beyond*. Chicago: CityFiles Press, 2011.

### Circling Back: *Subsurface Cisterns*

Dunnigan, Frank. "Streetwise—Water, Water, Everywhere." *Outside Lands* (blog), October 19, 2015.

Pabst, Greg. "In Case of Fire, Look to Twin Peaks." *San Francisco City Guides* (blog), accessed October 15, 2019.

Thompson, Walter. "Century-Old Auxiliary Water Supply System Gets New Ashbury Heights Tank." *Hoodline San Francisco* (blog), January 22, 2015.

Van Dyke, Steve. "San Francisco Fire Department Water Supply System." *Virtual Museum of the City of San Francisco* (blog), accessed October 12, 2019.

"Water Supply Systems." The San Francisco Fire Department website, accessed October 12, 2019.

### Apples to Oysters: *Flood Mitigation*

Environmental Protection Agency. *Summary of the Clean Water Act*. Washington, DC: Government Printing Office, 2019.

FitzGerald, Emmett. "282: Oyster-tecture." *99% Invisible* (podcast and MP3 audio), October 31, 2017.

Greenberg, Paul. *American Catch: The Fight for Our Local Seafood*. New York: Penguin, 2015.

Kurlansky, Mark. *The Big Oyster: History on the Half Shell*. New York: Random House, 2007.

Orff, Kate. *Toward an Urban Ecology*. New York: The Monacelli Press, 2016.

"Our Purpose." *Billion Oyster Project* (blog), accessed February 4, 2020.

## T E C H N O L O G Y
### Fine Lines: *Utility Poles*

Botjer, George. *Samuel F.B. Morse and the Dawn of Electricity.* Washington, DC: Lexington Books, 2015.
Bullard, Gabe. "The Heartbreak That May Have Inspired the Telegraph." *National Geographic,* April 26, 2016.
Lowndes, Coleman. "DC's abandoned fire and police call boxes, explained." Vox website, August 10, 2017.
Mulqueen, April. "A Natural History of the Wooden Telephone Pole." California Public Utilities Commission—Policy and Planning Division website, accessed October 23, 2019.
Updike, John. *Telephone Poles and Other Poems.* New York: Alfred A. Knopf, 1963.
Wildermuth, John. "Why S.F. still counts on street fire alarm." *San Francisco Chronicle,* February 7, 2012.

### Alternated Currents: *Power Grids*

"First Electricity in Los Angeles." *Water and Power Associates* (blog), accessed October 13, 2019.
"L.A. Confidential: Energy's Changing Landscape, Yesterday and Today." *Energy Today* (blog), July 25, 2018.
Masters, Nathan. "Before 1948, LA's Power Grid Was Incompatible with the Rest of the US." *Gizmodo* (blog), February 4, 2015.
Mingle, Katie. "263: You Should Do a Story." *99% Invisible* (podcast and MP3 audio), June 20, 2017.

### Moonlight Towers: *Street Lights*

*Dazed and Confused.* Directed by Richard Linklater. Universal City, CA: Universal Studios, 1993.
Freeberg, Ernest. *The Age of Edison: Electric Light and the Invention of Modern America.* New York: Penguin, 2014.
Oppenheimer, Mark. "Austin's Moon Towers, Beyond 'Dazed and Confused.'" *New York Times,* February 13, 2014.
Prince, Jackson. "The Complete Guide to Austin's Moonlight Towers." *The Austinot* (blog), March 26, 2018.
Thornby, Hanna. "Celebrate the 120th anniversary of Austin's moonlight towers." *All Ablog Austin* (blog), May 19, 2015.
Trufelman, Avery. "150: Under the Moonlight." *99% Invisible* (podcast and MP3 audio), January 27, 2015.

### Dialed Back: *Electricity Meters*

Evans-Brown, Sam, and Logan Shannon. "257: Reversing the Grid." *99% Invisible* (podcast and MP3 audio), May 2, 2017.
Johnstone, Bob. *Switching to Solar: What We Can Learn from Germany's Success in Harnessing Clean Energy.* Blue Ridge Summit, PA: Prometheus Books, 2010.
"Net Metering." Solar Energy Industries Association website, accessed November 9, 2019.

### Network Effects: *Internet Cables*

Burgess, Matt. "Ever wondered how underwater cables are laid? We take a trip on the ship that keeps us online." *Wired,* November 30, 2016.

Edwards, Phil. "A map of all the underwater cables that connect the internet." Vox website, updated November 8, 2015.
*A Journey to the Bottom of the Internet.* YouTube video, December 16, 2016.
"Secrets of Submarine Cables—Transmitting 99 percent of all international data!" NEC Global website, accessed January 4, 2020.
"Submarine Cable Frequently Asked Questions." TeleGeography website, accessed January 4, 2020.
*What's Inside the Undersea Internet Cable?* YouTube video, December 16, 2016.

## R O A D W A Y S
### Accelerating Change: *Painting Centerlines*

Chabot, Larry. "Highway Whodunit." *Marquette Monthly* (blog), May 9, 2018.
Highway Finance Data Collection. *Our Nation's Highways: 2011.* Washington, DC: Federal Highway Administration, 2011.
"Hines, Edward N. (1870–1938)." Michigan Department of Transportation website, accessed October 15, 2019.
Lehto, Steve. "The Man Who Invented 'The Most Important Single Traffic Safety Device.'" *OppositeLock* (blog), January 3, 2015.
*Manual on Uniform Traffic Control Devices.* Washington, DC: Federal Highway Administration, 2003.
Mars, Roman. "68: Built for Speed." *99% Invisible* (podcast and MP3 audio), December 12, 2012.
Robinson, John. "Michigan Hero: Edward N. Hines (1870–1938)." *99.1 WFMK* (blog), August 12, 2018.
Vanderbilt, Tom. *Traffic: Why We Drive the Way We Do (and What It Says About Us).* New York: Vintage, 2009.

### Shifting Responsibility: *Blaming Jaywalkers*

Dukes, Jesse. "76: The Modern Moloch." *99% Invisible* (podcast and MP3 audio), April 4, 2013.
Gangloff, Amy. "The Automobile and American Life (review)." *Technology and Culture* 51, no. 2 (April 2010): 517–518.
Goodyear, Sarah. "The Invention of Jaywalking." *Citylab* (blog), April 24, 2012.
"Nation Roused Against Motor Killings." *New York Times,* November 23, 1924.
Norton, Peter D. *Fighting Traffic.* Cambridge, MA: MIT Press, 2008.

### Key Indicators: *Crash Testing*

Alcorn, Stan. "287: The Nut Behind the Wheel." *99% Invisible* (podcast and MP3 audio), December 5, 2017.
Alcorn, Stan. "Trial and terror." *Reveal* (podcast and MP3 audio), June 24, 2017.
Nader, Ralph. *Unsafe at Any Speed.* New York: Grossman Publishers, 1965.
"Vehicle Safety Technology Has Saved Over 600,000 Lives Since 1960 Says NHTSA." *Global NCAP* (blog), January 26, 2015.

### Cemented Divisions: *Lane Separators*

Giblin, Kelly A. "The Jersey Barrier." *Invention & Technology* 22, no. 1 (Summer 2006).

Kehe, Andy. "Ridge Route history: The long and winding road." *Bakersfield Californian,* September 26, 2015.

Kozel, Scott M. "New Jersey Median Barrier History." Roads to the Future website, updated June 21, 2004.

Petrova, Magdalena. "This machine has eliminated head-on collisions on the Golden Gate Bridge." *CNBC,* February 8, 2018.

### Extra Turns: *Safer Intersections*

Hummer, Joseph E., and Jonathan D. Reid. "Unconventional Left-Turn Alternatives for Urban and Suburban Arterials." Urban Street Symposium website, accessed July 28, 2019.

"Jersey Left." Urban Dictionary website, accessed January 12, 2019.

Kendall, Graham. "Why UPS drivers don't turn left and you probably shouldn't either." *The Conversation* (blog), January 20, 2017.

Mayyasi, Alex. "Why UPS Trucks Don't Turn Left." *Priceonomics* (blog), April 4, 2014.

McFarland, Matt. "The case for almost never turning left while driving." *Washington Post,* April 9, 2014.

"Michigan Lefts." Michigan Department of Transportation website, accessed October 16, 2019.

Najm, Wassim G., John D. Smith, and David L. Smith. *Analysis of Crossing Path Crashes.* Springfield, VA: National Technical Information Service, 2001.

Prisco, Jacopo. "Why UPS trucks (almost) never turn left." *CNN,* February 23, 2017.

"There's Nothing Right About the 'Boston Left.'" *Boston Globe,* May 14, 2006.

### Circulating Logic: *Rotary Junctions*

Beresford, Kevin. "About Us—Roundabouts of Britain." UK Roundabout Appreciation Society website, accessed October 15, 2019.

"Brits Vote on the Best and Worst Roundabouts." *Easier* (blog), December 20, 2005.

Disdale, James. "World's worst junctions." *Auto Express* (blog), September 3, 2007.

"London road junction 'scariest.'" *BBC News,* December 12, 2007.

"The Magic Roundabout." Roads website, accessed October 15, 2019.

Metcalfe, John. "Why Does America Hate Roundabouts?" *Citylab* (blog), March 10, 2016.

"Roundabouts." City of Carmel, Indiana, website, accessed October 15, 2019.

Scott, Tom. *The Magic Roundabout: Swindon's Terrifying Traffic Circle and Emergent Behaviour.* YouTube video, posted January 12, 2015.

User: nick2ny. *Decoding the Magic Roundabout.* YouTube video, October 9, 2014.

### Incomplete Stops: *Calming Traffic*

"Cambridge 'ghost roundabout' attracts ridicule on social media." *BBC News,* November 22, 2016.

"Camcycle requests correction after misrepresentation of our views on Tenison Road scheme by County Council to BBC." *Cambridge Cycling Campaign* (blog), accessed October 19, 2019.

Collins, Tim. "What do YOU see? Optical illusions of speed bumps are being used in London to trick drivers into slowing down." *Daily Mail,* August 7, 2017.

Joyce, Ed. "Sacramento Traffic 'Calming' Takes Many Forms." *Capital Public Radio* (blog), August 20, 2014.

Rogers, SA. "Walk on the Wild Side: 13 Crosswalk Illusions & Interventions." *WebUrbanist* (blog), April 27, 2016.

"Urban Street Design Guide: Vertical Speed Control Elements." National Association of City Transportation Officials website, accessed December 15, 2019.

### Reversing Gears: *Changing Lanes*

Coley, Will. "215: H-Day." *99% Invisible* (podcast and MP3 audio), June 7, 2016.

Geoghegan, Tom. "Could the UK drive on the right?" *BBC News,* September 7, 2009.

"History of the Volvo Car: September 3, 1967. 40 years of driving on the right side in Sweden." The Volvo Owners' Club website, accessed January 16, 2020.

Kincaid, Robert. *The Rule of the Road: An International Guide to History and Practice.* Westport, CT: Greenwood, 1986.

"Samoa switches smoothly to driving on the left." *The Guardian,* September 8, 2009.

The Telstars. "Håll Dej Till Höger, Svensson." Song, 1967.

## PUBLIC

### On Verges: *Interstitial Spaces*

Briggs, Helen. "Roadside verges 'last refuge for wild flowers.'" *BBC News,* June 6, 2015.

"Designing Sidewalks and Trails for Access." Federal Highway Administration Bicycle and Pedestrian Program website, accessed October 16, 2019.

"Green Infrastructure." The City of Portland, Oregon, website, accessed October 19, 2019.

"Pavement History." Pavement Interactive website, accessed October 23, 2019.

### Crossing Over: *Pedestrian Signals*

"Ampelmännchen Is Still Going Places." *Deutsche Welle,* June 16, 2005.

Barkai, Maya. Walking Men Worldwide website, accessed October 19, 2019.

"The development of the East German Ampelmännchen." Ampelmann website, accessed October 19, 2019.

"East German Loses Copyright Battle over Beloved Traffic Symbol." *Deutsche Welle,* June 17, 2006.

Peglau, Karl. "Das Ampelmännchen oder: Kleine östliche Verkehrsgeschichte." Das Buch vom Ampelmännchen, 1997.

Pidd, Helen. "Hats off to Ampelmännchen, 50 today." *The Guardian,* October 13, 2011.

## Sharrowed Routes: *Cycling Lanes*

Alta Planning + Design for the San Francisco Department of Parking & Traffic. "San Francisco's Shared Lane Pavement Markings: Improving Bicycle Safety." Report, February 2004.

"Evaluation of Shared Lane Markings." Federal Highway Administration report, October, 2019.

Ferenchak, Nicholas N., and Wesley Marshall. "The Relative (In)Effectiveness of Bicycle Sharrows on Ridership and Safety Outcomes." Report for the Transportation Research Board's 95th Annual Meeting, 2016.

Getuiza, Cheryl. "Oakland introduces color to bike lanes to increase safety." California Economic Summit, September 25, 2013.

"How the SFMTA Invented—and Named—the Bike 'Sharrow.'" *San Francisco Municipal Transportation Agency* (blog), June 17, 2016.

Powers, Martine. "New 'sharrows on steroids' debut on Allston's Brighton Ave." Boston.com website, November 20, 2013.

Schmitt, Angie. "American Sharrow Inventor: 'I Was Always Under Pressure to Do Less.'" *StreetsBlog USA,* March 10, 2016.

## Congestion Costs: *Easing Gridlock*

Coffey, Helen. "Paris to Ban Cars in City Centre One Sunday a Month." *The Independent,* October 3, 2018.

"Congestion Charge." Transport for London website, accessed October 21, 2019.

"Great City Master Plan Chengdu." Adrian Smith + Gordon Gill Architecture website, accessed October 20, 2019.

"Grünes Netz." Hamburg.de website, accessed October 20, 2019.

Marshall, Aarian. "Downtown Manhattan Is the New Frontier of the Car-Free City." *Wired,* August 13, 2016.

*Paris Sans Voiture* (blog), accessed October 19, 2019.

Peters, Adele. "Paris Is Redesigning Its Major Intersections for Pedestrians, Not Cars." *Fast Company,* April 8, 2016.

Renn, Aaron M. "When New York City tried to ban cars—the extraordinary story of 'Gridlock Sam.'" *The Guardian,* June 1, 2016.

"Superblocks." Ajuntament de Barcelona—Ecology, Urban Planning and Mobility website, accessed October 21, 2019.

Willsher, Kim. "Paris divided: two-mile highway by Seine goes car-free for six months." *The Guardian,* September 9, 2016.

## Extravehicular Activities: *Naked Streets*

Edquist, Jessica, and Bruce Corben. "Potential application of Shared Space principles in urban road design: effects on safety and amenity." Monash University Accident Research Centre report to the NRMA-ACT Road Safety Trust, March 2012.

Frosch, Colin, David Martinelli, and Avinash Unnikrishnan. "Evaluation of Shared Space to Reduce Traffic Congestion." *Journal of Advanced Transportation* (2019).

Goodyear, Sarah. "Lots of Cars and Trucks, No Traffic Signs or Lights: Chaos or Calm?" *Citylab* (blog), April 2, 2013.

Haubursin, Christophe, Kurt Kohlstedt, and Roman Mars. "Road signs suck. What if we got rid of them all?" *99% Invisible* and Vox Media, November 24, 2017.

Mihaly, Warwick. "Naked streets." *Streets Without Cars* (blog), January 24, 2014.

Moody, Simon. "Shared space—research, policy and problems." *Proceedings of the Institute of Civil Engineers-Transport* 167, no. 6 (2014): 384–92.

Nyvig, Ramboll. "Shared Space >>> Safe Space: Meeting the requirements of blind and partially sighted people in a shared space." Report for the Guide Dogs for the Blind Association and Danish Building Research Institute, accessed October 2, 2019.

"'Shared' road schemes paused over dangers to blind people." *BBC News,* July 27, 2018.

Toth, Gary. "Where the Sidewalk Doesn't End: What Shared Space Has to Share." Project for Public Spaces website, August 16, 2009.

## CHAPTER 4: ARCHITECTURE

## LIMINAL

### Imperfect Security: *Locked Entries*

Greenspan, Sam. "160: Perfect Security." *99% Invisible* (podcast and MP3 audio), April 14, 2015.

Phillips, Bill. *Locksmith and Security Professionals' Exam Study Guide.* New York: McGraw Hill, 2009.

Towne, Schuyler. "Rethinking the Origins of the Lock." *Schuyler Towne* (blog), accessed October 21, 2019.

Vanderbilt, Tom. "Alfred C. Hobbs: The American who shocked Victorian England by picking the world's strongest lock." *Slate,* March 11, 2013.

### Open and Shut: *Revolving Doors*

Cullum, B. A., Olivia Lee, Sittha Sukkasi, and Dan Wesolowski. "Modifying Habits Towards Sustainability—A Study of Revolving Door Usage on the MIT Campus." Report for Planning for Sustainable Development, May 25, 2006.

"Deadliest U.S. nightclub fire influences safety codes, burn care." *CBS News,* November 28, 2017.

Grant, Casey E. "Last Dance at the Cocoanut Grove." *NFPA Journal* 101, no. 6 (2007): 46–71.

Greenspan, Sam. "93: Revolving Doors." *99% Invisible* (podcast and MP3 audio), November 6, 2013.

"The Story of the Cocoanut Grove Fire." Boston Fire Historical Society website, accessed July 2, 2019.

### Improved Egress: *Emergency Exits*

"Keep a Fire-Escape Under the Window-Sill." *Popular Science Monthly,* December 1918.

Lynch, Timothy D. "Deterioration of the Historic Construction & Prior Codes—How They Mesh." IES—Investigative Engineering Services course outline, October 22, 2015.

"Triangle Shirtwaist Factory Fire." The History Channel website, December 2, 2009.

Trufelman, Avery. "122: Good Egress." *99% Invisible* (podcast and MP3 audio), August 8, 2014.

"U.S. Census Bureau History: The Triangle Shirtwaist Fire." U.S. Census Bureau website, March 2016.

Young, Lauren. "The Creative and Forgotten Fire Escape Designs of the 1800s." *Atlas Obscura* (blog), December 9, 2016.

## MATERIALS

### Stolen Facades: *Recycling Brick*

Dyer, Zach. "283: Dollhouses of St. Louis." *99% Invisible* (podcast and MP3 audio), November 7, 2017.

Gay, Malcolm. "Thieves Cart Off St. Louis Bricks." *New York Times,* September 19, 2010.

Hayden, Liz. "St. Louis' Brick Paradox." *Urbanist Dispatch* (blog), January 28, 2014.

"The History of Bricks and Brickmaking." *Brick Architecture* (blog), accessed October 21, 2019.

### Aggregate Effects: *Cracking Concrete*

Beiser, Vince. *The World in a Grain: The Story of Sand and How It Transformed Civilization.* New York: Riverhead Books, 2018.

Courland, Robert. *Concrete Planet: The Strange and Fascinating Story of the World's Most Common Man-Made Material.* Buffalo, NY: Prometheus, 2011.

Davis, Nicola. "Why Roman concrete still stands strong while modern version decays." *The Guardian,* July 4, 2017.

Forty, Adrian. *Concrete and Culture: A Material History.* London: Reaktion Books, 2012.

Huxtable, Ada Louise. *On Architecture: Collected Reflections on a Century of Change.* New York: Bloomsbury Publishing, 2010.

Jackson, Marie D., et al. "Phillipsite and Al-tobermorite mineral cements produced through low-temperature water-rock reactions in Roman marine concrete." *American Mineralogist* 102, no. 7 (2017): 1435–50.

Mars, Roman. "81: Rebar and the Alvord Lake Bridge." *99% Invisible* (podcast and MP3 audio), June 7, 2013.

Mars, Roman. "361: Built on Sand." *99% Invisible* (podcast and MP3 audio), July 9, 2019.

Neyfekh, Leon. "How Boston City Hall was born." *Boston Globe,* February 12, 2012.

Pasnik, Mark, Chris Grimley, and Michael Kubo. *Heroic: Concrete Architecture and the New Boston.* New York: Monacelli Press, 2015.

Stewart, Andrew. "The 'living concrete' that can heal itself." *CNN,* March 7, 2015.

Trufelman, Avery. "176: Hard to Love a Brute." *99% Invisible* (podcast and MP3 audio), August 11, 2015.

### Hybrid Solutions: *Amassing Timber*

"Brock Commons Tallwood House: Design and Preconstruction Overview." Naturally:Wood website, 2016.

"CLT Gets Double Boost: ICC Clears Path for Taller Mass Timber Buildings in the U.S., Plus Overall Demand for CLT Predicted to Grow Significantly." *TimberLine,* March 1, 2019.

"Demonstrating the viability of mass wood structures." *Think Wood* (blog), accessed October 21, 2019.

"A Guide to Engineered Wood Products." The Engineered Wood Association website, accessed October 16, 2019.

Gul Hasan, Zoya. "Inside Vancouver's Brock Commons, the World's Tallest Mass Timber Building." *ArchDaily* (blog), September 18, 2017.

Kohlstedt, Kurt. "Branching Out: Sustainable Wood Skyscrapers Continue to Reach New Heights." *99% Invisible* (blog), October 30, 2017.

Pyati, Archana. "Faster Project Delivery Is a Hidden Feature of Sustainable Mass Timber." *UrbanLand,* May 3, 2017.

Quintal, Becky. "Wooden Skyscraper/Berg|C. F. Møller Architects with Dinnell Johansson." *ArchDaily* (blog), June 17, 2013.

## REGULATIONS

### Secular Orders: *Taxable Units*

"Brick Tax 1784–1850." Scottish Brick History website, accessed October 21, 2019.

Howell, Jeff. "On the level: building tax." *The Telegraph,* July 31, 2002.

Hurst-Vose, Ruth. *Glass.* New York: Collins, 1980.

Janse, Herman. *Building Amsterdam.* London: Egmont, 1994.

Kohlstedt, Kurt. "Vernacular Economics: How Building Codes & Taxes Shape Regional Architecture." *99% Invisible* (blog), January 22, 2018.

"The narrowest houses in Amsterdam." Holland.com website, accessed October 25, 2019.

Sullivan, Paul. *Little Book of Oxfordshire.* Cheltenham, UK: The History Press, 2012.

Theobald, Mary Miley. "Stuff and Nonsense: Myths That Should Now Be History." The Colonial Williamsburg Foundation website, accessed October 21, 2019.

"Window Tax." The National Archives website, accessed October 21, 2019.

### Formative Setbacks: *Mansard Roofs*

Bassett, Edward Murray. "Commission on Building Districts and Restrictions: Final Report." City of New York Board of Estimate and Apportionment, 1916.

Chey, Katy. *Multi-Unit Housing in Urban Cities: From 1800 to Present Day.* Milton Park, UK: Taylor & Francis, 2017.

Goodman, David C., and Colin Chant. *European Cities & Technology: Industrial to Post-industrial City.* Milton Park, UK: Routledge, 1999.

Stark, Stuart. "The Mansard Style: Politics, Tax Evasion and Beauty." *Old House Living* (blog), accessed October 25, 2019.

Willsher, Kim. "Story of cities #12: Haussmann rips up Paris—and divides France to this day." *The Guardian,* March 21, 2016.

### Heaven to Hell: *Property Limits*

"Airmail Creates an Industry: Postal Act Facts." Smithsonian National Postal Museum website, accessed October 22, 2019.

"A Brief History of the FAA." Federal Aviation Administration website.

"*Bury v Pope*: 1587." Swarb.co.uk website.

Goldberger, Paul. "Architecture View; Theaters and Churches Are the City's New Battleground." *New York Times,* May 30, 1982.

Kohlstedt, Kurt. "From Heaven to Hell: Exploring the Odd Vertical Limits of Land Ownership." *99% Invisible* (blog), June 19, 2017.

Kohlstedt, Kurt. "Selling the Sky: 'Air Rights' Take Strange Bites Out of Big Apple Architecture." *99% Invisible* (blog), June 23, 2017.

Lashbrook, Lora D. "Ad Coelum Maxim as Applied to Aviation Law." *Notre Dame Law Review* 21, no. 3 (1946).

Lowther, Ed. "Location, salvation, damnation." *BBC News,* January 29, 2014.

Quintana, Mariela. "What Are NYC Air Rights All About?" *StreetEasy* (blog), October 12, 2015.

"Special Purpose Districts." NYC Department of City Planning website, accessed October 22, 2019.

Tong, Ziya. *The Reality Bubble: Blind Spots, Hidden Truths, and the Dangerous Illusions That Shape Our World.* New York: Penguin, 2019.

*United States v. Causby,* 328 U.S. 256 (1946).

User: filthy light thief. "Cuius est solum, eius est usque ad coelum et ad inferos." *MetaFilter* (blog), July 16, 2018.

"What Are 'Air Rights' and Why Are They Important to Central?" *Los Angeles Public Library* (blog), February 10, 2017.

## TOWERS

### Braking Good: *Modern Elevators*

Carroll, Andrew. "Here Is Where: Elisha Otis rises out of small-town Vermont." HistoryNet website, accessed February 2, 2020.

DiMeo, Nate. "98: Six Stories." *99% Invisible* (podcast and MP3 audio), January 2, 2014.

"Facts & Figures." Burj Khalifa website, accessed February 14, 2019.

Robbins, Dan. "Founded in Yonkers, Otis Elevators Took American Industry to New Heights." *Westchester Magazine* website, accessed September 20, 2019.

### Cladding Skeletons: *Curtain Walls*

Dimeo, Nate. "27: Bridge to the Sky." *99% Invisible* (podcast and MP3 audio), June 3, 2011.

Gray, Christopher. "Streetscapes/The Tower Building: The Idea That Led to New York's First Skyscraper." *New York Times,* May 5, 1996.

"Monadnock Building." Chicagology website, accessed October 25, 2019.

Morris, Lloyd. *Incredible New York: High Life and Low Life from 1850 to 1950.* Syracuse, NY: Syracuse University Press, 1996.

### Topping Out: *Skyscraper Races*

Bascomb, Neal. *Higher: A Historic Race to the Sky and the Making of a City.* New York: Broadway Books, 2004.

Gray, Christopher. "Streetscapes: 40 Wall Street; A Race for the Skies, Lost by a Spire." *New York Times,* November 15, 1992.

Mars, Roman. "100: Higher and Higher." *99% Invisible* (podcast and MP3 audio), February 3, 2014.

### Unanticipated Loads: *Managing Crises*

Bellows, Alan. "A Potentially Disastrous Design Error." *Damn Interesting* (blog), April 12, 2006.

Morgenstern, Joe. "City Perils: The Fifty-Nine Story Crisis." *The New Yorker,* May 29, 1995.

"OEC—Addendum: The Diane Hartley Case." The Online Ethics Center website, accessed March 13, 2019.

Werner, Joel, and Sam Greenspan. "110: Structural Integrity." *99% Invisible* (podcast and MP3 audio), April 15, 2014.

### Perspective Matters: *Redefining Skylines*

"History." Transamerica Pyramid Center website, accessed October 20, 2019.

King, John. "An ode to the Transamerica Pyramid as a new tallest tower rises." *San Francisco Chronicle,* October 7, 2016.

King, John. "Pyramid's steep path from civic eyesore to icon." SFGate website, December 27, 2009.

Mars, Roman. "2: 99% 180." *99% Invisible* (podcast and MP3 audio), September 9, 2010.

### Beyond Above: *Engineering Icons*

"Experience the Skyslide at OUE Skyspace Los Angeles." Discover Los Angeles website, accessed February 2, 2020.

Poon, Dennis, Shaw-Song Shieh, Leonard Joseph, and Ching-Chang Chang. "Structural Design of Taipei 101, World's Tallest Building." Research paper presented at the Council on Tall Buildings and Urban Habitat 2004 Seoul Conference, October 10–13.

"Taipei Financial Center (Taipei 101)." C. Y. Lee & Partners website, accessed October 22, 2019.

Trufelman, Avery. "201: Supertall 101." *99% Invisible* (podcast and MP3 audio), April 19, 2016.

### Grouped Dynamics: *Street Canyons*

"Bridgewater Place lorry crush death referred to CPS by coroner." *BBC News,* February 10, 2012.

ChiFai, Cheung, and Ernest Kao. "Scientists examine the health risks of Hong Kong's notorious 'street canyons.'" *South China Morning Post,* October 13, 2014.

Kiprop, Victor. "What Is a Street Canyon?" World Atlas website, accessed October 22, 2019.

Kulig, Paul. "Seeking Sunlight in a Skyscraper City." *CityLab* (blog), May 1, 2017.

"London's 'Walkie Talkie' skyscraper reflects light hot enough to fry an egg." *The Guardian,* September 3, 2013.

Mullin, Emma. "No more Walkie Scorchie! London skyscraper which melted cars by reflecting sunlight is fitted with shading." *Daily Mail Online,* October 9, 2014.

Rao, Joe. "The Story of 'Manhattanhenge': An NYC Phenomenon Explained." Space.com website, May 19, 2018.

Spillane, Chris, and Eshe Nelson. "London's Walkie-Talkie 'Fryscraper' Draws Crowds in Heat." *Bloomberg,* September 6, 2013.

Stuart, Andrew. "Why does the Beetham Tower hum in the wind?" *Manchester Evening News,* March 2, 2018.

Tanner, Jane. "Sears Loses Windows in High Winds." *Chicago Tribune,* February 23, 1988.

Tyson, Neil deGrasse. "Manhattanhenge." *American Museum of Natural History* (blog), accessed October 22, 2019.

"Urban Street Canyons—Wind." MIT student projects, 2009.

Wainwright, Oliver. "'Killer towers': how architects are battling hazardous high-rises." *The Guardian Architecture and Design Blog,* August 14, 2014.

Ward, Victoria. "Walkie Talkie skyscraper blamed for creating wind tunnel on the street." *The Telegraph,* July 22, 2015.

## FOUNDATIONS

### Vernacular Enclaves: *International Districts*

Davis, Chelsea. "192: Pagodas and Dragon Gates." *99% Invisible* (podcast and MP3 audio), December 8, 2015.

Lee, Jennifer 8. *The Fortune Cookie Chronicles: Adventures in the World of Chinese Food.* New York: Hachette Book Group, 2009.

Reeves, Richard. *Infamy: The Shocking Story of the Japanese American Internment in World War II.* New York: Henry Holt and Co., 2015.

Trufelman, Avery. "182: A Sweet Surprise Awaits You." *99% Invisible* (podcast and MP3 audio), September 22, 2015.

Tsui, Bonnie. *American Chinatown: A People's History of Five Neighborhoods.* New York: Free Press, 2010.

### Reality Checks: *Service Centers*

Mars, Roman. "18: Check Cashing Stores." *99% Invisible* (podcast and MP3 audio), March 4, 2011.

McGray, Douglas. "Check Cashers, Redeemed." *New York Times Magazine,* November 7, 2008.

Nix, Tom. *Nixland: My Wild Ride in the Inner City Check Cashing Industry.* Irvine, CA: BusinessGhost Books, 2013.

### Approachable Ducks: *Commercial Signifiers*

Al, Stefan. *The Strip: Las Vegas and the Architecture of the American Dream.* Cambridge, MA: MIT Press, 2017.

DylanDog. "Ducks and decorated sheds." Everything2.com website, accessed October 2, 2019.

Green, Dennis. "Nobody wants to buy this $5 million basket-shaped building in Ohio." *Business Insider,* September 8, 2016.

Hill, John. "Of Ducks and Decorated Sheds: A Review of I Am a Monument." *Architect,* July 31, 2009.

Ketcham, Diane. "About Long Island; A Cherished Roadside Symbol of the Region." *New York Times,* July 30, 1995.

Mallett, Kate. "Longaberger empties famous basket building." *Newark Advocate,* July 8, 2016.

Trex, Ethan. "10 Buildings Shaped Like What They Sell." *Mental Floss* (blog), November 16, 2010.

Trufelman, Avery. "302: Lessons from Las Vegas." *99% Invisible* (podcast and MP3 audio), April 9, 2018.

Venturi, Robert, Steven Izenour, and Denise Scott Brown. *Learning from Las Vegas: The Forgotten Symbolism of Architectural Form.* Cambridge, MA: MIT Press, 1977.

## Competitive Starchitecture: *Contrasting Additions*

Dickinson, Elizabeth Evitts. "Louvre Pyramid: The Folly That Became a Triumph." *Architect,* April 19, 2017.

Jones, Sam. "'What the hell have they done?' Spanish castle restoration mocked." *The Guardian,* March 9, 2016.

Kohlstedt, Kurt. "Legible Cities: Fitting Outstanding Architecture into Everyday Contexts." *99% Invisible* (blog), August 25, 2016.

Loomans, Taz. "Why Fake Vintage Buildings Are a Blow to Architecture, Historic Neighborhoods and the Character of a City." *Blooming Rock* (blog), June 4, 2014.

TheOneInTheHat. "That's the last time we hire TWO architects." Reddit website, December 18, 2011.

Pavka, Evan. "AD Classics: Jewish Museum, Berlin/Studio Libeskind." *ArchDaily* (blog), November 25, 2010.

Pogrebin, Robin. "British Architect Wins 2007 Pritzker Prize." *New York Times,* March 28, 2007.

"Royal Ontario Museum opens Michael Lee-Chin Crystal Today." Royal Ontario Museum website, June 2, 2007.

Tschumi, Bernard. *Architecture and Disjunction.* Cambridge, MA: MIT Press, 1996.

Yasunaga, Yodai. "Old & New: Can Contemporary and Historical Architecture Exist?" *MKThink* (blog), August 1, 2014.

## HERITAGE

### Heathen's Gate: *Overlapping Narratives*

Downson, Thomas. "Three Ingenious Achaeological 'Re-Constructions.'" *Archaeology Travel* (blog), accessed October 2, 2019.

Kirsch, Jonathan. *God Against the Gods: The History of the War Between Monotheism and Polytheism.* New York: Viking, 2004.

Norris, Shawn T. "Carnuntum—A City of Emperors." Rome Across Europe website, October 4, 2015.

### Landmark Ruling: *Historic Preservation*

"About LPC." The New York Landmarks Preservation Commission website, accessed October 15, 2019.

"Action Group for Better Architecture in New York." The New York Preservation Archive Project website, accessed October 2, 2019.

Heppermann, Ann. "147: Penn Station Sucks." *99% Invisible* (podcast and MP3 audio), January 6, 2015.

Jonnes, Jill. *Conquering Gotham: Building Penn Station and Its Tunnels.* New York: Penguin Books, 2008.

Muschamp, Herbert. "Architecture View; In This Dream Station Future and Past Collide." *New York Times,* June 20, 1993.

*Penn Central Transportation Co. v. New York City,* 438 U.S. 104 (1978).

Quintana, Mariela. "What Are NYC Air Rights All About?" *StreetEasy* (blog), October 12, 2015.

Williams, Keith. "What Is That Spot on the Ceiling of Grand Central Terminal?" *New York Times,* June 7, 2018.

## Recrowned Jewel: *Complex Restoration*

"Bright look for ancient castle." *BBC News—Scotland,* October 19, 1999.

Bryson, Bill. *At Home: A Short History of Private Life.* New York: Anchor Books, 2011.

Mars, Roman. "178: The Great Restoration." *99% Invisible* (podcast and MP3 audio), August 25, 2015.

"Restoration work has turned the golden great hall into white elephant, claim townsfolk Stirling effort under fire." *Herald Scotland,* April 21, 1999.

"Stirling Castle: Castle Wynd, Stirling, FK8 1EJ." Historic Environment Scotland website, accessed November 28, 2019.

"Stirling Castle Timeline." Stirling Castle website, accessed October 11, 2019.

Talbot, Margaret. "The Myth of Whiteness in Classical Sculpture." *The New Yorker,* October 29, 2018.


## Architectural License: *Faithless Reconstruction*

Drozdowska, Amy, and Dave McGuire. "72: New Old Town." *99% Invisible* (podcast and MP3 audio), February 5, 2013.

Gliński, Mikołaj. "How Warsaw Came Close to Never Being Rebuilt." *Culture.pl* (blog), February 3, 2015.

McCouat, Philip. "Bernardo Bellotto and the Reconstruction of Warsaw." *Journal of Art in Society,* 2015.

Mersom, Daryl. "Story of cities #28: how postwar Warsaw was rebuilt using 18th century paintings." *The Guardian,* May 11, 2018.

"Trakt Królewski." Zabytki w Warszawie website, accessed October 29, 2019.

Zarecor, Kimberly E. "Architecture in Eastern Europe and the Former Soviet Union." In *A Critical History of Contemporary Architecture, 1960–2010,* edited by Elie G. Haddad and David Rifkind. Farnham, UK: Ashgate Publishing, 2014.


## Unnatural Selection: *Subjective Stabilization*

Cooper, Paul. "Rome's Colosseum Was Once a Wild, Tangled Garden." *The Atlantic,* December 5, 2017.

Dickens, Charles. *Pictures from Italy.* London: Bradbury & Evans, 1846.

FitzGerald, Emmett. "289: Mini-Stories: Volume 3: The Green Colosseum." *99% Invisible* (podcast and MP3 audio), December 19, 2017.

"Issues Relevant to U.S. Foreign Diplomacy: Unification of Italian States." Office of the Historian website, accessed January 5, 2020.

Poe, Edgar A. "The Coliseum." In *The Works of Edgar Allan Poe, The Raven Edition,* vol. 5. New York: P. F. Collier and Son, 1903.


## Faded Attraction: *Alluring Abandonments*

"A History of the Sutro Pleasure Grounds and Merrie Way Stands." Sonoma State University website.

Martini, John A. *Sutro's Glass Palace: The Story of Sutro Baths.* Bodega Bay, CA: Hole in the Head Press, 2013.

*Sutro Baths.* Directed by James H. White. San Francisco: Edison Manufacturing Company, 1897.

"Sutro Baths History." National Park Service website, updated February 28, 2015.

Trufelman, Avery. "112: Young Ruin." *99% Invisible* (podcast and MP3 audio), April 29, 2014.


## Runed Landscapes: *Peripheral Traces*

Cooper, Paul M. M. "The Mysterious Landscapes of Heat-Scorched Britain." *New York Times,* August 15, 2018.

Dockrill, Peter. "Brutal Heat in the UK Is Revealing Hidden Footprints of Historic Civilisations." Scient Alert website, July 11, 2018.

"Hidden landscapes the heatwave is revealing." *BBC News,* July 25, 2018.

"UK heatwave exposes ancient Chatsworth House gardens." *BBC News,* July 25, 2018.

Victor, Daniel. "Drought and Drone Reveal 'Once-in-a-Lifetime' Signs of Ancient Henge in Ireland." *New York Times,* July 13, 2018.


## Unbuilding Codes: *Premeditated Deconstruction*

Brasor, Philip, and Masako Tsubuku. "Japan's 30-year building shelf-life is not quite true." *Japan Times,* March 31, 2014.

"High-Tech Demolition Systems for High-rises." *Web Japan—Trends in Japan* (blog), March 2013.

"The Kajima Cut and Take Down Method." Kajima Corporation website, accessed October 23, 2019.

Kohlstedt, Kurt. "Earth Defense: Shaking Buildings in the World's Largest Earthquake Simulator." *99% Invisible* (blog), March 20, 2017.

Nuwer, Rachel. "This Japanese Shrine Has Been Torn Down and Rebuilt Every 20 Years for the Past Millennium." *Smithsonian,* October 4, 2013.

Townsend, Alastair. "Testing Buildings to Destruction." *Alatown* (blog), February 19, 2015.

"Why Japanese houses have such limited lifespans." *The Economist,* March 15, 2018.


## CHAPTER 5: GEOGRAPHY

### DELINEATIONS

## Points of Origin: *Zero Markers*

"Cuba's Famous Diamond Stolen from Capital." *The Barrier Miner,* March 27, 1946.

Grout, James. "Milliarium Aureum." Encyclopedia Romana website, accessed October 20, 2019.

Kohlstedt, Kurt. "Point Zero: Circling the Globe with Central City 'Zero Stones.'" *99% Invisible* (blog), August 11, 2016.

"Nuestra Señora de Luján, Patrona de la República Argentina." Agencia Informativa Católica Argentina website, accessed October 20, 2019.

Rubenstein, Steve. "SF marks the very middle of town, more or less." SFGate website, June 8, 2016.

Saperstein, Susan. "Sutro's Triumph of Light Statue." *Guidelines Newsletter,* accessed October 20, 2019.

Weingroff, Richard F. "Zero Milestone—Washington, DC." National Highway Administration website, June 27, 2017.

## Edge Cases: *Boundary Stones*

"Boundary Stones of the District of Columbia." Boundary Stones website.
Manaugh, Geoff. "Boundary Stones and Capital Magic." *BLDGBLOG,* May 20, 2017.
*Records of the Columbia Historical Society of Washington, D.C.* Vol. 10. Washington, DC: Historical Society of Washington, DC, 1907.
St. Onge, Tim. "Modest Monuments: The District of Columbia Boundary Stones." *Geography and Map Division of the Library of Congress* (blog), May 17, 2017.
Vitka, William. "Quest to save DC's 1st federal monuments: Boundary stones." *Washington Times,* April 15, 2018.

## Defining Moments: *Standardized Time*

Bartky, Ian R. *Selling the True Time: Nineteenth-century Timekeeping in America.* Redwood City, CA: Stanford University Press, 2000.
*Dinsmore's American Railroad and Steam Navigation Guide and Route-Book.* New York: Dinsmore & Co., 1800.
Myers, Joseph. "History of legal time in Britain." Polyomino website.
Powell, Alvin. "America's first time zone." *Harvard Gazette,* November 10, 2011.
"Railroads create the first time zones." The History Channel website, updated July 17, 2019.
Reed, Robert Carroll. *Train Wrecks: A Pictorial History of Accidents on the Main Line.* Prineville, OR: Bonanza Books, 1982.
"Russia Turns Clocks Back to 'Winter' Time." Sputnik News website, October 26, 2014.
"Time Standardization." The Linda Hall Library Transcontinental Railroad website, accessed October 20, 2019.
"Uniform Time." US Department of Transportation website, updated February 13, 2015.
"Why Do We Have Time Zones?" Time and Date website.

## Road Boosters: *National Highways*

"Futurama: 'Magic City of Progress.'" The New York Public Library's website, accessed October 20, 2019.
Hirst, AR. "Marking and Mapping the Wisconsin Trunk Line Highway System." *Good Roads: Devoted to the Construction and Maintenance of Roads and Streets* 55, no. 2 (1919).
"History and Significance of US Route 66." National Park Service's website, accessed December 26, 2019.
Lawson, Wayne. "The Woman Who Saved New York City from Superhighway Hell." *Vanity Fair,* April 14, 2017.
Pfeiffer, David A. "Ike's Interstates at 50." *Prologue Magazine* 38, no. 2 (2006).
Weingroff, Richard F. "From Names to Numbers: The Origins of the U.S. Numbered Highway System." Federal Highway Administration website, updated June 27, 2017.

## CONFIGURATIONS

### Rounding Errors: *Jeffersonian Grids*

California Land Title Association's Claims Awareness Committee. "Filling the Holes in a 'Swiss Cheese Parcel': Correcting Flawed Metes & Bounds Descriptions." Wendel Rosen website, March 7, 2018.
Corner, James. *Taking Measures Across the American Landscape.* New Haven, CT: Yale University Press, 1996.
Delpeut, Peter. *Gerco de Ruijter: Grid Corrections.* Rotterdam: nai010 publishers, 2019.
Knight, Paul. "A History of the American Grid in 4 Minutes." *The Great American Grid* (blog), January 9, 2012.
Land Ordinance of 1785. May 20, 1785.
Manaugh, Geoff. "Mysterious Detour While Driving? It Could Be Due to the Curvature of the Earth." *Travel + Leisure,* December 10, 2015.

### Unassigned Lands: *Patchwork Plans*

Anderson, Sam. *Boom Town: The Fantastical Saga of Oklahoma City, Its Chaotic Founding, Its Apocalyptic Weather, Its Purloined Basketball Team, and the Dream of Becoming a World-class Metropolis.* New York: Crown Publishing Group, 2018.
Blackburn, Bob L. "Unassigned Lands." Encyclopedia of Oklahoma History and Culture website, accessed October 20, 2019.
Mars, Roman. "325: The Worst Way to Start a City." *99% Invisible* (podcast and MP3 audio), October 16, 2018.
"Removal of Tribes to Oklahoma." Oklahoma Historical Society website, accessed February 5, 2020.

### Rectilinear Revelations: *Coordinated Layouts*

Dagenais, Travis. "Why city blocks work." *Harvard Gazette,* January 9, 2017.
Dalrymple II, Jim. "Urban designers in Salt Lake City praise innovations of the 'Mormon Grid.'" *Salt Lake Tribune,* June 13, 2013.
"Granary Row: Shipping Container Pop-up Market Jump-Starts Industrial Neighborhood in Salt Lake City." *Inhabitat* (blog), August 31, 2013.
Greenspan, Sam. "240: Plat of Zion." *99% Invisible* (podcast and MP3 audio), December 12, 2016.
Speck, Jeff. *Walkable City: How Downtown Can Save America, One Step at a Time.* New York: North Point Press, 2013.
Williams, Frederick G. "Revised Plat of the City of Zion, circa Early August 1833." The Joseph Smith Papers website, accessed October 20, 2019.

### Good Eixamples: *Reconfigured Superblocks*

Bausells, Marta. "Superblocks to the rescue: Barcelona's plan to give streets back to residents." *The Guardian,* May 17, 2016.
De Decker, Kris. "The solar envelope: how to heat and cool cities without fossil fuels." Low-Tech Magazine website, accessed January 20, 2020.
Roberts, David. "Barcelona's radical plan to take back streets from cars." Vox website, updated May 26, 2019.

Soria y Puig, Arturo. "Ildefonso Cerdà's general theory of 'Urbanización.'" *The Town Planning Review* 66, no. 1 (1995).
Southworth, Michael, and Eran Ben-Joseph. *Streets and the Shaping of Towns and Cities.* Washington, DC: Island Press, 2013.
"The Urban Mobility Plan of Barcelona." The Urban Ecology Agency of Barcelona website, accessed September 22, 2019.
"The Visionary Urban Design of the Eixample District, Barcelona." *Latitude 41* (blog), January 10, 2019.

### Standard Deviations: *Growth Patterns*

"8 Mile Road is eight miles from where?" Michigan Radio website, October 4, 2014.
*Detroit's Pattern of Growth.* Directed by Robert J. Goodman and Gordon W. Draper. Detroit: Wayne State University Audio-Visual Utilization Center, 1965.
"The Explorers: Antoine Laumet dit de la Mothe Cadillac 1694–1701." Canadian Museum of History website, accessed October 20, 2019.
Sewek, Paul. "Woodward Plan Part II: Dawn of the Radial City." *Detroit Urbanism* (blog), April 25, 2016.

## DESIGNATIONS

### Citations Needed: *Informal Geonyms*

"Busta Rhymes Island." Wikipedia entry, accessed January 6, 2020.
Cole, Sean. "105: One Man Is an Island." *99% Invisible* (podcast and MP3 audio), March 11, 2014.
"House Approves Renaming Cape Kennedy." *Daytona Beach Morning Journal,* May 19, 1973.
Reed, James. "Sound off." *Boston Globe,* March 13, 2009.
"U.S. Board on Geographic Names." United States Geological Survey website, accessed October 28, 2019.

### Hybrid Acronames: *Neighborhood Monikers*

Carroll, Ruaidhri. "How Did London's Soho Get Its Name?" *Culture Trip* (blog), updated June 7, 2018.
"Graduate Hospital." Visit Philadelphia website, accessed October 12, 2019.
"Hell's Hundred Acres." *New York History Walks* (blog), March 14, 2012.
Mahdawi, Arwa. "Neighbourhood rebranding: wanna meet in LoHo, CanDo or GoCaGa?" *The Guardian,* January 15, 2015.
Nigro, Carmen. "A Helluva Town: The Origins of New York's Hellish Place Names." *New York Public Library—NYC Neighbors* (blog), April 22, 2011.
NOBENeighborhood.com (website). Inaccessible.
*South Park,* episode 3, season 19, "The City Part of Town." Directed by Trey Parker, aired September 30, 2015, on Comedy Central.
Trufelman, Avery. "204: The SoHo Effect." *99% Invisible* (podcast and MP3 audio), March 15, 2016.
Zaltzman, Helen. "32: Soho." *The Allusionist* (podcast and MP3 audio), March 18, 2016.

### Calculated Omissions: *Unlucky Numbers*

"How Many Floors Does the 51-Floor Rio Have?" *Las Vegas Blog,* May 1, 2012.
Kohlstedt, Kurt. "Floor M: Avoiding Unlucky Numbers Amounts to Design by Omission." *99% Invisible* (blog), April 4, 2016.
Lee, Jeff. "New Vancouver tower Burrard Place caters to luxury buyers." *Vancouver Sun,* October 7, 2015.
Mitra, Anusuya. "Lucky Numbers and Unlucky Numbers in China." *China Highlights* (blog), updated September 27, 2019.
"Superstitious Chinese Willing to Pay for Lucky Address: Vancouver Study." *Huffington Post,* March 26, 2014.
Wells, Nick. "Days of Vancouver developers skipping 'unlucky' floor numbers are numbered." *CTV News,* November 5, 2015.

### Deliberated Errors: *Fictitious Entries*

"Errors on Road Maps." Petrol Maps website, 2006. Inaccessible.
Green, John. *Paper Towns.* New York: Dutton Books, 2008.
Krulwich, Robert. "An Imaginary Town Becomes Real, Then Not. True Story." *Krulwich Wonders* (NPR), March 18, 2014.
Youssef, Sharif. "242: Mini-Stories: Volume 2: Fictitious Entry by Sharif." *99% Invisible* (podcast and MP3 audio), December 19, 2017.
Zaltzman, Helen. "7: Mountweazel." *The Allusionist* (podcast and MP3 audio), March 25, 2015.

### Misplaced Locations: *Null Island*

Hill, Kashmir. "How an internet mapping glitch turned a random Kansas farm into a digital hell." *Splinter* (blog), April 10, 2016.
St. Onge, Tim. "The Geographical Oddity of Null Island." *Geography and Map Division of the Library of Congress* (blog), April 22, 2016.
"Station 13010—Soul." National Ocean and Atmospheric Administration's National Data Buoy Center website, accessed January 20, 2020.

### Paved Ways: *Tucson Stravenues*

Edwards, Phil, and Gina Barton. "How streets, roads, and avenues are different." Vox website, November 14, 2016.
Kelly, Andrea. "'Stravenue': Is it unique to Tucson?" *Road Runner* blog at Tucson.com, March 3, 2008.
"Most Common U.S. Street Names." National League of Cities website.
"Official USPS Abbreviations." United States Postal Service website, accessed January 14, 2020.
Rudd, Damien. *Sad Topographies.* London: Simon & Schuster, 2017.

### Accessible Voids: *Nameless Places*

Coreil-Allen, Graham. "The Typology of New Public Sites." Graham Projects website, 2010.

Greenspan, Sam. "60: Names vs the Nothing." *99% Invisible* (podcast and MP3 audio), August 6, 2012.

"What Is the Gore Area in Driving?" Legal Beagle website, updated October 14, 2019.

## LANDSCAPES

### Graveyard Shifts: *Pastoral Parks*

Branch, John. "The Town of Colma, Where San Francisco's Dead Live." *New York Times,* February 5, 2016.

"Colma History: The City of Souls." City of Colma website, accessed January 20, 2020.

Cranz, Galen. "Urban Parks of the Past and Future." Project for Public Spaces website, December 31, 2008.

Eggener, Keith. *Cemeteries.* New York: W. W. Norton & Company, 2010.

Greenfield, Rebecca. "Our First Public Parks: The Forgotten History of Cemeteries." *The Atlantic,* March 16, 2011.

Trufelman, Avery. "258: The Modern Necropolis." *99% Invisible* (podcast and MP3 audio), May 9, 2017.


### Trailing Spaces: *Converted Greenways*

"About the Greenway." Midtown Greenway Coalition website, accessed October 20, 2019.

Berg, Madeline. "The History of 'Death Avenue.'" *The High Line* (blog), October 22, 2015.

Beveridge, Charles E. "Frederick Law Olmsted Sr.: Landscape Architect, Author, Conservationist (1822–1903)." National Association for Olmsted Parks website, accessed February 1, 2020.

Bilis, Madeline. "The History Behind Boston's Treasured Emerald Necklace." *Boston Magazine,* May 15, 2018.

"Garden Bridge should be scrapped, Hodge review finds." *BBC News,* April 7, 2017.

Hynes, Sasha Khlyavich. "The Story Behind the High Line." Center for Active Design website, accessed October 20, 2019.

"Lowline: About/Project." The Lowline website, accessed October 20, 2019.

National Trails System Act Amendments of 1983, Pub. L. No. 98-11, 97 Stat. 42 (1983).

Rogers, SA. "Rail to Trail: 12 U.S. Park Projects Reclaiming Urban Infrastructure." *WebUrbanist* (blog), October 9, 2017.


### Courting Palms: *Street Trees*

Carroll, Rory. "Los Angeles' legendary palm trees are dying—and few will be replaced." *The Guardian,* September 29, 2017.

Dümpelmann, Sonja. "Not so long ago, cities were starved for trees. That inspired a fight against urban warming." *PBS NewsHour,* January 25, 2019.

Farmer, Jared. *Trees in Paradise: A California History.* New York: W. W. Norton Company, 2013.

Greenspan, Sam. "155: Palm Reading." *99% Invisible* (podcast and MP3 audio), March 3, 2015.

Pinkerton, James. "Palm tree poachers plaguing the Valley." *Houston Chronicle,* May 30, 2004.

Schulz, Bailey. "Campus evergreens sprayed with fox urine to prevent theft." *Daily Nebraskan,* October 8, 2015.


### Lawn Enforcement: *Owned Backyards*

Barnard, Cornell. "Bay Area homeowners turn to paint to cover brown lawns." *ABC7 News,* June 1, 2015.

"Boys mow lawn to keep elderly Texas woman out of jail." *CBS News,* June 12, 2015.

Downing, Andrew Jackson. *The Architecture of Country Houses.* New York: Dover Publications, 1969.

*Gimme Green.* Directed by Isaac Brown and Eric Flagg. Yulee, FL: Jellyfish Smack Productions, 2006.

"Gov. Jerry Brown Issues Calls for Mandatory 25 Percent Water Reduction with No End in Sight for Drought." *CBS SF,* April 1, 2015.

"Grand Prairie man goes to jail for overgrown lawn." *WFAA 8 News,* April 6, 2015.

Greenspan, Sam. "177: Lawn Order." *99% Invisible* (podcast and MP3 audio), August 18, 2015.

"More Lawns Than Irrigated Corn." NASA Earth Observatory website, November 8, 2005.

Pollan, Michael. "Why Mow? The Case Against Lawns." *New York Times,* May 28, 1989.

Robbins, Paul. *Lawn People: How Grasses, Weeds, and Chemicals Make Us Who We Are.* Philadelphia: Temple University Press, 2007.

Vogt, Benjamin. "Our Gardens Are at the Center of Vanishing Bees and Butterflies—and in Saving Nature." *Medium* (blog), February 4, 2019.

Wilson, Kirby. "Dunedin fined a man $30,000 for tall grass. Now the city is foreclosing on his home." *Tampa Bay Times,* May 9, 2019.

"Xeriscaping." National Geographic Resource Library website, accessed October 20, 2019.


### Lofty Treescrapers: *Ungrounded Plants*

Capps, Kriston. "Are 'Treescrapers' the Future of Dense Urban Living?" *CityLab* (blog), November 16, 2015.

De Chant, Tim. "Can We Please Stop Drawing Trees on Top of Skyscrapers?" *ArchDaily* (blog), March 21, 2013.

Kohlstedt, Kurt. "Parisian Treescraper: Vertical Mixed-Use Planter Will Also Have Room for People." *99% Invisible* (blog), November 27, 2017.

Kohlstedt, Kurt. "Renderings vs. Reality: The Improbable Rise of Tree-Covered Skyscrapers." *99% Invisible* (blog), April 11, 2016.

"La Forêt Blanche and Balcon sur Paris win the Marne Europe—Villiers sur Marne competition." Stefano Boeri Architetti website, October 20, 2017.

"Nanjing Vertical Forest." Stefano Boeri Architetti website, accessed October 28, 2019.

Onniboni, Luca. "Vertical Forest in Milan—Boeri Studio." *Archiobjects* (blog), accessed October 20, 2019.

Sun, Yitan, and Jianshi Wu. "New York Horizon." Conceptual urban design, winner of the eVolo Skyscraper Award, 2016.

"Vertical Forest." Stefano Boeri Architetti website, accessed October 28, 2019.

## SYNANTHROPES

### Naturalized Denizens: *Common Squirrels*

Benson, Etienne. "The Urbanization of the Eastern Gray Squirrel in the United States." *Journal of American History* 100, no. 3 (2013): 691–710.

Carrington, Damian. "Return of pine martens could save Britain's red squirrels, say scientists." *The Guardian,* March 7, 2018.

"Central Park Squirrel Census—2019 Report." The Squirrel Census website, accessed October 28, 2019.

Gilpin, Kenneth N. "Stray Squirrel Shuts Down Nasdaq System." *New York Times,* December 10, 1987.

Greig, Emma. "Analysis: Do Bird Feeders Help or Hurt Birds?" The Cornell Lab of Ornithology's All About Birds website, January 11, 2017.

Ingraham, Christopher. "A terrifying and hilarious map of squirrel attacks on the U.S. power grid." *Washington Post,* January 12, 2016.

Metcalfe, John. "The Forgotten History of How Cities Almost Killed the Common Squirrel." *CityLab* (blog), December 20, 2013.

Schwalje, Kaitlyn. "352: Uptown Squirrel." *99% Invisible* (podcast and MP3 audio), April 30, 2019.

Sundseth, Kerstin. *Invasive Alien Species: A European Union Response.* Luxembourg: Publications Office of the European Union, 2017.

Zuylen-Wood, Simon van. "Philly Was the First City in America to Have Squirrels." *Philadelphia Magazine,* December 12, 2013.

### Ghost Streams: *Fish Stories*

Bliss, Laura. "The Hidden Health Dangers of Buried Urban Rivers." *CityLab* (blog), August 5, 2015.

Chan, Sewell. "Fishing Under the City." *New York Times Empire Zone* (blog), May 16, 2007.

Gasnick, Jack. "Manhattan Reminiscence: Fishing in 2d Ave." *New York Times,* Letters to the Editor, August 22, 1971.

Kadinsky, Sergey. "Sunfish Pond, Manhattan." *Hidden Waters Blog,* May 11, 2016

"A lively subterranean riverlet." *Urbablurb* (blog), May 18, 2007.

Manaugh, Geoff. "Deep in the basement of an ancient tenement on Second Avenue in the heart of midtown New York City, I was fishing." *BLDGBLOG,* May 5, 2008.

O'Donnell, Bryan. "'Ghost Streams' Sound Supernatural, but Their Impact on Your Health Is Very Real." *Popular Science,* February 5, 2019.

### Home to Roost: *Unloved Doves*

Bryce, Emma. "Why Are There So Many Pigeons?" Live Science website, October 27, 2018.

Clayton, Indya. "Spikes on branches of tree in Oxford to stop bird droppings on parked cars." *Oxford Mail,* April 24, 2019.

Johnson, Nathanael. *Unseen City: The Majesty of Pigeons, the Discreet Charm of Snails & Other Wonders of the Urban Wilderness.* New York: Rodale Books, 2016.

Mars, Roman. "210: Unseen City: Wonders of the Urban Wilderness." *99% Invisible* (podcast and MP3 audio), April 26, 2016.

Primm, Arallyn. "A History of the Pigeon." *Mental Floss* (blog), February 3, 2014.

### Raccoon Resistance: *Trash Pandas*

Bowler, Jacinta. "Raccoons Have Passed an Ancient Intelligence Test by Knocking It Over." Science Alert website, October 23, 2017.

Dempsey, Amy. "Toronto built a better green bin and—oops—maybe a smarter raccoon." *Toronto Star,* August 30, 2018.

Hsu, Jeremy. "Why Raccoons Didn't Cut It as Lab Rats." Live Science website, September 15, 2010.

Kohlstedt, Kurt. "MPR Raccoon: Exploring the Urban Architecture Behind an Antisocial Climber." *99% Invisible* (blog), June 15, 2018.

Main, Douglas. "Raccoons are spreading across Earth—and climate change could help." National Geographic website, July 29, 2019.

Mingle, Katie. "330: Raccoon Resistance." *99% Invisible* (podcast and MP3 audio), November 27, 2018.

Nelson, Tim. "Social climber: Raccoon scales St. Paul skyscraper, captures internet." *MPR News,* June 12, 2018.

Pettit, Michael. "Raccoon intelligence at the borderlands of science." *Monitor on Psychology* 41, no. 10 (2010): 26.

### Unmanned Lands: *Wildlife Corridors*

"Adult Upstream Passage on the West Coast." NOAA Fisheries website, updated September 27, 2019.

"European Green Belt Initiative." European Green Belt website, accessed January 28, 2020.

FitzGerald, Emmett. "197: Fish Cannon." *99% Invisible* (podcast and MP3 audio), January 26, 2016.

Groves, Martha. "Caltrans proposes wildlife overpass on 101 Freeway." *Los Angeles Times,* September 2, 2015.

McKenna, Phil. "Life in the Death Zone." PBS NOVA website, February 18, 2015.

Montgomery, David. *King of Fish: The Thousand-Year Run of Salmon.* New York: Basic Books, 2004.

Rogers, SA. "Urban Rewilding: Reverse-Engineering Cities to Save Nature—and Ourselves." *WebUrbanist* (blog), August 6, 2018.

"Wildlife Corridors." New South Wales Department of Environment and Conservation website, August 2004.

## CHAPTER 6: URBANISM

## HOSTILITIES

### Loved Park: *Dubious Skateblockers*

Bracali, Anthony. "Thanks, Le Corbusier (... from the skateboarders)." AnthonyBracali.com (website). Inaccessible.

Madej, Patricia. "LOVE Park reopens after renovations." *Philadelphia Inquirer,* May 30, 2018

McQuade, Dan. "A Farewell: LOVE Park, Skateboard Mecca." *Philadelphia Magazine,* February 12, 2016.

Norton, Andrew. "71: In and Out of LOVE." *99% Invisible* (podcast and MP3 audio), January 23, 2013.

"Philly mayor shows love to skateboarders, lifts ban in Love Park." *The Morning Call* (Allentown, PA), February 10, 2016.

Rafkin, Louise. "Sea Life Skate Stoppers." *New York Times,* December 3, 2011.

"Rob Dyrdek/DC Shoes Foundation Skate Plaza." City of Kettering Recreation Department website, accessed October 1, 2019.

## Urine Trouble: *Discouraging Spikes*

Halliday, Josh. "Tesco to remove anti-homeless spikes from Regent Street store after protests." *The Guardian,* June 12, 2014.

Jackson, Lee. "Urine Deflectors in Fleet Street." *The Cat's Meat Shop* (blog), July 23, 2013.

McAteer, Oliver. "'Anti-homeless' spikes are 'ugly, self-defeating and stupid', says Boris Johnson." *Metro* (UK), June 9, 2014.

Nelson, Sara C. "Anti-Homeless Spikes Outside Tesco Vandalised with Concrete." *Huffington Post,* June 12, 2014.

"On Human Exuviae and Soil Holes." *The Farmer's Magazine* 10 (1809).

"Residents of Hamburg's St Pauli nightclub district use pee repellent paint against public urination." Australian Broadcasting Corporation website, March 5, 2015.

Rogers, SA. "Hostile Urbanism: 22 Intentionally Inhospitable Examples of Defensive Design." *WebUrbanist* (blog), January 1, 2018.

## Obstinate Objects: *Discomforting Seats*

Andersen, Ted. "What happened to SF's controversial 'sit-lie' ordinance?" SFGate website, October 18, 2018.

Bastido, Danielle de la. "The Sinister Story Behind the Design of McDonald's Chairs." *Loaded* (blog), August 12, 2016.

"Great Queen Street, Camden." Factory Furniture website, accessed October 28, 2019.

Kohlstedt, Kurt. "Hostile Architecture: 'Design Crimes' Campaign Gets Bars Removed from Benches." *99% Invisible* (blog), February 9, 2018.

Mars, Roman. "219: Unpleasant Design & Hostile Urban Architecture." *99% Invisible* (podcast and MP3 audio), August 5, 2016.

Norman, Nils. "Defensive Architecture." Dismal Garden website, accessed October 3, 2019.

Savić, Selena, and Gordan Savičić, eds. *Unpleasant Design.* Berlin: GLORIA Publishing, 2013.

Swain, Frank. "Designing the Perfect Anti-Object." *Medium* (blog), December 5, 2013.

## Cities of Light: *Dissuasive Illumination*

"Blue streetlights believed to prevent suicides, street crime." *Seattle Times—Yomiuri Shimbun,* December 11, 2008.

"Crime statistics for Buchanan Street/streets with blue street lighting in Glasgow before/after they were installed and the recent situation." What Do They Know website, updated January 18, 2011.

Heathcote, Edwin. "Architecture: how street lights have illuminated city life." *Financial Times,* March 13, 2015.

"History of Street Lighting." History of Lighting website, accessed October 15, 2019.

Jacobs, Jane. *The Death and Life of Great American Cities.* New York: Random House, 1961.

Mikkelson, David. "Blue Streetlight Crime Reduction." Snopes Fact Check website, May 2015.

"Pink Cardiff street lights plan 'to deter Asbo yobs.'" *BBC News—Wales,* March 5, 2012.

Roberts, Warren. "Images of Popular Violence in the French Revolution: Evidence for the Historian?" American Historical Review website, accessed October 29, 2019.

Schivelbusch, Wolfgang. "The Policing of Street Lighting." *Yale French Studies,* no. 73, Everyday Life (1987): 61–74.

## Targeting Demographics: *Disruptive Sounds*

Campbell, Sarah. "Now crime gadget can annoy us all." *BBC News,* December 2, 2008.

Conan, Neal. "Mosquito Targets Teens with Audio Repellent." *Talk of the Nation* (NPR), September 1, 2010.

"EU rejects bid to ban Mosquito." *The Herald* (Plymouth, UK), September 14, 2008.

Lawton, B. W. "Damage to human hearing by airborne sound of very high frequency or ultrasonic frequency." An Institute of Sound and Vibration Research report for the UK's Health and Safety Executive, 2001.

Lyall, Sarah. "What's the Buzz? Rowdy Teenagers Don't Want to Hear It." *New York Times,* November 29, 2005.

Ng, David. "Classical music still effective at dispersing loitering teens." *Los Angeles Times,* April 4, 2011.

## Exterior Motives: *Deceptive Deterrents*

Groover, Heidi. "Seattle Uses Bike Racks to Discourage Homeless Camping." *The Stranger: Slog* (blog), December 19, 2017.

Kohlstedt, Kurt. "Unpleasant Design in Disguise: Bike Racks & Boulders as Defensive Urbanism." *99% Invisible* (blog), February 5, 2018.

Mark, Julian. "Defensive boulders arrive at a cleared SF homeless encampment." Mission Local website, December 20, 2017.

Monahan, Rachel. "Oregon Officials Deter Portland Homeless Campers with a Million Dollars' Worth of Boulders." *Willamette Week,* June 19, 2019.

Smith, Joseph. "Anti-homeless sprinklers installed by Bristol tanning salon could be 'a death sentence' for rough sleepers." Bristol Live website, January 30, 2018.

# INTERVENTIONS

## Guerrilla Fixation: *Unsanctioned Shield*

Aaron, Brad. "Refused by His City, Man Jailed for Painting a Crosswalk." *Streetsblog NYC,* February 7, 2008.

Ankrom, Richard. "Freeway Signs: The installation of guide signs on the 110 Pasadena freeway." Ankrom website, accessed October 19, 2019.

Bednar, Adam. "Hampden's DIY Crosswalks." *Patch* (blog), February 1, 2012.

Burchyns, Tony. "Police: Vallejo man arrested for spray-painting crosswalk." *Vallejo Times-Herald,* May 31, 2013.

*California Manual on Uniform Traffic Control Devices.*
Caltrans website, updated March 29, 2019.

Noe, Rain. "The Efficient Passenger Project vs. the MTA: Is Good Signage a Bad Idea?" *Core77* (blog), February 12, 2014.

Stephens, Craig. "Richard Ankrom's Freeway Art: Caltrans Buys into the Prank." *LA Weekly,* December 30, 2009.

Weinberg, David. "288: Guerrilla Public Service Redux." *99% Invisible* (podcast and MP3 audio), December 12, 2017.

### Drawing Attention: *Viral Signage*

Badger, Emily. "Raleigh's Guerrilla Wayfinding Signs Deemed Illegal." *CityLab* (blog), February 27, 2012.

Lydon, Mike, and Anthony Garcia. *Tactical Urbanism: Short-term Action for Long-term Change.* Washington, DC: Island Press, 2015.

"Matt Tomasulo—From Pedestrian Campaigns to Pop-Ups, This 'Civic Instigator' Makes His Mark." *Next City* (blog), March 25, 2015.

Rogers, SA. "Guerrilla Wayfinding: User-Powered Signs Aid Exploration." *WebUrbanist* (blog), September 30, 2013.

Stinson, Liz. "A Redesigned Parking Sign So Simple That You'll Never Get Towed." *Wired,* July 15, 2014.

Sylianteng, Nikki. "Parking Sign Redesign." NikkiSylianTeng .com, accessed October 28, 2019.

### Asking Permission: *Open Hydrants*

"Busy Street Deluged; A Little Boy's Prank; He Loosened the Hydrant on a Fifth Avenue Corner." *New York Times,* May 17, 1904.

"City H.E.A.T. Campaign Warns of Dangers of Illegally Opening Fire Hydrants." NYC Department of Environmental Protection website, July 26, 2019.

"Department of Environmental Protection Launches 2014 Summer Fire Hydrant Abuse Prevention Campaign." NYC Department of Environmental Protection website, July 23, 2014.

Fernandez, Manny. "Cracking the Locks on Relief." *New York Times,* August 6, 2010.

Kohn, Edward P. *Hot Time in the Old Town: The Great Heat Wave of 1896 and the Making of Theodore Roosevelt.* New York: Basic Books, 2011.

Nosowitz, Dan. "New Yorkers Have Been Illicitly Cracking Open Fire Hydrants for Centuries." *Atlas Obscura* (blog), July 30, 2015.

### Seeking Forgiveness: *Embattled Boulders*

Baskin, Danielle (@djbaskin). "Some neighbors pooled together $2000 to dump 24 boulders into the sidewalk as a form of 'anti-homeless decoration.' The city won't remove them, so I put their rocks on the Craigslist free section." Twitter, September 26, 2019.

Cabanatuan, Michael, Phil Matier, and Kevin Fagan. "Anti-tent boulders trucked away from SF neighborhood—may be replaced by bigger ones." *San Francisco Chronicle,* September 30, 2019.

Nielsen, Katie. "'Boulder Battle' in Response to Homeless Crisis Continues on San Francisco Street." *CBS SF,* September 29, 2019.

Nielsen, Katie (@KatieKPIX). "SF native Wesley House writes 'and in the end the love you take is equal to the love you make' on the sidewalk near Clinton Park where neighbors put boulders on the sidewalk to prevent encampments. It's an ongoing neighborhood battle that now involves SF Public Works." Twitter, September 29, 2019.

Ockerman, Emma. "Some San Franciscans Are Trying to Get Rid of Homeless People with Boulders. Here's How That's Going." VICE website, September 30, 2019.

### Legitimizing Action: *Middle Way*

*Buddha of Oakland.* Video by Oakland North posted on Vimeo, October 24, 2014.

Judge, Phoebe, and Lauren Spohrer. "119: He's Still Neutral." *Criminal* (podcast and MP3 audio), August 19, 2019.

Lewis, Craig. "The 'Buddha of Oakland' Transforms California Neighborhood." *The Buddhist Next Door* (blog), December 20, 2017.

Silber, Julie. "How a cynic, Vietnamese immigrants, and the Buddha cleaned up a neighborhood." *Crosscurrents* (KALW), November 6, 2014.

## CATALYSTS

### Ramping Up: *Cutting Curbs*

Dawson, Victoria. "Ed Roberts' Wheelchair Records a Story of Obstacles Overcome." *Smithsonian,* March 13, 2015.

@DREAMdisability. "Ed Roberts and the Legacy of the Rolling Quads." *Medium* (blog), January 29, 2018.

Gorney, Cynthia. "308: Curb Cuts." *99% Invisible* (podcast and MP3 audio), May 22, 2018.

Iman, Asata. "'We Shall Not Be Moved': The 504 Sit-in for Disability Civil Rights." Disability Rights Education & Defense Fund website, June 1, 1997.

Ward, Stephanie Francis. "Disability rights movement's legislative impact sprang from on-campus activism." ABA Journal website, January 1, 2018.

"What Is the Americans with Disabilities Act (ADA)?" ADA National Network website.

Worthington, Danika. "Meet the disabled activists from Denver who changed a nation." *Denver Post,* July 5, 2017.

### Cycling Through: *Clearing Cars*

Alcindor, Yamiche. "A Day Without the Detriments of Driving." *Washington Post,* September 22, 2009.

"Bird Cages." YARD & Company website, accessed February 4, 2020.

Crawford, J. H. "The car century was a mistake. It's time to move on." *Washington Post,* February 29, 2016.

Dixon, Laura. "How Bogotá's Cycling Superhighway Shaped a Generation." *CityLab* (blog), October 2, 2018.

Ellison, Stephen, and Terry McSweeney. "Two Cyclists Killed in Separate Hit-and-Runs in San Francisco: Police." NBC Bay Area website, June 22, 2016.

Fucoloro, Tom. "New York guerrilla bike lane painters hope city takes cue from Seattle." *Seattle Bike Blog,* September 26, 2013.

Goodyear, Sarah. "Are Guerrilla Bike Lanes a Good Idea?" *CityLab* (blog), September 25, 3013.

Hernández, Javier C. "Car-Free Streets, a Colombian Export, Inspire Debate." *New York Times,* June 24, 2008.

Jenkins, Mark. "How a Colombian Cycling Tradition Changed the World." *Bicycling* (blog), August 17, 2015.

Metcalfe, John. "San Francisco Makes a Guerrilla Bike Lane Permanent." *CityLab* (blog), October 12, 2016.

SF Transformation (@SFMTrA). "We've transformed two sections of bike lanes at JFK and Kezar in Golden Gate Park. #DemandMore." Twitter, posted September 11, 2016.

SFMTA San Francisco Municipal Transportation Agency. "We always look for opportunities to more comfortably separate bike lanes from motor traffic using low-cost measures like plastic 'safe-hit' posts." Facebook post, October 8, 2016.

Willsher, Kim. "Paris divided: two-mile highway by Seine goes car-free for six months." *The Guardian,* September 9, 2016.

## Driving Away: *Appropriating Parklets*

Bialick, Aaron. "In Park(ing) Day's Seventh Year, Parklets Now a San Francisco Institution." *Streetsblog San Francisco,* September 20, 2012.

"Case Study: Pavement to Parks; San Francisco, USA." Global Designing Cities Initiative website, accessed October 19, 2019.

Douglas, Gordon C. C. *The Help-Yourself City. Legitimacy and Inequality in DIY Urbanism.* Oxford, UK: Oxford University Press, 2018.

Kimmelman, Michael. "Paved, but Still Alive." *New York Times,* January 6, 2012.

Marohn, Charles. "Iterating the Neighborhood: The Big Returns of Small Investments." Strong Towns website, October 3, 2019.

Mars, Roman. "372: The Help-Yourself City." *99% Invisible* (podcast and MP3 audio), September 30, 2019.

Rogers, SA. "Free of Parking: Cities Have a Lot to Gain from Recycling Car-Centric Space." *99% Invisible* (blog), March 1, 2019.

Schneider, Benjamin. "How Park(ing) Day Went Global." *CityLab* (blog), September 15, 2017.

Spector, Nancy. "Gordon Matta-Clark: Reality Properties: Fake Estates, Little Alley Block 2497, Lot 42." Guggenheim Museum website, accessed October 19, 2019.

Veltri, Bridget. "San Francisco's Weird and Wonderful Parklets." The Bold Italic website, September 23, 2016.

## Grafting On: *Grassroots Gardening*

Broverman, Neal. "See Scott, One of LA's Guerrilla Gardeners, in Action." *Curbed—Los Angeles* (blog), July 12, 2010.

Dotan, Hamutal. "Not Far from the Tree, Very Close to Home." *Torontoist* (blog), November 3, 2009.

"History of the Community Garden Movement." New York City Department of Parks & Recreation website, accessed February 4, 2020.

"How to Make Moss Graffiti: An Organic Art Form." Sproutable website, accessed October 19, 2019.

Kelley, Michael B. "Crazy Invention Lets Gardeners Plant Seeds with a Shotgun." *Business Insider,* December 17, 2013.

"Manual." *Guerrilla Grafters* (blog), accessed October 29, 2019.

Marshall, Joanna. "Remembering Liz Christy on Earth Day." The Local East Village website, April 22, 2013.

Range. "Flower Grenades: For Peaceful Eco-Terrorists." *Technabob* (blog), July 24, 2011.

Robinson, Joe. "Guerrilla gardener movement takes root in L.A. area." *Los Angeles Times,* September 16, 2014.

Rogers, SA. "Hack Your City: 12 Creative DIY Urbanism Interventions." *WebUrbanist* (blog), March 12, 2014.

Shavelson, Lonny. "Guerrilla Grafters Bring Forbidden Fruit Back to City Trees." *The Salt* (NPR blog), April 7, 2012.

Wilson, Kendra. "DIY: Make Your Own Wildflower Seed Bombs." *Gardenista* (blog), May 16, 2019.

## Bumping Out: *Collaborative Placemaking*

"Dirt paths on Drillfield to be paved." *Virginia Tech Daily* (blog), August 5, 2014.

"Earls Court Project Application 1: The 21st Century High Street." Royal Borough of Kensington and Chelsea website, June 2011.

Geeting, Jon. "Readers: Brave the snow and send us your sneckdown photos." WHYY website, January 26, 2015.

Jennings, James. "Headlines: 'Sneckdown' Post Leads to Real Changes on East Passyunk Avenue." *Philadelphia Magazine,* May 11, 2015.

Kohlstedt, Kurt. "Least Resistance: How Desire Paths Can Lead to Better Design." *99% Invisible* (blog), January 25, 2016.

Kohlstedt, Kurt. "Undriven Snow: Activists Trace Winter Car Routes to Reshape City Streets." *99% Invisible* (blog), January 29, 2018.

Kohlstedt, Kurt. "Leafy Neckdowns: Cornstarch, Water & Leaves Reshape Unsafe Intersection." *99% Invisible* (blog), December 8, 2017.

Lydon, Mike, and Anthony Garcia. *Tactical Urbanism: Short-term Action for Long-term Change.* Washington, DC: Island Press, 2015.

Malone, Erin, and Christian Crumlish. "Pave the Cowpaths." *Designing Social Interfaces* (blog), accessed October 19, 2019.

Mesline, David. "Last week I got together with some neighbors and we temporarily re-designed a dangerous intersection near our homes." Facebook post, November 29, 2017.

Sasko, Claire. "How Snowstorms Help Philadelphia Redesign Its Streets." *Philadelphia Magazine,* March 10, 2018.

Schmitt, Angie. "The Summer Heat Can't Melt This Famous Philly 'Sneckdown'—It's Here to Stay." *Streetsblog USA,* August 14, 2017.

Walker, Alissa. "'Desire Lines' Are the Real Future of Urban Transit." *The Daily Grid* (blog), April 22, 2014.

## OUTRO

*99% Invisible* (podcast and blog), https://99pi.org, accessed 2010–2020.

# INDEX